The Future of Work is Human

───◆───

The Future of Work is Human

———————————————✦

TRANSFORMING COMPANY CULTURE
FOR A POST-PANDEMIC WORLD

BY HANNAH L. UBL
AND
LISA X. WALDEN

The Future of Work is Human © copyright 2023 by Hannah L. Ubl and Lisa X. Walden. All rights reserved. No part of this book may be reproduced in any form whatsoever, by photography or xerography or by any other means, by broadcast or transmission, by translation into any kind of language, nor by recording electronically or otherwise, without permission in writing from the author, except by a reviewer, who may quote brief passages in critical articles or reviews.

ISBN 13: 978-1-63489-639-9

Library of Congress Catalog Number has been applied for.
Printed in the United States of America
First Printing: 2023
27 26 25 24 23   5 4 3 2 1

Cover design by Courtney DeRuiter
Illustrations by Elliott Aleksander — www.elliottaleksander.com
Interior design by Vivian Steckline

Wise Ink is a creative publishing agency for game-changers. Wise Ink authors uplift, inspire, and inform, and their titles support building a better and more equitable world. For more information, visit wiseink.com

To order, visit itascabooks.com or call 1-800-901-3480. Reseller discounts available.

For media inquiries and information on speaking engagements, contact the authors at GoodCompanyConsulting.com.

Contents

INTRODUCTION 1 Stepping Through the Portal	**CHAPTER 6** 179 Caring for Caregivers
CHAPTER 1 17 Humans, Not Robots	**CHAPTER 7** 201 A Culture of Connection
CHAPTER 2 49 Defeating Perfectionism	**CHAPTER 8** 231 Meaning Matters
CHAPTER 3 75 The Power of Empathetic Communication	**CHAPTER 9** 255 Leading with Compassion, No Matter Your Role
CHAPTER 4 107 Our Burnout Emergency	**CONCLUSION** 289 A More Human Workplace
CHAPTER 5 149 Flexibility or Bust	**REFERENCES** I.

INTRODUCTION

Stepping Through the Portal

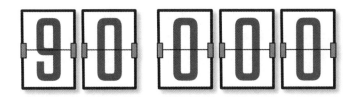

Ninety thousand hours.

That's how long the average person will spend at work over their lifetime. To put it another way, it's roughly one-third of our lives. Which is a whole heck of a lot.

When you think of your time spent at work, what words and feelings come to mind?

In our experience, the answer to this question is honestly . . . depressing. We hear words like *frustrating, stressful, overworked, overwhelming, monotonous, bureaucratic, unbalanced,* and *draining.* One time, someone answered the prompt with *heartbreaking.*

We know, we know. Bleak, right? And that's precisely why we wrote this book. It's why we started our business. Because with every fiber of our beings, we stand by this statement: *It doesn't have to be this way.* We can forge a different path toward a workplace where people feel joy, fulfillment, and even calm.

Let us show you how.

OUR WORKPLACE ORIGIN STORIES

We've both had our fair share of workplace ups and downs. For Hannah, a big low was when she landed her dream internship. The role (and the organization) intrigued her with its rich sense of mission and purpose. That notion was quickly corrected when she found her days filled with meaningless projects and tedious phone calls with IT to troubleshoot her prehistoric computer at a desk with mousetraps beneath it. Lisa's big low was a role fresh out of college where the owner regularly overshared and crossed professional boundaries. And don't even get us started about how Lisa had to buy a flyswatter to manage the fly infestation that management refused to do anything about. (True story!)

We laugh at these tales of workplace woe now, but in all truth we consider ourselves lucky. Because while we had our job lows, we were both lucky enough to experience an extreme high when we—as sprightly twentysomething Millennials—landed jobs that seemed almost too good to be true as generational speakers and researchers at a boutique consulting firm.

There's a key moment from our time there that sticks out for both of us. During onboarding, our boss Debra said, "If you ever get that pit-in-your-stomach, sinking feeling on a Sunday night because you have to go to work on Monday morning, I need you to tell me. Because if that's happening, then I'm doing something wrong."

Cue the dance music. This was seriously the most inspiring thing either of us had ever heard from a boss! And it wasn't the only time she said it to us. It came up during check-ins and performance reviews so we could course correct if needed. It was, for lack of better words, effing great.

That's not to suggest that everything was perfect. There is no such thing. Mixed in with the good were a lot of exhausting, trying moments. But most of the time, it really was amazing. Our leader valued us as individuals and honored the human side in each of us. After Lisa adopted two kittens—the oh-so-adored Pan and Lyra—Debra gave her a day off for "caternity" leave (she didn't call it that, we did) so that Lisa could spend a day acclimating the new additions to her family. And one time, when Hannah had an especially jam-packed speaking week, Debra gathered the rest of the team to secretly put together a curated care package for her. When Hannah returned from her travels, she found on her desk a collection of her favorite things: a vase of calla lilies, a package of Peeps (Hannah has an unstoppable sweet tooth), and a Shakespeare-themed tote bag.

We were constantly encouraged to share our ideas and explicitly asked to iterate and innovate on research methods, strategic initiatives, and client projects. We celebrated wins all the time with bonuses, shared meals, and impromptu fro-yo outings. And when we inevitably experienced failures, we met as a team to learn from them without blame or shame. Our projects were fun more often than not, we supported our teammates and felt supported, and our clients frequently shared feedback about how our work had positively impacted their organizations.

All in all, it was a pretty idyllic situation. But for our family and friends, it might've been too much of a good thing—or at least a painful reminder about how unhappy they were in their roles. Whenever we would (often) tell stories about something funny, interesting, or inspiring that happened at work, we'd be greeted with some variation of "Oh, cool, that must be nice" and maybe a poorly concealed eye roll.

These responses always brought us back to earth. They served as reminders that most people don't have jobs they love so much that they can't stop raving about them. In fact, it's quite the opposite. Because in reality, "work sucks" is the norm, and "work rocks" is the exception.

This uncomfortable truth didn't just show up in our personal lives. In our interviews and research, the resounding theme was deep unhappiness bordering on resentment about the toll that work exerted. From "toxic" workplaces and colleagues, to unrealistic expectations around work hours, to overbearing and micromanaging leaders, there was no shortage of reasons for all the negativity—and it grew increasingly tough to hear.

At one point, the cognitive dissonance that came with loving our jobs, while everyone else seemingly hated theirs, became too much. We decided that the topic of generations, though useful and so fun (who doesn't love talking about MTV music videos and AOL Instant Messenger?), didn't address the root causes of all the workplace unhappiness.

Thus, Good Company Consulting was born. And so was the sacred (to us) mission of identifying the major issues at play so that we could help people and organizations build people-first workplaces that are life enriching instead of soul crushing.

THERE'S WORK TO BE DONE AT WORK

As we already said, Debra was a leader committed to preventing the Sunday Scaries (i.e., that pit-in-your-stomach feeling she first mentioned to us during onboarding). Unfortunately, for most people, those Sunday Scaries are all too common. Everyone knows someone—or has been the someone—who feels the Scaries so strongly that Sundays become one long, painful countdown to starting the work week all over again. Some have told us that the aversion to returning to work can be so intense that it triggers panic attacks.

There are countless memes capturing the feeling of Sunday Scaries or Monday Blues. And how many of you have bonded over crappy jobs and annoying bosses? (It's okay to admit it. We've done it, too. Don't get Lisa started on the flyswatter experience!)

It's actually not surprising that so many of us have felt this way. Sadly, many people are operating in workplaces built more for the bottom line than the employees. There are shared experiences about burnout, overwork, the pressure to live to work, and frustrating workplace dynamics. For decades, there's been this consensus, spoken and unspoken: Work kind of sucks. That's the way it is. And that's the way it's always going to be.

But the consequences of having less-than-awesome workplaces as the norm are becoming glaringly obvious:

- Only 15 percent of the world's one billion full-time workers are engaged at work.[1]

- During the pandemic, 95 percent of US workers said that they were considering leaving their jobs.[2] (Yikes!)

- About 70 percent of people at work say we need a new definition of what a leader is in today's world.[3]

Perhaps we have a little bit of work to do. No—a lot of work to do! The workplace has been ripe for disruption for a *long* time.

A WHOLE NEW WORLD OF WORK

With the pandemic years, we saw a long-flawed work system put to the test. And under the pressure, much of the structure buckled. Previously held assumptions had to be thrown out the window as organizations embraced rapid change and dynamic decision-making in a bid to weather the storm. We were all swept along on that roller coaster o' change: Companies shifted from in-person work to remote, then switched to hybrid or full-time back to the office, and sometimes back again, trying to adapt quickly to each new condition. They were pushed to re-examine expectations around employee productivity, standards for good communication, and which leadership characteristics they really wanted to uphold.

Enter The Great Resignation, aka The Big Quit. While there are many theories as to what caused this wave of mass resignations, we have our own. Employees experienced an existential crisis. After months of witnessing the seemingly endless suffering, constant bad news, and unending political turmoil, people turned inward. Life is painfully short, and they bore witness to that daily. So they started asking the big questions: "What am I doing with my time? Am I spending it the way I should? What is the point of it all? What is my purpose here on this planet? And at the end of my life, whenever that comes around, will I regret those eighty-hour work weeks? The sleepless nights? The constant worrying? And for what? *For what?*"

The pandemic years jolted people out of autopilot, and they began to seriously consider what they were willing to sacrifice for a job or career. And because this movement was about so much more than quitting your job, we prefer to call it **The Great Reassessment**, a term coined by journalist Heather Long.[4] Regardless of what phrase you use, there's no question that we witnessed a shift in the balance of power at work from the employer to the employee. People demanded change, and their conviction was palpable in where they chose to work (or where they chose not to work). This period tangibly shifted not just how work works, but also how people think work should work. This marked an inflection point in our communal professional history.

STEPPING THROUGH THE PORTAL

There is no returning to what was before. There's no putting the toothpaste back in the tube. We proved, collectively, that working from home is not only possible but also can be even more efficient than working at an office. (Let's be honest: Many of us knew this beforehand, but it was hard to convince others!) We saw how compassion and camaraderie are powerful resilience tools that motivate far more effectively than blame and hypercompetition ever could. We saw that no matter how hard we try to show up as professionals who don't let the personal bleed into our work lives, sometimes it's impossible to compartmentalize. And that maybe doggedly adhering to that standard was damaging in the first place. We're but mere humans, after all.

While change was undoubtedly thrust upon us, it has become clear that some are embracing the lessons of this time and are seeking to use them as a guide to building our new, better world of work. Others are eager to "return to normal." They're having a harder time letting go of what once was, and they continue to cling to the past, similar to how Blockbuster clung to its outdated rental model (and we all know how that story played out).

For all of us, these pandemic years have opened the door of possibility to a meaningful, long-term overhaul of the working world.

Author Arundhati Roy has described this pandemic as a portal. While we've pondered over the future of work, we have returned to her words over and over again. In her *Financial Times* article "The pandemic is a portal," she writes:

> Historically, pandemics have forced humans to break with the past and imagine their world anew. This one is no different. It

is a portal, a gateway between one world and the next. We can choose to walk through it, dragging the carcasses of our prejudice and hatred, our avarice, our data banks and dead ideas, our dead rivers and smoky skies behind us. Or we can walk through lightly, with little luggage, ready to imagine another world. And ready to fight for it.[5]

While Roy's words encapsulate much more than just the world of work, for us they're an excellent analogy to frame what comes next in the evolution of the professional world. And to be clear, the portal isn't a quick hop, skip, and jump from one world (and one version of work) to another. It's a tunnel—one we're still walking through, and one we'll continue to traverse for some time. The way will not be smooth. We've never trodden this path before. It will be littered with new challenges. We will fail as we try things for the first time, tweak them, and try them again. We're like children learning to walk, falling and tripping (sometimes painfully) but oh so determined to keep getting up, because the world at the end is worth all the blundering along the way.

A BETTER WORK FUTURE FOR US ALL

The future of work is human.

That's what we see at the other end of this portal. That's our dream for what the future of work can (and should) look like.

It's a world where people are valued as individuals, motivated to meet their potential, and celebrated for their unique contributions.

It's one where the Sunday Scaries are rare, people feel supported by their colleagues and leaders, and sentiments like "I really enjoy my work/job/company" are the new norm.

It's one where people can look back at those 90,000 hours spent at work with peace and maybe even pride, knowing that, for the most part, it was time well spent.

It's a work world that unwaveringly puts people first.

A GUIDE FOR THE PAGES AHEAD

Here are some important things to know as you venture onward.

SOME MORE INFO ABOUT US

A quick formal hello! We're Lisa and Hannah, the authors of this book, the founders of Good Company Consulting, and humans who are passionate about populating this planet with more awesome workplaces. We are researchers, speakers, and consultants who thrive on helping people and organizations build workplaces that don't suck.

An important part of us sharing who we are includes acknowledging the limitations of our perspective. We are products of our own lived experiences, and that creates blind spots and biases. Hannah is a white, cisgender, heterosexual, Midwestern, middle-class female. Lisa is a white Hispanic, cisgender, heterosexual, British Colombian (yes, we spelled that correctly—half-British, half-Latina), middle-class female. When we're writing about a topic we have not lived or are not experts in, we lean on others' research and encourage you—the reader—to find works, articles, or talks from sources whose expertise far outweighs our own. We are but two voices in the world of work, and reading our thoughts without reading others is not recommended.

This is one book of many on work. It is intended to be complementary to other extremely important lenses of workplace culture.

OUR UNIQUE RESEARCH PROCESS

As trendspotters, our journey is one of constant learning. We scour a diverse range of resources to gain insights and formulate theories. Our sources include publications in the vein of *Harvard Business Review* (HBR), *Stanford Social Innovation Review*, and *MIT Sloan Management Review*. We also study the latest reports from large and small research firms. In addition to the more traditional sources, we tap into the collective consciousness by including social media like TikTok, LinkedIn, and Twitter in our content scans.

Most importantly, though, we're constantly conducting interviews and focus groups with real working humans. (Shout-out to the upcoming chapter, "Humans, Not Robots"!) For just shy of a decade, we've been interviewing people. People who operate at all levels, within organizations of different sizes, and across a wide variety of industries. It has allowed us to keep a pulse on what's really happening in the world of work (and to sort the wheat from the chaff in all those buzzworthy studies and articles). This ongoing qualitative research allows us to unearth the stories behind the data. And those stories are what matter.

For this book, we conducted an informal survey across our networks in the US and the UK, and held in-depth one-on-one interviews with professionals working during the pandemic. We are not ourselves a traditional research house, but rather the aforementioned trendspotters who are also quasi-futurists and thought leaders in the realm of workplace culture.

Put simply, we're here to cut through the noise you're hearing about the future of work.

LINGO AND VERBIAGE

Certain phrases and words will be repeated throughout the book. Here's what we mean when we use them:

Pandemic

The use of the word pandemic is intentional. When preparing to write this book, we were cautioned against using it because, as many advised us, "Everyone is tired of hearing about the pandemic" and "We're ready to move on." We've chosen to go against that advice and embrace the usage from a both/and place. We can be both sick of hearing about the pandemic and understanding of how it served as a major catalyst for organizational change.

Pandemic Years

This phrase is a catchall for the years of tumult and uncertainty in the wake of March 2020, when the pandemic really started changing our world. Almost every area of our lives—health care, politics, the economy, global affairs, the workplace, our personal lives, and more—was touched by an upheaval of some sort. This period includes the murder of George Floyd and the civil rights movement it ignited, the contentious US presidential election, and the attack on the US Capitol. It includes inflation, lockdowns, and painful separations from family and friends. Globally, we saw Russia's invasion of Ukraine and the resulting global and economic unrest. There are so many events, moments, and movements that occurred during this time; and we acknowledge that a single phrase can't capture the enormity of everything that occurred, but the "pandemic years" will be our attempt at a shorthand. And when needed, we'll specify the event or moment influencing the work world. Otherwise, we'll lean on this broader definition.

GCC

When we use this acronym, we're referring to our company, Good Company Consulting.

A SPLASH OF GENERATIONS

For years, we immersed ourselves in studying workplace dynamics through a generational lens. We still see great value in addressing generational theory in certain contexts. So from time to time, when we refer to a generational cohort, these are the associated age brackets:

- Traditionalist: Born before 1946
- Baby Boomer: Born between 1946 and 1964
- Generation X, or Gen X: Born between 1965 and 1979
- Millennial: Born between 1980 and 1995
- Generation Z, or Gen Z: Born between 1996 and 2010

WHO THIS BOOK IS FOR

This work is not written for or about leadership. Instead, it's designed to apply to people at all levels within an organization (or even to those who have yet to dip their toes into the professional world!). While leaders have a stronger capability to influence organizational change, we believe that nonmanagerial employees also have the power to effect change within their sphere of influence. Creating awesome workplaces may start at the top, but it only happens when everyone is on board and working toward something greater together.

The inverted pyramid above captures how we see the burden of influence and the capability to manifest change within a company. Think of it as an impact pyramid. The maximum impact is found at the top, with the standards set by the organization at large, then tapers down to the individual employee. But individuals still play a huge role. Underneath that broader organizational and leadership umbrella, employees define their daily approach to work and directly impact team dynamics. And, of course, individuals collectively make up organizations! Without them, there is no culture.

Top: The organization. Sets the overarching standards for company culture. Responsible for soliciting feedback from the other layers.

Middle: Leadership. Models the organizational standards. Guides teams and individuals that operate within that framework. Serves as the mediator between the organization and its employees.

Bottom: The individual. Lives out the company values in their behavior and daily work. Creates culture with their colleagues, and influences up.

We also note that we wrote this book with the traditional office environment in mind. If you're in a non-office workspace, know that some of the tips, insights, and suggestions may be less applicable. However, people are still people no matter where or how they work, so chances are high that you'll find useful information here regardless of your work environment. Take what works, and leave behind what doesn't.

WHAT YOU'LL FIND IN THIS BOOK AND HOW TO NAVIGATE IT

Within this book, we've captured what we've identified as the essentials to creating more people-first workplaces. Each chapter speaks to a specific theme or concept that we believe is critical to embrace if we want to make the world of work one where our human side does not have to be locked in a battle with our professional self.

Each chapter has been organized using subsections we've titled "Pre-Portal," "The Portal," and "Now What?". "Pre-Portal" is a sweep of the status quo before the pandemic years occurred. "The Portal" explores how the pandemic years ushered in change and what the future might look like. "Now What?" offers actionable tools to help you act on that opportunity for change.

Our proposed ideas and solutions range from big, sweeping mindset shifts to more tangible, practical tools. Admittedly, the shifts in perspective will require deep thought work and learning to retrain our brains to think differently. We recognize that this is a long-term, big-picture effort. This is why we've paired those mindsets with more immediately implementable tools that can help move the needle closer toward that mindset shift.

Within these pages, you'll also find case studies, either taken directly from our work with clients or from excellent examples we've come across in our research. We include stories and anecdotes from our many years of consulting and speaking, as well as relevant personal tales of our own.

Lastly, know that there is no one "correct" way to read this book. Feel free to absorb the whole thing on a rainy Saturday afternoon while your cat dozes in your lap (Lisa's preferred way of reading). Or, you can be like Hannah, and consume it in small, meaningful doses, jumping around to the parts that suit your needs most. Either approach will do the book justice, so make it work for you!

OUR ASK OF YOU

As you read, we invite you to pause, ask questions, and process. When we present a challenging or "uncomfy" concept, sit with the emotions that come to the surface rather than jump to a reaction. What are you feeling? Where is it manifesting in your body? Why might you be feeling that way? Is your initial response one of defensiveness? Why? What is so uncomfortable about what we've presented? In what ways do you agree or disagree? Give yourself the time you need.

As you process the information within these pages, we also ask that you read with a critical eye to seek the areas of opportunity. Find the ways that you can contribute your uniquely human skills to better the workplace for everyone.

READ ON!

In your hands, you hold the result of years of our research and thought work. It's our best effort to help us all redesign work so that it serves us, the people, as much as we serve it.

Because that all-too-common, depressing, and decidedly "meh" reaction to work-life we mentioned earlier? Turning that narrative around is why we founded GCC in the first place. That not-insubstantial one-third of our time spent on this planet doesn't have to be spent in miserable, toxic, dehumanizing environments. We want to help people build workplaces that inspire positivity, not dread. One where work and life aren't opposing, competing forces, but rather coexist in harmony (and maybe even support and complement one another!). Rather than associating work with words of negativity like those we mentioned earlier, we envision a world that inspires words like *joy*, *pride*, *warmth*, *connection*, *potential*, *calm*, and even *happiness* and *satisfaction*.

While accomplishing this feat might feel at first like a daunting, mythic quest—desperately searching for that holy grail of company culture—we believe that this seemingly elusive goal is well within our reach.

So we humbly offer ourselves as your guides along this quest. Within these pages, you'll find the answer to why the time is ripe for a workplace transformation to people-first cultures, as well as the road we need to tread—along with the actions we must take—to get there.

A new, reimagined world of work is here. We all deserve it, and we're all a part of designing it. You're already taking a big step by reading this book.

What's next?

CHAPTER 1

HUMANS, NOT ROBOTS

The big "workplace of the future" fear has been that artificial intelligence (AI) will take our jobs. What should really scare us is that we're being treated like the very robots we worry might replace us.

Employees should be valued as complex, nuanced, distinct human beings. Simple enough concept, right? Pretty obvious standard? The baseline, even? Most people would probably agree. But the truth is that in practice, people at work tend to be treated more like producers rather than . . . well, people.

In our interviews for this book, we asked this pair of questions:

1. "Do you feel like a valued employee in your workplace?"

2. "Do you feel like your workplace values you as a person?"

The first time we ventured down this line of questioning, an interviewee named Mara took a very long pause. (Not a great sign.) She was taken aback and said, "Wow. I guess I hadn't thought about it like that before. But am I valued as a person in my workplace? No, I don't feel that I am."

This was not surprising to us. We've found that strategic conversations around employees at work can take on a very—shall we say, practical—bend, with topics like how to get the most out of human capital, ideas to squeeze more productivity out of each individual, and exploring ways to optimize work environments so that leaders get the most out of their staff. The work world has normalized this way of thinking and talking about human beings. But if we take a step back and look at this kind of language with a more objective, fresh set of eyes, it sounds less like it's about people and more like a nod to machines. And, to be clear, whenever we hear this language, we cringe.

The root of this line of thinking hearkens back to the Industrial Revolution. Don't worry, this isn't about to turn into a History 101 lesson. But it's important to note that the mechanization of work, with its focus on constantly improving output and using humans to help run machines more effectively, has left a deep groove in how the world thinks about work and the people getting that work done.

These days, employees' proximity to machines has moved from primarily production line machinery to the modern technology that enables our current workflow. Computers, smartphones, Wi-Fi—our reliance on work tools is more ubiquitous and intimate than it's ever been. In the early 1900s, factory workers couldn't take the factory home with them. These days, it's as easy as folding up your laptop and bringing it back to your home. Wearable technology like smartwatches has made it effortless for us to stay plugged in around the clock, with a handy *ping* alerting you every time an email lands in your inbox (oh joy!).

When the tech that facilitates work and the humans who actually do the work become so interlinked, is it any wonder that humans are treated more like robots than actual people?

Let's explore this concept a little further, first by looking at how this showed up in the pre-pandemic years (what we'll refer to as pre-portal, as described in the introduction) before examining the opportunities in a post-portal world. Remember that you'll find this framework repeated throughout each of the following chapters. First, we'll show you how this has shown up in the past. Then, we'll show you what the portal taught us. Finally, we'll provide solutions for creating a more human-centric workplace future.

✦ PRE-PORTAL

To be clear, we don't think leaders or organizations intentionally frame their thinking about employees and employee output in a "robots, not humans" way. That would be terribly sad (and false!). It's more of a subconscious throughline, a background hum in the professional world that has become so normalized it hasn't been sufficiently challenged.

Before the COVID-19 pandemic, many embraced the common wisdom of "leave your personal life at home, and show up as your professional self." From a communication standpoint, there was an unspoken rule that the golden standard was near-instantaneous responses and constant accessibility. Managers often behaved as though flattening people's performance into data and measurable metrics was the most important performance management tool, without giving enough thought to what lies behind those numbers. We worked with clients who still used "rank and yank" appraisals, the handy method to compare employee output and then fire those who ended up last (eek!). Whether intentionally or not, employees were being treated like cogs in a machine.

Once you know to look for it, the "people equal robots" formula shows up time and again. Here are some of the versions we find most destructive.

DEHUMANIZING OUTPUT EXPECTATIONS

Productivity has been the buzzword of the past decade—or decades—and boy oh boy has it taken up a good deal of our brain space! Productivity listicles and hacks are everywhere, offering up the latest idea, tool, or app to squeeze more work into the same twenty-four hours of a day. It's not so uncommon to look back on our day, review a completed to-do list, and think, *Yes! I feel amazing! I was SO productive!*

But when we look at the language used around productivity—"improving efficiencies," "streamlining workflow," "optimizing output," and so on—it all sounds a bit too "system upgrade" for our liking. Phrases like "human capital" shrink employees down to two-dimensional resources. (That one is our least favorite phrase within corporate jargon.)

With these norms in place, it's easy to forget the human part of the employee equation. Employers start asking questions like, "How can I do more with less?" The people who produce the most with minimal friction are the ones who are rewarded and promoted. "Unnecessary frills" and moments for connection are reduced in order to focus on what's going to improve output and thereby grow the profit line. Opportunities for offhand conversations and non-work-related team interactions fade into the background because they're seen as distractions from the work at hand. Development opportunities are strictly based on job descriptions and vertical growth. Compassion and grace take a backseat as the "results-oriented mindset" is embraced a bit too literally.

When productivity and output reign supreme, it's a pretty clear sign that the people doing the work are shrinking themselves to fit a mold that doesn't make allowances for the human experience.

CALLOUT: JUST THE FACTS

Taylor and the Scientific Principles of Management

Let's hop into ye ol' time machine for a moment and look at Taylorism and *The Principles of Scientific Management*. Frederick Winslow Taylor published *Principles* back in 1911; and in that monograph, he laid out a scientific way to analyze, standardize, and streamline workflow. The theory was originally developed specifically for the manufacturing industry, and this is reflected in its focus on the assembly line theory of work. Taylor's scientific management technique aimed to refine the supply chain to make work faster, better, and more efficient. The primary objective was to optimize for speed; and to accomplish that, he took a mechanical approach to the optimization process that didn't center on the human element. Essentially, it focused on mandating each employee's work, rather than allowing for self-determination or the capability to self-regulate. The idea was that through scientific precision, you could maximize individual output.[1] Thus, the seeds of "humans equal robots" thinking bloomed, and we see the implications of this principle still in play today.

DEHUMANIZING DATA FOCUS AND SURVEILLANCE TOOLS

If the hyperfocus on productivity and the language used to refer to employees kicks off the flattening of humans into two-dimensional beings, then the job is finished off by what we call "data diminishment." Now, don't get us wrong. Data is good. We love it. Hannah is a giant stat nerd. She's that person who brings up the latest report findings at Saturday brunch to gauge the friend group's reactions (nothin' like mimosas and the latest from FiveThirtyEight). But without the story behind the statistics, the why behind the numbers, then we're only getting part of the story. And sometimes this attempt to collect data (often to increase output, as noted above) ventures into questionable territory.

From the few (but still alarming) number of companies that microchip employees[2] so they can "easily" punch in and out, to the many that install surveillance programs on employees' laptops to ensure they don't stray from their tasks, technology is being used in a way that strips autonomy and decision-making away from individual contributors. It also strips away the human side of management, reducing managers to mere interpreters of statistics.

Then there are the metrics used to inform decision-making. When numbers are utilized for hiring, firing, and promotions, and treated as an end in and of themselves, leaders can miss out on the bigger picture. What if there's an incredibly innovative and outspoken employee who might not hit target goals every quarter but contributes massively to the organization with their ideas and input? How do we make allowances for the person who is going through a rough patch in their life and needs a month or two of grace? And if we're promoting only those who look good on paper, what talent is being left behind? What skills aren't we recognizing because they don't show up in the data? And what behavior might we be allowing that hurts the team but helps the bottom line?

DEHUMANIZING EXPECTATIONS OF CONSTANT ACCESS

Technology has made it possible to reach employees in a multitude of ways, 24/7. We answer emails on our phones. We text in lieu of sending a short email. And because most of us keep our smartphones within three feet at all times, we're all (in theory, at least) a simple phone call away. Add to that the preponderance of easy-to-use messaging platforms like Slack and Microsoft Teams, and we have a picture of constant contact.

This convenience that technology initially offered workers has led to an undesirable, unintended consequence. There's an expectation—sometimes explicit, other times unspoken—that people should be responsive and available at all times. Back in pre-pandemic days, Lisa had a manager who determined whether someone was a dedicated employee by their choice to take their laptop home after work every day (to be available for—you guessed it!—more work). Availability and responsiveness are held up as a measure of your dedication to the job; and the closer you are to embodying living, breathing chatbots, instantaneously responding to an email or request, the higher you seem to be held in esteem.

These are just a few of the ways in which humans can be treated like robots at work. There are obviously issues aplenty with this norm. It damages the individual through disconnection, lack of motivation, and chronic stress—and, perhaps counterintuitively, it hurts organizations as well. Because as Margaret Heffernan, author of *Uncharted: How To Map The Future*, once said, "When you start treating people like machines, they start acting like them."[3] That means there's less creativity and innovation, fewer people speaking up when something is bad or broken, and even less joy. It's a recipe for monotony, complacency, overwork, and—eventually—attrition and burnout.

✦ THE PORTAL

The pandemic years, kicked off by the now-infamous 2020, have been full of paradoxical truths and experiences that both amped up and stripped away the "humanity" at work. All of a sudden, much of the American workplace was connecting strictly via computers, webcams, and phones, showing up to work as a conglomeration of pixels on screens instead of their embodied in-person selves. At the same time, there was no denying the real grief and hardships experienced collectively (as a society whose routines and coping mechanisms were stripped away in one fell swoop) and as individuals (carrying painful stories of personal suffering). Also, when your boss's cat leaps onto her shoulders in the middle of a team meeting, and your boss squeaks, "Milo, your claws!" it's a pretty instantaneous reminder that "hey, Rachael might be my leader, but she's also a human being with needy cat problems."

Questions about productivity and work performance took a backseat to questions like "How do we take care of our employees during this crisis?" and "Are you okay?" One smaller tech organization we worked with started taking a weekly happiness survey to measure overall wellness. When they noted a continuous downward trend in employee happiness and satisfaction, they decided to implement a company-wide shutdown for two days. It was a pretty bold (and pretty awesome) move, and the employees we spoke to were emphatic in their praise for the decision. They felt that they'd been given the chance to regularly give feedback, and that the feedback was properly addressed and acted upon. Most importantly, there was an overwhelming sense of gratitude that leaders had recognized that, rather than just looking at productivity and output, it was worth checking in on people to see if they were doing all right. The employees at this organization told us that, for them, this act of mid-pandemic compassion wouldn't soon be forgotten.

That tech company acted early, but other organizations soon followed suit. In 2021, Bumble, Hootsuite, LinkedIn, Nike, and others closed their offices for a week to manage rising rates of burnout. While these shutdowns are not a long-term solution, they did show that these companies were willing to make a huge investment toward employee well-being.

Others made more permanent changes. After noting alarming results in quarterly pulse surveys, SAP, a global software corporation, made the call to designate April 27 as Mental Health Day, a company-mandated holiday. They wanted to not only recognize the importance of giving employees a day off to focus on their mental well-being, but they also hoped to demonstrate their commitment to helping employees live a well-rounded life by making it an annual PTO day. Former SAP North America president, DJ Paoni, said, "It's not just another day off. It's a clear message from the company that it's okay to relax. Healthier employees mean happier customers, so there is a business benefit in the long run."[4]

On the other side of the spectrum, some chose to bypass the opportunity to reflect, reassess, and create a more human work environment. Instead, they pushed forward without adjusting expectations or deadlines, sometimes even when the company was on target to have a record-breaking year. They might have done what we consider the bare minimum, offering resources like mental health webinars or perhaps calling out a few articles on their intranet. Otherwise, they proceeded with business as usual.

In some cases, rather than help employees navigate the pressures of the crisis, companies tried to get more out of them because of the crisis. We were told about one organization where the messaging from management was, "Well, what else are people going to do in the evenings or on the weekends? This is the time to put your energy toward work . . . and our dedicated employees are doing just that." In other words, because there was nothing "better to do," they felt that people should put their time and effort into the company. A pretty stark illustration of treating people as productivity robots, instead of as human beings.

As you might imagine, employees reacted negatively to organizations that seemed to ignore the real human struggles, stress, and grief that the workforce was facing. Some people we spoke to mid-pandemic expressed an overwhelming sense of desperation. Despite being disappointed by their organization's way of handling the pandemic, they couldn't afford to lose their jobs. They had to go through the motions and play by unrealistic expectations of longer hours and increased focus and devotion to work because for the first half of the pandemic, a prevailing thought was, "Well, I'm lucky to just have a job."

But change was already in the air. One interviewee, Sean, an academic administrator, said "I will never in my whole life forget how this company treated me and my colleagues this year. The first chance I get, I'm jumping ship and never looking back." Cue the Great Resignation of 2021, and a call to action (and a call to change) unlike anything we've seen in decades.

✦ NOW WHAT?

The future of some work might be AI. However, the future of the workplace and corporate culture is *human*, one that is steeped in more humane, balanced ideologies about the role work plays in people's lives in general as well as the role that organizations play in enriching their employees' lives. The kicker of this whole debate is that when work is humanized, the benefits extend far beyond employee wellness. When people are treated with compassion, kindness, respect, and consideration, we can truly increase productivity—or, as we prefer to call it, efficiency—far beyond the "humans equal robots" framework.

As we continue to refine workplace culture and step into this new world of work, we at GCC have outlined some of the ways we can stop the intentional (or unintentional) "humans equal robots" policies and behaviors and instead validate the human experience.

As with all of our advice, we know that your role at the company matters. That's why we've split up our recommendations, where relevant, into organization, leader, and employee levels. While we believe that everyone deserves the chance to be the leader of their own career (and that leadership can happen in any position regardless of official title), we also want to be honest about the role that hierarchy often plays in organizations and provide solutions that will work for everyone.

CALLOUT: Toolbox

Turning Traditional Workplace Norms on Their Head

Take five minutes and answer these questions. Then study your responses and gut-check them against your organization's current policies, culture, and unwritten rules. Is your company supporting the "humans equal robots" equation? If so, what changes can you make within your sphere of influence to encourage a more human-centric approach to work?

- What might happen when "employee quality of life" is bumped up in line with "profit" as a company's major driving goal? Is your company clear in communicating support for one or the other? How so?

- How does the nature of work change when you work to live rather than live to work?

- Which of these is the bigger individual motivator at your company: the desire to keep up with peers and be viewed as a productive employee? Or the desire to deliver excellent work? How does that show up in the day-to-day?

- What are the driving motivators at your workplace? Are people motivated because they're trying to win the productivity award? Or are they striving toward the collective company goal, mission, and/or purpose? Are there potentially harmful behaviors that emerge in pursuit of one or the other? Conversely, what positive behaviors do you observe?

- What kinds of qualities are rewarded and praised? Selflessness, dedication, or loyalty? Balance, calm, or boundary-setting? What message does this send to employees and/or colleagues?

HUMANS EXPERIENCE EMOTIONS (AND ROBOTS DON'T)

You know those people who are Bob at home and Robert at work? Bob—or Bobby to his innermost circle—may be goofy, loud, and fun with friends and family. But at work, he's Robert, and Robert is a consummate professional. If Bob's having a bad day personally, at work Robert acts as if everything is going swimmingly. When Bob is going through a rough patch in his life, you wouldn't know it because Robert would never let a glimmer of hardship slip through in his work persona.

This sort of double life has been normalized and even encouraged. It mandates that if we're good employees, we don't let life and emotions get in the way of our work. And while it makes sense in some ways to keep emotions under control because the office (virtual or physical) shouldn't be the place where all emotions and feelings are processed, completely shutting them off or simply acting as if emotions don't exist . . . well, that's not the solution either. Because we're processing our feelings throughout the day, whether it's from frustration that we ran out of granola for our morning yogurt or joy at being recognized as a top salesperson of the year.

Feelings aren't inherently "unprofessional." Leaving aside the personal component, people experience feelings at work all the time. Negative feelings can arise when someone is overlooked for a promotion, talked over, talked down to, or frustrated by team dynamics. Positive feelings can arise when a big sale is landed, a launch runs smoothly, or a bonus is awarded. Rather than trying to suppress or box up the feelings that naturally arise as we human beings navigate the world, becoming skilled at naming, processing, and working through emotions is a much better use of time and effort. Employees who can do this, and who embody high emotional intelligence, are more likely to succeed.[5]

Also, leaders with higher emotional intelligence tend to have happier employees. A study by the Yale Center for Emotional Intelligence found that, for employees whose supervisors lack emotional intelligence, 70 percent of "their primary feelings about work were negative." On the flip side, when employees had supervisors with a high EQ (emotional intelligence), "nearly two-thirds of the words they used to describe work were positive."[6]

FOR THE ORGANIZATION

Normalize conversations about mental health.

- ✦ The year 2020 somehow took what was once considered a taboo topic, especially at work, and made it accessible. In a client conversation, one leader said that 2020 was "the year that made mental health cool." Much like emotions shouldn't be kept at bay, conversations about mental health shouldn't be hush-hush or considered shameful. Addressing the importance of mental health openly and honestly is a meaningful step toward a more human workplace.

- ✦ For leaders specifically, this might look like being open about your struggles. Not trauma dumping or venting, but also not pretending you've always got it all under control. Organizationally, you might create space for events that explicitly address mental health.

Offer EQ training at all levels.

- ✦ Emotional intelligence training will make building a culture where emotions are healthily embraced possible. Emotional intelligence is all about managing one's own emotions and those of others. It's an essential workplace skill, but it's often overlooked for other, more technical training. Investing in EQ education means fewer microaggressions, more opportunities for connection, and laying the groundwork for an organization where feelings can peacefully coexist with the work getting done.

> **FOR LEADERS AND INDIVIDUALS**

Make it a practice to regularly check in on each other.

- ✦ This doesn't mean being intrusive or nosy, but it does mean leaving space to ask how people are really doing (not the throwaway exchange of "How are you doing?" and "I'm fine") regularly. To make these check-ins extra powerful, think through your follow-up plan before checking in. How will you address what you hear if something comes up that requires action or solution-finding? Who's holding people accountable? What resources can you point people to if what you hear is outside of your influence?

HUMANS BENEFIT FROM GRACE (AND ROBOTS DON'T)

When a computer shuts down or a machine stops working, we might grumble some four-letter words under our breath, wonder if any system updates are needed, and proceed to reboot (which is sometimes accompanied by a frustrated keyboard smash). When we humans aren't performing at top capacity, though, there isn't a simple system upgrade that can be installed. It's more complicated than that.

Because humans are not machines, there's not going to be one solution that works for all employees.

Because humans are not machines, you might not see them "shut down" when they hit surge capacity and choose to hide their exhaustion and pending burnout.

Because humans are not machines, almost every "system error" can benefit from a heavy dose of humanity and grace.

It doesn't matter how much grace you give a broken copy machine. It won't suddenly fix itself. For human beings, time to recharge and reconfigure can be the difference between burnout and success. In practice, this means being open to giving people the benefit of the doubt when they are struggling to meet demands or aren't performing to the level they used to.

Malik, one of our interviewees, told us a story about lack of grace in a previous workplace. For a couple of weeks, he'd been showing up five to ten minutes late to work. He'd done his best to arrive on time, but he was going through some personal challenges that were making it really tough. Rather than ask how he was doing or if he was okay, his manager scheduled a meeting where Malik was reprimanded and told that if he didn't fix his behavior ASAP, he'd be put on an improvement plan. But what was actually happening behind the scenes? His daughter had been diagnosed with a debilitating health condition, and Malik was making trips from the hospital to home, then to school for his other kids. This made it hard for him to arrive at work on time like he used to. The meeting with his manager was a major reason why he eventually chose to leave that organization.

This story gets us to the crux of the point. There are real, negative consequences to withholding empathy and grace from employees who need it. Because while robots might be interchangeable, great employees are not so easily replaced. To shift into a more grace-filled work environment, it's critical to lead with compassion, follow up with communication, and always remember that context is key. There is no way to know what someone is going through, where they're coming from, and what they might have recently experienced. As one of our mentors put it when encouraging us to be kind even in the face of frustrating situations, "You just never know if someone's just gotten back from adopting a new puppy or burying their mother."

FOR EVERYONE

Extend grace by responding with curiosity.

- ✦ Before jumping to negative conclusions, default to asking questions like "Is everything okay?" or "Can I help?" It's possible that there's a simple performance issue, but it's also possible that something challenging or distracting is going on in that person's life. Extend some grace, ask if you can help, and go from there. Don't immediately seek to solve a problem. Instead, be open to listening and learning. When you show up—as a manager, leader, or colleague—with the intention to listen instead of problem-solve and learn instead of dictate, that can often be the grace needed to help someone get through a rough patch.

- ✦ A note for leaders: Be aware that some employees may not feel comfortable sharing the details of their personal life or struggles with their manager or leader. And that's okay! Part of extending grace is letting people share what they feel comfortable with while meeting them where they are emotionally.

Courageously squash the small, uncomfy conversations to lessen the need for the big ones.

- ✦ Grace can mean saying the hard things upfront so that they don't spiral into trickier conversations. Too often at work, people can default to passive-aggressiveness with "per my last email" comments or gossipy chats behind people's backs. In fact, during the pandemic years, we received many requests for presentations and workshops on civility in the workplace! Rather than engaging in these damaging behaviors, address issues head-on by being direct with heart. It's the difference between letting resentment build and build, and simply dissipating it with a quick conversation.

Take the story of Arielle, for example. Arielle was working on a project with a colleague who required daily Zoom meetings. When they met, this person was always making lunch or fixing a snack. While Arielle didn't mind, the frequency of dishes clanking, the banging of the fridge door, and the lack of focused attention got on her nerves. After noticing she herself was becoming sharp and passive-aggressive, Arielle raised the issue. She communicated that "the constant meal-making and snack-grabbing is distracting and making me feel like I'm unimportant and not worthy of your full attention."

The response? Arielle's colleague genuinely thought that Arielle wouldn't mind. Because of the other person's grueling Zoom meeting schedule, their hours with Arielle were when they felt comfortable taking a moment to multitask and fuel up while getting work done. They'd never intended to give the impression that they were taking Arielle's

CALLOUT: Story Time

A Note on That Pesky Desire to Solve Others' Problems

Lisa has always taken pride in being someone who's great to come to for advice because she considers herself a problem-solver extraordinaire. You know what's much harder? Listening to a person's problems without offering a solution. That means making space for their pain without trying to make it better (and thereby making yourself feel better) by coming up with a fix. THIS IS HARD. But it's needed. And hey, sometimes people will come to you and actually want a solution (Lisa's favorite!). The trick is to ask what they need and when. Lisa has now made it a habit, when brought an issue or complaint, to ask: Is this a venting and validating moment, a problem-solving moment, or just a listening moment? That little question makes all the difference.

time for granted, and they actually very much valued their meetings. Even this level of awareness melted the frustration that Arielle initially felt, and her colleague was mindful to not always default to "Arielle meeting time equals food time." It was a simple conversation that began with candor and ultimately stopped mounting tension in its tracks.

HUMANS CRAVE RECOGNITION AND APPRECIATION (AND ROBOTS DON'T)

Getting mad at our machines is a normal part of living in a tech-connected world. It helps us deal with the frustration of the spinning wheel of death to scream "Ya dumb hunk of metal!" at our lagging computer. It's probably much rarer for people to dole praise upon a well-functioning smartphone or printer ("well-functioning printer" may be an oxymoron). And no matter how many times I thank Alexa for giving me the weather, it doesn't change her feelings about having to play Lizzo's "About Damn Time" on loop every day.

With humans, on the other hand, recognition and appreciation are not just desired but also required. They're a way to honor the creativity, innovation, and collegial spirit that people are capable of bringing to the table. They're a way to value people as people, not just employees.

Being valued as an employee can look like being valued as a productive worker bee and appreciated as someone who does good work, meets goals, behaves professionally, etc. But to be valued as a person? To be seen as a person? That means to be recognized for individual contributions, to be appreciated for the quirks and individualities that make us distinct, important members of the team. It means being honored for who we are, not just what we do. This acknowledgment shouldn't just be something that comes from leaders or is reserved for once-a-year 360s. It should be embedded into the very fabric of an organization's culture. We should strive to nurture cultures of appreciation.

Remember that neither recognition nor appreciation need to be grand

HUMANS, NOT ROBOTS

gestures or actions that require tons of energy or mental effort. At GCC, this lesson was reconfirmed to us when we sent a small batch of cookies to our accountant, Jude, as thanks for shepherding us through a particularly hairy tax season. It was such a simple gesture, but his reaction reminded us how even the smallest acts can have big payoffs. Here's a snippet of his effusive response. The all caps are his flourish, not ours. We hope it makes you smile the way it did for us!*

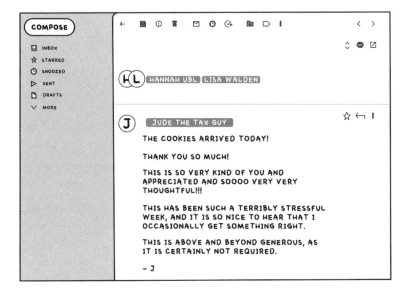

FOR THE ORGANIZATION

Promote praise as a cultural practice, and establish easy methods and systems for recognition.

✦ If people within a company are tuned in to the idea of praise as a practice, it creates so many opportunities to give and receive genuine, authentic feedback. When that practice is baked in as a cultural expectation, praise and recognition (where and when

---

* Yes, we're happy to share Jude's contact info upon request. He's the best. :-)

appropriate) become the norm. Might you build a company value around praise and recognition? Are you including this expectation on the "Careers" page of your company's website?

+ Beyond messaging, the way you facilitate the cultural expectation for praise is to make it really easy to give it. Try using a specific Slack channel for positive callouts, a section on your intranet dedicated to sharing kudos, a corkboard in the lunchroom for handwritten messages of appreciation, or a "Monday Morning Shout-out" tradition at weekly meetings. There are even apps that allow employees to give colleagues a +1 in real time to recognize them for stand-out work or for being a supportive team member.

+ Remember, these celebratory moments are not just for the big wins! The small ones matter just as much, if not more. Call out the person who has great ideas during brainstorming, asks for help, sets a boundary, steps outside their comfort zone, or courageously gives tough feedback. These moments may seem inconsequential or minor, but they could be monumental to the person who is recognized.

FOR LEADERS

Be generous in your praise.

+ What's the opposite of death by 1,000 cuts? Life by 1,000 compliments! So don't skimp on the praise. Really. Don't. This doesn't mean you have to be inauthentic or weird about it. But if a nice thought comes to mind about someone's work or attitude on a project, spread the love. It doesn't have to be a large, public display of appreciation complete with baked goods and champagne. Little compliments stack up. It can be helpful to think about the five-to-one ratio for building positive relationships at work (and at home). Relationship researcher John

Gottman discovered that we should be giving five positive comments or interactions for every one negative one.[7] (Also, a later study found that teams who followed this ratio of feedback showed higher productivity rates![8]) While this is especially true for leaders, it's important for all colleagues to keep it in mind as well.

FOR INDIVIDUALS

Don't rely on leaders to dole out praise—and be specific!

+ There is something really powerful about living up to the expectations of your peers. It can be a driving factor behind why people behave the way they do at work. In a toxic way, this plays out when others aim for unhealthy standards of productivity after comparing themselves to their workaholic coworkers. But if harnessed in a healthy way, this looks like individuals who are motivated by a desire to do great work and be a contributing member of the team.

+ As you embrace the praise practice and recognize your peers more consistently, know that praise lands best when it's specific and recognizes the individual for their contribution. What did they bring to the table that no one else could have? Maybe someone approached a challenging project with unwavering positivity and support for the team. Perhaps another person was tenacious in pursuing a sale, using their particular brand of humor as a way to connect with the client. Call these things out! And remember, it doesn't always have to be focused on work. Recognizing the human is also about honoring personal wins and accomplishments. If someone just completed their GED, that's huge—and definitely a cause for celebration. Did a colleague adopt a new puppy? Time for a puppy party! Again, these recognitions don't need to be big or formal. They can be as simple as a handwritten card or a quick celebratory IM or text (GIFs and emojis welcomed).

HUMANS CRAVE COMMUNITY (AND ROBOTS DON'T)

This will be addressed more robustly in chapter 7, which focuses on connection. But it's worth noting here as well. One of the main motivators for doing work—and doing it well—is the interpersonal bonds created at work. When we started asking questions about the transition to 100 percent work from home (WFH), it became indisputably clear that what people missed most about working in the office was their colleagues. Those friendships and that sense of camaraderie are some of the most satisfying things about work. A Gallup poll found that "close work friendships boost employee satisfaction by 50%, and people with a best friend at work are seven times more likely to engage fully in their work."[9]

At GCC, we live this every day. We both could have easily embarked on our solo careers as keynote speakers, but we knew it wouldn't be nearly as satisfying (or, let's face it, fun) as doing it with a BFF by your side. We are lit up by our duo brainstorming sessions, laugh at inside jokes on the regular, indulge in playful gibing (which is more of Lisa's expertise, as her family's eldest child), share often-bizarre and always-entertaining tales of our travels to and from events, and show up to support each other. Are there hard days? Heck yeah. But a vast majority of the time, having a friend working alongside you to experience both the rough patches and the joyful moments makes work infinitely better. And our work product is better for it, too.

Truly great work cultures emphasize the fact that, in some capacity or another, employees are building something great together. A robot doesn't care if it's tasked with a solo project or linked up to 500 other robots. A human does. There's such gratification in accomplishing something big and doing it with your peers. Leaders and employees alike underestimate the power of community at work at their peril, and organizations should make sure to leave space for that community to thrive. Nourishing a community spirit can be a meaningful differentiator between robot-minded workplaces and human-centric ones.

FOR THE ORGANIZATION

Establish a "helping culture."

- Much like how promoting a culture of recognition centers on the humans doing the work, establishing a helping culture encourages the human-to-human connection and makes for stronger community ties. One of the best ways to build meaningful bonds with others is to operate within a network of help. That means if you need help, ask. And when others ask, volunteer. (This is advised with the obvious caveats. First, people shouldn't volunteer to help if they're at capacity. Second, boundaries are amazing. And finally, don't constantly ask for help without helping yourself first.) The best kind of environment you can work to create is one where people say, "I know my team has my back if I need their help." For an organization or a leader, this may mean actively soliciting and rewarding people who help their colleagues.

FOR THE LEADERS

Intentionally create space for impromptu connections.

- ✦ This one may be hard if you have a virtual or hybrid work environment. But those organic moments of connection that happen in the office, like bumping into a coworker in the hallway or chatting while you're heating leftovers for lunch, are the invisible glue that holds organizations together. In a virtual setting, it can be hard to replicate but not impossible. For leaders, it's important to be attentive to how you can create space for this to happen. It will require planning and intentionality. Leave a few extra minutes at the top of meetings for folks to chat. Or set up virtual work cafés for your team (standing Zoom meetings where people can log in to work with their peers in a collective "space" and place). In this way, employees can show up to work together for accountability and/or connection. Or consider a virtual watercooler channel on Slack with new prompts every day.

FOR THE INDIVIDUALS

Show up authentically (but respectfully).

- Remember Robert from the earlier example? Why not show up as Bob instead? Bob is so much more relatable than Robert. If we allow some of the personal touch to bleed into our work lives, we have more meaningful ways to connect as human beings outside of a love for Excel hacks.

- In case you're wondering what "respectfully" means, here's a quick checklist. While you won't always be 100 percent accurate in your assessment of the following, it should help prevent you from straying too far from authenticity and into the land of inappropriate:

    1. Am I being kind to and inclusive of others?

    2. Could my behavior be perceived as harmful or hurtful?

    3. Do the thoughts or anecdotes I'm sharing have the potential to make others uncomfortable?

    4. Am I frequently distracting or keeping others from their work?

HUMANS WANT HUMANE LEADERS (AND ROBOTS DON'T)

If employees are sometimes treated like robotic productivity machines, leaders face their own unrealistic standard: They're expected to be all-knowing, infallible beings. The old-school mentality of what made for a good boss included words like strong, outspoken, charismatic, knowledgeable, driven, forward-thinking, and tough. These are good words, but the ones that came up in our research when we asked about desired characteristics in leaders were compassionate, authentic, transparent, humble, good listener, mentor, open, and kind.

It's a big move away from the strict, traditional boss prototype to one who acts more like a coach. And what's harder than controlling

CALLOUT: Rethink the Norm

Old versus New: A Fresh Take on Professionalism

Take a few minutes and read through this list, noting where you land: the old way, or the new way. Which do you prefer? If you're more old-school, what value can be found in the new approach? What steps can you take to shift toward the new-way mentality?

THE OLD WAY	THE NEW WAY
Shut down the feelings.	Process the feelings, and take mental health days when needed.
Don't talk about personal stuff.	Share personal information as you feel comfortable. For leaders, create a space where the personal can naturally and authentically be shared (if desired).
The suit and tie show you care about your job.	Doing great work and supporting your colleagues shows you care about your job.
Your productivity output measures your worth as an employee.	Your worth as an employee encapsulates your EQ, your helping behaviors, and your productivity.

or leading? Motivating and inspiring. Turns out that one of the most compelling ways to model a more motivating, inspiring style of leadership is to steer away from the "perfect, has-it-all-together" kind of persona to a more grounded, "I'm a human being, just like you" type of mindset.

FOR THE LEADERS

Don't be afraid of admitting your mistakes.

+ Employees don't want to see leaders as an "other" or someone who's on a pedestal. They want to be led by a person who isn't afraid of showing that they're fallible and is willing to own up to their mistakes. A characteristic of a post-portal leader will be one who takes the opportunity to show where their logic may have failed and use them as coaching tools for their employees.

Invite employees to be a part of the solution.

+ Leaders are not repositories for all the organization's (or world's) best practices and solutions. They might carry a heap of institutional wisdom, but they're still bound by their leadership perspective. This means it can often disconnect them from what's really happening within the organization and the work that's being carried out. (In our client work, we find this is the case more often than not.) Inviting employees to be part of the solution means being humble enough to admit that you might not know it all.

Create standing opportunities for feedback on leadership performance.

- ✦ Opportunities for feedback are extremely important and need to be multidirectional. What that means is it's not just leaders giving feedback to employees, but also employees trickling that feedback back up to the organization (and its leaders). Computers don't need to tell people how to better operate them (though we're sure that if they were sentient beings, they'd have a lot to say). But people need that opportunity; and for an organization to function smoothly, it's essential to create regular, standing opportunities for employees to tell leaders where and how they could improve (without fear of being punished for their candor). This is another point that may seem fairly obvious, but we don't see it put into practice nearly as often as it should be.

- ✦ To create a culture where feedback flowing up is even a possibility, some heavy lifting is required to make sure employees feel safe about being candid. Leaders can help create this precedent by actively soliciting feedback and accepting it without getting defensive or making excuses. From a procedural perspective, organizations can create safeguards for their people through anti-retaliation policies.

There is so much more to work than productivity or just being good at your job. The connections we nourish, the feelings we navigate, the wins we collectively celebrate, the little pockets of laughter in our day-to-day—they're all wrapped into the experience of being a human at work. If we can stop seeing these things as secondary, or as nice but nonessential, and instead embrace them as the very essence of being a human at work (and necessary ingredients to doing great work), then we can move toward creating an environment where we see and value the person first.

Yes, it's still important to assess people by the work they're producing and how they contribute to the organization. But as the new workplace culture evolves, our hope is that strategy and policies will be informed as much by care for humans as they are by the bottom line. Idealistic, perhaps? Overly optimistic? Unrealistic to the real demands of the business world? We don't think so.

──────── ✦ **THE GIST** ✦ ────────

PRE-PORTAL STANDARD

The "humans equal robots" formula has become embedded in our ways of working; and it's ultimately detrimental to retention, burnout prevention, and the overall health of the organization (and the individual!).

PORTAL LESSONS

The coronavirus pandemic pushed people into questioning the role of work in their lives. Many resented that the organizations they worked for didn't make accommodations for the challenges the pandemic presented. Others felt great gratitude and loyalty for the companies that did show compassion. Most felt that this time period revealed how the overall standard of work is unsustainable for human beings and requires deep redesign to put humans first.

NOW WHAT? STEPPING THROUGH THE PORTAL

We all need to honor and consider each individual's humanity in these key ways:

- ✦ **Humans experience emotions**, and there needs to be space made for these emotions to exist (and not simply be shut down) at work. We can do that by checking in on each other, and (for organizations) offering mental health support.

- ✦ **Humans need grace**, so let's respond to moments of conflict with curiosity and have small, uncomfy conversations upfront rather than letting them sit and fester.

- ✦ **Humans are fueled by recognition and appreciation**, which means promoting praise as a cultural practice and establishing easy systems to encourage appreciation to be shared by all levels.

✦ **Humans crave community**, which can be actively fostered by establishing a helping culture and creating space for authentic connections.

✦ **Humans want and need humane leaders** who admit their mistakes and invite employees to be a part of the solution.

CHAPTER 2

Defeating Perfectionism

> *We chase toward a standard of perfection we've been told is the ideal. We strive to "arrive." But people are starting to wonder: Arrive where, exactly? And why?*

For a long time, Lisa wore the badge of perfectionism as one of honor. It was something she loved about herself. It proved that she cared so deeply that her efforts went beyond the big win or moment of success. She was also passionate about getting the details, the minutiae, right. You could always count on Lisa to do a great job at whatever you asked of her. A really, really great job. When she crafted her résumé, the word *perfectionist* topped her list of skills.

Being a perfectionist was part of her core identity. She always tried to work that word into job interviews. When asked, "Can you tell us about one of your flaws?" she'd coyly laugh, flick her hair behind her shoulder, and say, "I guess I can be a bit of a perfectionist." To her, perfectionism was never really a flaw. It was something to be proud of, an asset, and (or so she thought) a crafty way of answering that "gotcha" interview question. Nowadays, if someone we interviewed were to tell us they're a perfectionist, we'd have serious reservations. Or, at the very least, many follow-up questions.

Because, oh sweet former self of Lisa, how wrong she was. The truth is, perfectionism is a huge barrier to building an awesome workplace. In its worst forms, it can cause serious harm not just to the individual, but also to teams, company culture, and even organizational growth. A topic that's often reserved for self-help books and personal development journeys, perfectionism needs to be addressed from a more holistic perspective. If left unchecked, it seeps into every corner of life and undermines efforts at company growth and self-actualization. From poisoning team dynamics and stunting innovation and creativity, to creating feelings of marginalization and a sense of otherness, perfectionism has no home in a healthy company.

Lisa lived this reality. The same impulse that made her deliverables excellent also held her back from engaging in projects out of fear that she would fail, even outside of work. Lisa has always dreamed of being a novelist, and she has spent years (actually decades, at this point) in a state of perfectionism paralysis. Procrastination, perfectionism's evil twin, has been a clingy, unwanted friend for much of her life; and she

is only just now learning how to pry herself out of the clutches of that state of fear-fueled inaction. This change began with recognizing that "I'm a perfectionist!" actually isn't a desirable descriptor. Instead, it's a challenge to overcome.

Lisa now refers to herself as a recovering perfectionist. Getting past that perfectionistic tendency may be a lifelong effort, but it's one well worth making. The pandemic years made many of us question our previously accepted beliefs, one of them being that all-too-common standard of perfection. For some, the years sparked a journey of liberation from the perfectionist cage. Unfortunately, for others, this period simply reinforced those deeply ingrained grooves.

We believe that moving away from perfectionism is a crucial component of building nourishing, supportive, happy workplaces. Every level of work is informed (and weakened) by a perfectionist mindset, so much so that we felt it was worthy of devoting an entire chapter to exploring the importance of dismantling perfectionist tendencies—and, of course, how to actually do that.

In the wise words of Anne Lamott, "Perfectionism is the voice of the oppressor, the enemy of the people. It will keep you cramped and insane your whole life."[1] With the following, we hope to help silence that oppressive voice and create space for us to stretch to our full individual and organizational potential.

✦ PRE-PORTAL

For decades, perfectionism has been on the rise. Especially in a highly individualistic Western culture, unrealistic standards of achievement and the constant striving for bigger and better have created a society that glorifies aiming for perfection.

In a groundbreaking and oft-cited study on the rise of perfectionism among college students in the US, Canada, and the UK, lead author Thomas Curran, PhD, broadly defines *perfectionism* as "an irrational desire to achieve along with being overly critical of oneself and others."[2] More specifically, the study breaks down perfectionism into three categories:

- **Self-Oriented Perfectionism**: The desire to be perfect (Constantly driving to meet higher and higher standards for oneself)
- **Other-Oriented Perfectionism**: Placing unrealistic standards on others (Constantly criticizing others for their mistakes)
- **Socially Prescribed Perfectionism**: Perceiving excessive expectations from others (Fear of making mistakes because of outside judgment)

Within these categories, the study found that "between 1989 and 2016, self-oriented perfectionism rose by 10%, other-oriented rose by 16%, and socially prescribed rose by 33%."[3]

While there are many theories as to why this may be the case, a big one comes down to ease of comparison (or, as a friend of ours once put it, comparisonitis). Through Instagram, Facebook, TikTok, and other social media platforms, opportunities to compare ourselves to others are available at a scale and rate unseen at any other time in our history. Facetune and selfie filters render these comparison tools even more nefarious. Technology has made it possible for us to make comparisons not just to other people, but also in what our lives might be like if we were as successful or beautiful as them. Now, we're in competition with the "best" filtered version of ourselves.

Comparisonitis plays out at work too. It's common—and natural even—to compare career and life milestones with those of our peers.

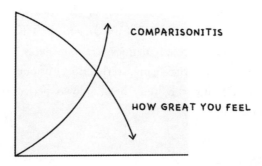

But social media yet again rears its ugly head to make it that much easier for us to contrast our lows to (as already written about by others at length) everyone else's highlight reels. (Example inner monologue: *Thank you, LinkedIn, for reminding me that my college classmate is now a senior executive at her firm while I'm still a "specialist" at the company I've been working at since I turned twenty-four. *sigh**) Even without social media, comparisons to colleagues happen daily, often in regard to how much and how hard people are working. Emails from peers coming through at 10:00 p.m. may prompt us to ask, "Am I working enough hours? Should I also be putting in some time right now?" When juxtaposed with what others are doing, good just never seems good enough.

This comparison game happens on personal and professional fronts, bolstered by the meritocracy narrative that tells the (false) story that the harder you work and the more time you put in, the more you'll level up your skills and the more successful you'll become. Through grit and determination, anything is possible. Except . . . that's not actually how it works. Maybe for some lucky people. But for others, it's just not that simple.

If society—and U.S. workplace cultural norms—operated on a completely level playing field where things like class, wealth disparities, and discrimination didn't play into decision-making, then meritocracy might be a cool (and valid) idea. But meritocracy is as much a fairy tale as leprechauns or unicorns. One person can work just as hard as another and, for reasons completely out of their control, miss out on an important opportunity or be seen as less worthy of promotion than someone else.

This plays out with startling clarity when race and gender are added to the conversation. Black employees often feel that they need to go above and beyond the expectations set for their white counterparts to even get a seat at the table. For them and other minority groups, trying to live by the mostly white-male-prescribed version of perfection

CALLOUT: A GENERATIONAL MOMENT

The Kids: Are They All Right?

Gen Z, those born between 1996 and 2010, are true digital natives. They're the first generation to spend their teen years not just comparing themselves to actors and models on covers of magazines, but also to Facetuned Insta influencers and (worst of all) filtered versions of themselves. They're developing a sense of self in which social evaluation plays an oversized role. How many likes did they get on that pic they shared? How many comments on that uploaded TikTok video? How many new subscribers on YouTube?

A 2018 article by *The New York Times* bearing the title "More College Students Seem to Be Majoring in Perfectionism" shared that colleges and universities were hiring professionals to teach college courses on how to fail.[4] Yes. College courses on how to fail.

It may be easy to scoff at such a course, but the consequences of perfectionism on this generation are squarely in the not-funny camp. Rates of anxiety, depression, and even suicide skyrocketed with the Millennial generation[5]; and now the American Psychological Association states that an "alarming" increased number of young people suffer from perfectionism, "leading to soaring rates of depression and suicide."[6] In this case, perfectionistic tendencies don't just defeat progress. They can also defeat (sometimes temporarily, other times indefinitely) the person.

at work is an oversized burden that can also mean they have to bend over backward or act inauthentically.[7] One need look no further than standards of professional attire to see this point in action. Black hairstyles like locs and Afros have long been frowned upon, if not outright banned, in the workplace. To show up as the "perfect professional," Black employees have had to literally change their appearance to match the version prescribed by the white majority.

So not only can perfectionism be a practice in futility, but the damage it inflicts is also very real. Rather than helping people and organizations flourish, it impedes progress and corrodes relationships.

How Perfectionism Harms the Individual:

- Shuts down creativity and innovation
- Makes people more prone to stress, burnout, anxiety, and depression
- Leads to procrastination paralysis
- Inspires imposter syndrome and a sense of insecurity
- Leads to workaholism

How Perfectionism Harms the Team:

- Breeds a competitive rather than collaborative environment
- Creates a dynamic of resentment and finger-pointing
- Hinders the development of trust and psychological safety
- Favors shortsighted, "safe" (rather than innovative) work

- Promotes the idea of "perfect" peers, making others believe they should be the same

How Perfectionism Harms the Company:

- Alienates people from different backgrounds who don't fit the pre-established mold

- Creates a culture of silence or, even worse, "yes" (to everything) people

- Promotes a standard of "flawless" leadership that makes climbing the ladder seem impossible

- Leads to procrastination paralysis, which means both efficiency and productivity suffer

- Promotes a culture of burnout

BEING A PERFECTIONIST DOESN'T MAKE ANYONE A BETTER EMPLOYEE

Probably the worst thing about being a perfectionist is that the loudest troll and cruelest critic is often the inner voice that every perfectionist carries around. And yes, we can't forget the social component, the constant worrying about what others will think and say. But often the most damaging opinion is actually our own. Cue the villainous Shakespearean soliloquies inside our minds (can you tell we're former theater nerds?). The negative self-talk can start even before we've created anything to critique, leading us into that painful state of procrastination and paralysis. We resort to all-or-nothing thought patterns, with very little room for the gray:

- "I'm the weakest link on this team."
- "I can never catch up to my peers."
- "I'm awful in meetings."
- "I have nothing valuable to contribute."

For Lisa, this fear-inspired paralysis meant almost turning down the opportunity to write our first book, *Managing Millennials for Dummies*.[8] She was so deeply afraid that it would turn out to be a massive failure. Lisa could vividly imagine the hecklers showing up to throw rotten tomatoes and yell "Boo, for shame!" at her every morning (a rather unlikely scenario, we now agree). In her self-admittedly somewhat neurotic mind, she was preemptively preventing future pain by, in the present, turning down a huge opportunity. She took the "no pain, no gain" saying to heart, but the wrong way around: trying to duck the (imagined) pain at the cost of the gain. Luckily, Lisa overcame this broken thinking, and we did indeed write that book. And even wrote another (this one)!

The point is, perfectionist tendencies did not make Lisa better at her job. This example illustrates how perfectionism almost stopped her from embarking on a pretty big, pretty great opportunity. But perfectionism held her back in the more regular, day-to-day tasks as well. Sure, her deliverables were always great, but she produced way less than others. She also had to put in more hours than her peers to meet the volume of the workload at her unrealistically high standard. She also stressed a lot more while she was working, which frustrated and frazzled others along the way.

Lisa is not alone. Perfectionist employees can have a harder time getting started on projects. They may produce excellent work, but it's possible that they'll produce a lot less than those whose work isn't impeccable but still great. Perfectionists can also spend a lot of time spinning their wheels, stuck in that aforementioned purgatory-like place of procrastination paralysis. They'll chip away at the small stuff, emails, minor to-dos, even tidying up their space, before finally attempting to climb the Mount Everest-like mountain they've built up for themselves in their heads.

BEING A PERFECTIONIST DOESN'T MAKE ANYONE A BETTER TEAMMATE

This seems so counter to logic, right? Everyone seems eager to have perfectionists on their teams! They're the people who are dependable and truly detail-oriented, and they won't let anything fall through the cracks! In reality, perfectionists can be viewed by their peers as nit-picky, obsessively detailed, and people who carry unreasonably high expectations of others.

Because not only will a perfectionist bust their butt to make sure they're contributing their all to a given task or initiative, but they'll also make sure absolutely every *i* is dotted and every *t* is crossed. One only needs to hearken back to *The Brady Bunch* and recall that the iconic perfectionist Marcia was not endearing to all. But seriously, those overachieving go-getters may favor perfection and achievement over fostering team connection. And their teammates can tell—so much so that "all perfectionists, especially the other-oriented perfectionist, received significantly lower ratings on social skills and attraction than the non-perfectionist colleague."[9]

One of our clients, Katherine, is also a recovering perfectionist. In her mind, when she was assigned to a team project or initiative, she'd give her all to make sure she was pulling her fair share of the work and being an excellent team player. There was a sense of pride in carrying her weight and going that extra mile to show her dedication to the team, the project, and her work. For her, that meant taking on the brunt of the project-related assignments, reviewing colleagues' work, and putting in extra hours to make sure the team was on track. Later, during performance reviews, Katherine was shocked to see that, of the group, she'd been the one singled out with the lowest marks from her peers.

Her manager explained that people suspected she was looking out for her own interests and trying to set herself apart from others by taking on so much more work. They also felt that she was being nitpicky of errors they made along the way. Perhaps worst of all, because she was so steeped in what she was doing, they never connected with her as a human and coworker. The trust ties they had developed with each other simply didn't exist with her. For Katherine, this experience was a loud wake-up call. Here she was, thinking that she was being a team player, when in reality the perception was that she'd behaved with her own needs front and center.

BEING A PERFECTIONIST DOESN'T MAKE ANYONE A BETTER LEADER

We'd argue that it actually makes for a worse leader, because the volume on the leader bus is ten times louder than any other. Leading with perfectionist tendencies means that, very likely, other leaders (and employees) will try to emulate that style of work. These perfectionistic leaders can be frustrating to work for, because employees worry that they'll never live up to their leader's extremely high standards. In the worst-case scenarios, these leaders become hypercritical of everyone and everything. They embody the "If I want something done right, I've got to do it myself" thought pattern.

Enter the micromanaging boss, who wants to see every email that goes out to a client, inserts themselves into every new initiative (even if they are near burnout), and clearly shows favoritism to other perfectionist-minded employees in the office. But that's the worst-case scenario. Even well-intentioned leaders who know that their perfectionistic tendencies need some curbing can cause their staff harm. Constantly asking for more proof of their ideas may shut people down and prevent those prone to perfectionism from feeling inspired to bring new ideas forward. Having a critique for every small project or email that crosses the leader's desk (even if it's about an insubstantial detail) may signal to someone that their work will never be good enough. A perfectionistic leader's goal for incessant improvement, if overdone, can quickly morph a company's collaborative culture into one of fear.

Add all these pieces together, and it's not hard to conclude that perfectionism is harmful to companies as a whole, affecting everything from work quality and employee morale, to peer relationships and overall organizational health. And on an individual level, it's not at all good for our careers, connections, or health.

✦ THE PORTAL

The year 2020 inspired self-reflection in more ways than one, including scrutiny of things we'd once considered normal. Perfection as a concept did not stand up to that scrutiny. As Katherine said when we asked her how 2020 affected her idea of perfectionism, "Ha! Made me come to terms with it. As in, it obliterated that cute notion of mine."

To be clear, 2020 didn't obliterate perfectionism as a workplace tendency. Arguably, in some cases, it exacerbated it. People who were worried about losing their jobs started putting in more hours and performing at higher levels than pre-pandemic (despite the drain on themselves) to try and carve out some sense of job security or regain a sense of control.

For other people, there was simply no way to keep up with perfectionist tendencies. With kids' schooling now taking place through a computer screen in the family living room, routines in flux, schedules totally rearranged, and the very real threat of illness or death (and, for too many of us, all while bearing the heavy burden of grief), it became impossible to continue living up to expectations that were unrealistic even before the pandemic years took hold.

For yet others, these years inspired a serious existential crisis, one that made them question all sorts of things: the need to be everything to everyone, the desire to perform at excruciatingly high levels, and the actual value in engaging in these perfectionist tendencies.

On the other hand, organizations—many of which were used to measured, slow change—were forced to move quickly to stay afloat. Changes that would typically require years of planning and loads of buy-in were fast-tracked in a "done is better than perfect" kind of way.

Take these for example:

- **Pre-Portal**: We can never work remotely. It just won't succeed in our organization!

    Portal: It's either shut down the business or figure this out. So we're going to figure it out.

    Portal, Two Months Later: Wow. this actually turned out okay.

- **Pre-Portal**: Flexible schedules don't make sense for us. We need synchronous work.

    Portal: You know what? Flexible schedules aren't so bad!

- **Pre-Portal**: All conferences must be in person. That's the whole point!

    Portal: Huh, virtual and hybrid conferences can be just as engaging if done right.

- **Pre-Portal**: We need in-person meetings to do our best creative work.

    Portal: Actually, we can develop and deliver great ideas and pitches via Zoom.

- **Pre-Portal**: Stress management is something people need to take care of on their own.

> **Portal**: Quick! Find tips, webinars, or tricks to help our people. Their mental well-being is at stake!

The biggest takeaway from the pandemic years, from a perfectionism standpoint, is that life does go on even when things fall short of perfect. And sometimes—maybe even oftentimes—aiming for perfect is a big waste of time, energy, and emotional reserves. Rather than trying to be the best colleague, leader, or company, perhaps the aim should be for momentum, moving toward goals, enjoying the process, and understanding that perfection is not only impossible but—in many instances—a colossal waste of time and effort.

✦ NOW WHAT?

We understand how damaging perfectionism can be. We've lived it. We continue to work through it. Heck, we felt it while writing this book, including this chapter. It can feel like a negligible little thing, a pebble in the shoe toward building an awesome workplace culture. But if anyone tries walking ten miles with a pebble in their shoe, it starts to feel like a dagger—and at some point, it becomes intolerable.

As always, any actionable change needs to start with awareness followed by embracing key mindset shifts. Here are some shifts to consider when transitioning from a "perfect" mindset to a "progress" mindset.

ADOPT ANTI-PERFECTIONIST MINDSET SHIFTS

If you are a perfectionist, try shifting your thoughts to transform how you go about your day:

- ✦ I'm my biggest critic. → I'm my loudest cheerleader!
- ✦ My job defines my worth. → My job is only one part of me. It doesn't define my value.

- Aim for perfection. → Aim for good enough.
- Lead with a fixed mindset. → Lead with a growth mindset.

To be clear, we're not saying that striving for excellence is a bad thing. Ambition and a drive to perform well are great qualities in people and in organizations. But when that drive is all-consuming and begins to negatively affect other areas of your life (and your colleagues' lives), then it's no longer an asset. Focusing on progress toward excellence can help shift this into a more positive approach.

PERFECTIONISM	PROGRESS TOWARD EXCELLENCE
Experiences a paralyzing fear of failure	Views failure as a growth opportunity
Engages in constant self-criticism	Engages in relentless grace
Is risk-averse	Is risk-tolerant
Has desire to win at all costs	Views progress as a win
Believes that results are most important	Believes that process is most important

SHUT DOWN PEER-FECTIONISM

Peer-fectionism (a term we coined thanks to a happy typo accident—see how wonderful mistakes can be!?) captures the feeling when co-workers pressure their peers either intentionally or unintentionally, overtly or covertly, into fulfilling unhealthy standards of perfectionism at work. Of course, there's nothing wrong with having high standards and pushing peers to excel and grow. But when the weight of those expectations is crushing—and when falling short of those expectations leads to disappointment, resentment, and even gossip and side talk from others—then it's no longer healthy.

Leaders and individual contributors alike can put a stop to peer-fectionism by examining perfectionistic tendencies in and of themselves, working to diminish how those tendencies show up at work, and embracing the concepts laid out in the rest of this chapter. To give these

---

CALLOUT: A Space for Grace

The Deviously Pervasive Imposter Syndrome

There is an imposter among us! And it's you. It's always you. Or so people think. Like perfectionism and comparisonitis, imposter syndrome and perfectionism are part of the wretched "drain your self-esteem down to nothing" club. And it's a club with esteemed (and probably unexpected) members: Michelle Obama, Penelope Cruz, Tom Hanks, and Lady Gaga, to name a few. The quest to be perfect often means worrying that you're never quite good enough, which can make you feel like you're one big phony, a big ol' fake. It makes you work even harder to achieve the highest possible level of expertise, knowledge, and skillset so that you can *finally* not feel like an imposter.

Spoiler: If this is you, you will never get there. And we don't mean that in a bad way. We mean that in a great way. Free yourself from this debilitating syndrome so that you can recognize your highly capable self now and share your skills with those who need them.

peer-fectionsim deflection strategies a fighting chance, organizations that encourage peer comparisons have an obligation to ensure they don't promote impossible standards that encourage toxic competitiveness within company walls.

DEFINE WHAT SUCCESS LOOKS LIKE FOR YOU

It's all too easy to move through life in default mode. We tend to tread in the steps that came before us, because why not? It's logical, it's obvious, and—in many ways—it's more effortless to follow what's been done before than to forge a new path. Lisa originally thought she wanted to join a huge organization, prove her mettle, climb the corporate ladder, and really crush it in the professional world. Just like she'd seen her dad do. Just like she'd seen her friends and relatives do. She burned herself out trying to achieve this goal, though; and in the ashes of exhaustion, she realized that she was chasing the wrong dream—the dream she thought she wanted, not the one she actually wanted.

Perfectionism is a state of being that the average American worker can take on in pursuit of dreams of success that may or may not be authentic to who they are and what they really want. If you're prone to the perfectionist mindset, it may be worthwhile to look beyond the how of your workflow (perfectionism) to the why (what you're chasing, or your metric for success) and release yourself from the "tyranny of the should."[10]

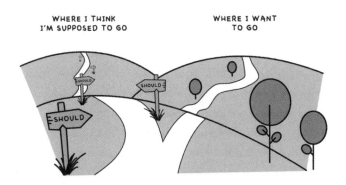

Here are questions for a recovering perfectionist to ask themself:

- How do I define success?
- Is this a success metric I've created for myself?
- Why is it so important to me to achieve this?
- How does this align with my values?
- Am I comfortable spending one-third of my life in pursuit of this goal?
- What other goals or dreams am I leaving behind in favor of this one?

GET COMFY WITH BEING A BIT UNCOMFY

Perfectionism is the pursuit of greatness, but also the pursuit of comfort. It's a perceived safeguard against failure. If you're a perfectionist, you may think that by aiming for perfection, you can steer clear of the shame and embarrassment of failing. You'll hew close to your cozy comfort zone and hesitate to stray too far from it, because it means you might do something poorly and draw criticism from others. People live out entire lives like this, playing it safe, doing what's comfortable for fear of stepping out and messing up.

One of our friends, imposter syndrome coach Heather Whelpley, shared a wise insight she'd unearthed in her work with clients. She told us, "People will often choose unhappiness over discomfort." That was a mind-blowing, "oh my gosh the truth can feel uncomfy" moment for both of us. Because being stuck in an often destructive loop of perfectionism means far more unhappiness in the long run than learning to veer and venture away from what's familiar. Getting comfortable with going out of one's comfort zone, that safe bubble of what is known and predictable, can be a game changer when it comes to leveling up careers and leaning into personal growth. As our former boss Debra would say, "You'll have far more regrets about what you didn't do than what you did." (How lucky are we to have these wise people in our circle?)

If reading this feels like a harsh spotlight on your existence, try breaking the perfectionism cycle in microways. Attend a class where you know you'll make mistakes or feel a tad foolish. Hannah's currently working on making it to a salsa lesson, something she's been avoiding for fear of failing. Try something new just to do it, not to improve yourself, be more productive, or be really good at it. Notice how trying something new and being really bad at it can make you feel. What thoughts race through your head? Small doses of discomfort can eventually turn into a healthy life of embracing potential failures.

LEARN TO GET HYPED ABOUT FAILURE (NO, REALLY)

Failure, like feelings (especially in a work context), is another one of those f-words that gives people the heebie-jeebies. But it doesn't have to. Consider how A. P. J. Abdul Kalam, the late president of India, defines failure as a "first attempt in learning." While it's easy to give in to the urge to run from your fears—ahem, potential to fail—learning to stay the course despite that potential failure is integral to individual and company growth. They're called growing pains for a reason. Growth hurts. Failure hurts. When people can acknowledge it simply as a part of the process, as a data point, they turn the volume down on feelings of shame or embarrassment and turn up the gratitude.

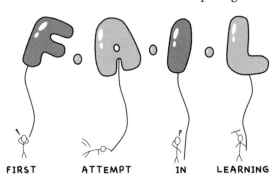

CELEBRATE AND ACKNOWLEDGE THE PROCESS, NOT JUST THE RESULTS

For those of us who've heard the idea of a "results-oriented" workplace praised over and over again, this might feel a bit surprising. Because at this point, most people are familiar with ROWE (Results Only Work Environment)—if not by name, then by practice. With the shift to virtual work, the core tenets of ROWE (namely measuring employees by the work they produce, not the hours they're putting in) have helped forward-thinking employers release the micromanaging vice-like grip on their employees, letting them achieve results via whatever path makes sense for each one.

The danger is, with the shift to remote and hybrid-heavy work environments, there can be a pull toward transactional work and placing an oversized emphasis on results. While there are tons of pros to result-oriented environments, there's one pretty big con that needs to be addressed: It can mean that we overemphasize the importance of results and demote the value of effort and process. Which, unsurprisingly, can lead to a culture that (intentionally or unintentionally) encourages perfectionistic tendencies.

Leaders and colleagues alike must not only pay attention to *what* is produced, but also give weight (and praise, when praise is due) to the *how*. If someone has laid out a thoughtful system but the initial result was subpar, a thoughtful leader will recognize that attempt and help with system revisions so that the next try is more successful. It's equally important to acknowledge effort, because behaviors that are praised will be repeated. If leaders only recognize the wins and not the good attempts at a win, then employees will eventually feel less comfortable drawing outside the lines. They'll stick to what's safe—to a fault.

Oh, and one final note, in case you're thinking, *Classic Millennials. Here they are, saying we should all be handing out participation trophies.* Psychologists suggest that participation trophies at certain ages can be excellent at encouraging collaboration and teamwork, as well as promoting the value of helping others and the importance of process and growth over singular "winning or achievement."[11] (Also, can we point out that we weren't giving those participation trophies to ourselves? Food for thought.)

CALLOUT: THE REAL WORLD – A CASE STUDY

Failure Cards

Tim, a speaking client of ours and the director of a large school system in the northeastern US, has implemented a brilliant way of encouraging failure. At the beginning of each semester, he hands out a failure card to each of the school's teachers and tells them, "I want you to hand this in to me when you fail at some point this semester. And if I don't get this back, that means you're doing something wrong." On the back of those failure cards are a few simple prompts: *1.) How I failed 2.) Why I think it failed 3.) What I learned from this failure.*

To be clear, Tim isn't giving his colleagues permission to fail in some catastrophic way that will harm the school or students permanently. He is, however, giving them the freedom to try things out. Beyond that, he is actively asking them to take calculated risks that might lead to failure sometimes but could also become innovations.

EMBRACE IMPERFECT LEADERSHIP

There is no such thing as a perfect leader, no matter how polished, knowledgeable, or capable one may be. Plus, trying to appear as if you are will earn you negative numbers on the "Is this actually helpful?" scale of leadership qualities. A study of over 300 global executives found that about 35 percent of execs fail "because of a tendency toward perfection."[12] While the idea of perfect leadership might seem good in theory (who doesn't want a high-achieving leader who models excellence for others?), in practice those leaders not only set the stage for a culture of peer-fectionism but can actually end up shutting their people down.

So, to the perfection-leaning leaders out there:

- **STOP** responding defensively when someone pushes back on one of your ideas or critiques how the business or organization is run.

    START freely admitting you're not always right, and openly solicit feedback from contributors at all levels of the organization. (Also, don't always demand the perfect amount of proof on the spot. Let people ideate.)

- **STOP** giving employees secret tests in the form of off-the-cuff questions to see if they get the "right" or "perfect" answer (i.e., your answer).

    START inviting them to speak up (to you, their colleagues, or in meetings) when they have questions or need help.

- **STOP** casually sprinkling employees with your harsh criticism, even if at times it may be valid.

    START leaning into (authentic) praise and offering criticism only in a safe way—and only when it's truly necessary.

✦ **STOP** being overly tough on yourself and your performance, including using self-disparaging talk in front of others.

START being kind about your failures in addition to those of your reports and framing failure as a learning opportunity.

PRACTICE RELENTLESS SELF-COMPASSION

This right here is one of the most important concepts when it comes to overcoming perfectionistic tendencies and quieting the inner saboteur. And yet it's one of the hardest things to put into practice. It takes work to switch our inner narrative from mean girl/boy/person, an inner troll berating us at every turn, to a more Mr. Rogers-esque vibe, speaking in soft, dulcet tones and encouraging us as effusively when we rise as when we fall. But it is *the* work. The hard but necessary work. Self-compassion begets compassion for others begets a culture where compassion is the norm, and perfectionism has no home in a culture of compassion.

If you find yourself doling out self-blame and criticism instead of compassion, one simple trick is to ask yourself, "Would I talk to my friend this way if they were in a similar situation?" The answer will almost always be an aghast, "I WOULD NEVER!" If you wouldn't treat your friend that way, then don't treat yourself that way. The philosopher Marcus Aurelius sagely said, "What you throw on top of the fire is fuel for the fire." Fuel yourself with compassion and grace, not self-flagellation and frustration.

Now, what would a perfectionist do upon finishing this chapter? Probably what Lisa did (at first): Think that she could embrace and implement all of these concepts from one day to the next, then rain down a storm of negativity on herself for failing to meet that impossible goal. Don't do this! Know that when we say "recovering perfectionists," we mean it. For individuals, it's not going to happen overnight. It will instead be an extended practice of learning how to sit in the discomfort of imperfection. The same is true on a much larger scale when talking about shifting an organization's culture. Embrace the process, practice that grace, and focus on small, implementable chunks of changed behaviors and mindsets. And if you can, always, always, *always* uphold progress over perfection.

─────────── ✦ **THE GIST** ✦ ───────────

PRE-PORTAL STANDARD

Perfectionism has been a barrier to great work for too long, contributing to a fear-based culture that leads to overwork, unrealistic expectations, and burnout. Long upheld as a desirable standard, perfectionism actually doesn't make anyone a better employee or teammate, it limits creativity, and it can lead to behaviors like shaming and micromanaging.

PORTAL LESSONS

The pandemic showed us that life keeps on trucking even when we fall short of being perfect, and that perhaps instead of aiming for that impossible standard of perfection, we should embrace progress (not perfection) as our goal.

NOW WHAT? STEPPING THROUGH THE PORTAL

Adopt these perfectionism mindset shifts:

- ✦ Shut down perfectionism's evil siblings, peer-fectionism and comparisonitis.
- ✦ Define your personal vision of success.
- ✦ Get comfy with being uncomfy.
- ✦ Learn to get hyped about failure.
- ✦ Embrace imperfect leadership.
- ✦ Practice relentless self-compassion.

CHAPTER 3

The Power of Empathetic Communication

✦ *Great communication is not innate or effortless. It's a skill that requires thoughtfulness, intentionality, and a willingness to flex our empathy muscles.*

Communication is foundational to the success of any business. And yet it's such a deeply ingrained part of daily life that it's easy to take for granted. Many of us feel we can communicate almost by instinct, without needing to pause and consider whether our communication is actually effective. In fact, we'd hazard a guess that most people don't often (if ever) pause to think about how they're communicating, take stock of their effectiveness in connecting with other humans (both at work and at home), or make an effort to develop skills that might be lacking.

This means that this critical part of how we all navigate the world, a key piece to how we innovate and exchange ideas and one of the—if not *the*—most important ways to maintain a thriving, successful business, goes unattended to with unnerving frequency. We operate with basic comprehension instead of real connection and understanding, and then we are surprised when clashes and miscommunications at work are rife.

Moments of miscommunication can range from the snort- or laugh-inducing (like the autocorrect mishaps that make us say, "Oh duck!") to the annoying (like when people fail to answer all the questions in a painstakingly constructed email), to the harmful (when feedback is taken as a personal affront instead of a take on performance). Left unchecked, poor communication means that many, many people are collectively working very, very hard to achieve an unclear goal. It also means that day-to-day work lives are filled with frustrating encounters and missed opportunities for connection.

As humans, one of our greatest drivers is the desire to be understood by our fellow humans. The main way we accomplish this is through communication. Nonverbals, conversational skills, how we write, even how we text and the emojis or GIFs we choose to send—they're all part of expressing ourselves and trying to understand others' perspectives.

Good communication is more than moving projects along or improving productivity. It's about building community, aligning around a core set of goals and values, learning about and from one another, and creating a work environment where the points of connection outweigh the frustrating moments of disconnect. Building up communication acumen, from the starting point of thoughtfulness and empathy, can be . . . well, transformative. Without it, we'd argue that attempts at creating a truly exceptional workplace will be incomplete at best.

✦ PRE-PORTAL

One of our favorite nuggets of wisdom comes from playwright George Bernard Shaw. He once wrote, "The single biggest problem in communication is the illusion that it has taken place." At work, this illusion runs rampant. As soon as words have left our mouths or we've hit the Send button on an email, it's like we mentally check off that microcommunication task as completed, without giving it a second thought. It's assumed that others will know what we mean. Then we likely physically check off that email on our to-do list and feel an oh-so-wonderful boost of dopamine that motivates us to take on the next task.[1]

Psychologists call this phenomenon "signal amplification bias." Fancy phrase, but all it means is that while people are generally super confident that they've supplied enough information and communicated effectively, in reality the receivers of said information are often left trying to fill the gaps. This overconfidence in communication skills is really common; and to some degree, it makes sense. When we craft a message, we do so using our own lens and experience. Individual preferences—from the level of formality and the tone of messaging, to the platform or tool of choice—all define a person's distinct communication style. When we default to our own style, it can make it hard to see that others might not be picking up what we're putting down.

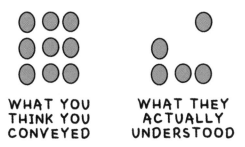

A classic example we share with our audiences is one form of punctuation: the ellipsis. Take this email that a friend of Hannah's actually called her about in a panic:

Hi Reece,

Good job today, we'll talk more about the meeting next week . . .

Thanks.

T

To Reece, the ellipsis meant that she was in trouble or getting fired. Our audience members usually quickly point out, "What?! No, it just means 'to be continued.'" And then someone else chimes in, "But an ellipsis almost always means something ominous is being left unsaid!"

Here's the takeaway: Micromoments of communication we think are clear likely aren't to someone else. (Reece got a promotion the following week, in case you're curious.)

The paradox of choice adds an extra challenge to the mix. There is an ever-evolving, ever-growing list of communication tools and platforms to choose from. As a society, we went from using actual carbon copies for sending memos, to cc-ing people in emails and tagging in instant messaging platforms. And now, some of the newer generation in the workplace are even using social media to communicate about work tasks. (One client, Tara, told us—with an understandable dash of frustration—that Snapchat is her direct report's platform of choice.)

Daily interpersonal communication challenges aside, managers, leaders, and organizations as a whole face even more pressure to ensure their communication is on point. Managers have to walk the fine line of delivering feedback constructively, in a way that inspires but doesn't shut down. CEOs and leaders are expected to cast visions of the future while being transparent and realistic about what's happening in the present. Organizations have to do their best to maintain a united workforce amid constant change and upheaval.

No matter how hard we all try, we're bound to experience at least one of these communication woes:

- Feeling our voice isn't heard—or maybe not until someone else says the same thing in a slightly different way (aka idea theft)

- A perceived lack of transparency (cue the "Am I going to get fired?" or "Are they going to quit?" panic)

- Careless written communication habits (my name Katherine is in my signature and sign-off, so why did they call me Katie?)

- Relevant people, including you, being left out of the loop

- Difficulty locating important resources within shared files (seriously, why does it take fifteen minutes to find one spreadsheet?!)

- Frustration over ego-driven communication styles (the thesaurus skills doth not crystallize the composition, but rather perpetuate estrangement)

- Lack of communication etiquette, especially with regards to younger employees (text norms don't always equal email norms)

- Inconsistent messaging from leadership and managers (sometimes it feels like they're all saying something different even though they walked out of the same meeting)

- Infrequent or ineffective feedback (how do we know how to fix something if we aren't yet aware of what needs fixing?)

- Meeting overload (couldn't this meeting have been an email?)

Communication, it turns out, is not as simple as we might think. And poor communication comes with a hefty price tag. Yes, actual dollars. One study cited the collective annual cost of poor communication as being around $37 billion.[2] Another estimated an annual $62.4 million loss for companies with over 100,000 employees and $420,000 for companies with less than 100.[3] Yet another suggests the cost incurred may be up to $26,000 per employee each year.[4] These costs manifest in various ways, depending on the company. Rebecca, a project manager, told us about days so full of unproductive meetings that she didn't have time to actually deliver projects. She spoke about projects that were forced to go back to the starting point because the right person's feedback wasn't solicited early enough, wasting thousands of dollars and tons of employee time. Ask any leader or project manager about how poor communication impacts the company's bottom line, and you'll likely be flooded with example after example.

Besides the dollars at stake, it's also necessary to note the interpersonal toll that miscommunication can take on us: increased levels of stress, low overall morale and happiness, missed opportunities for promotion, frayed team dynamics. . . . For so many reasons, bad communication is no good.

✦ THE PORTAL

During the pandemic years, any gaps in communication skill sets, both individually and organizationally, became impossible to ignore. Because with the pandemic years, change—fast and furious—was pushed on all of us, whether we liked it or not.

Almost overnight, work became a Zoom (or Teams, or one of the other many video platforms) world. Communication shifted from in-person to behind-screen. For many of us, meetings now happened via video. One-on-one with a manager? Time to set up a Zoom. Quick project check-in? Video. All-hands meetings? Yep, switch on that camera.

Enter Zoom fatigue! The need for thoughtful consideration around the communication platform of choice became startlingly clear.

Even those who weren't working from home had to learn to navigate the unfamiliar. Previously open, buzzing spaces became closed-door, socially distanced environments. Masks and staying six feet away from each other made reading nonverbal cues super hard. (*Is that person angry at me? Are they smiling? Are they not? What does that expression mean? Gah!!*) And even if one office or company kept its doors open for whatever reason (e.g., industries like health care and manufacturing), at least a segment of their staff, along with clients or customers, still found themselves trying to figure out the new world of virtual communication.

With this sudden shift to virtual, some of the elements that had previously made workplace communication better and easier (even if it might not have been noted at the time) disappeared. There were no more "popping by someone's office" or casual, impromptu encounters. Unreliable home Wi-Fi went from being annoying to an almost unbearable barrier to getting work done. We both had a time or two when, mid-call with a client, one of our cats (we own four between us!) loudly sang the song of their people in a bid to be fed (again). Embarrassing? Absolutely. But also entirely relatable.

All of these challenges are before we even add emotions to the mix. Fear was one that reigned supreme. Uncertainty, anxiety, grief, depression, loneliness, exhaustion, boredom, and ennui also made for a terrible soup of fraught feelings that certainly did not establish a solid baseline for strong communication.

Employees who went without consistent, regularly scheduled messaging from leadership were left to make up stories in all the blank space. And human minds don't tend to fill that space with good news. As a survival mechanism, we expect the worst to protect ourselves from the worst. ("The company is going under!" "I'm going to be fired or

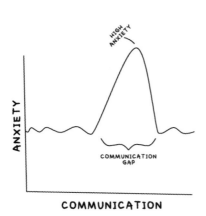

furloughed!" "They're going to dock our pay!") The employees we spoke to said that when there was a gap in communication, lag time between emails from leadership, or any other unexpected break in messaging, anxiety would spike and they would jump to the most dire conclusions.

To be fair, maintaining regular messaging mid-pandemic was understandably challenging. All the uncertainty and unprecedented circumstances meant that leadership simply didn't have answers. In the scramble to keep things moving, some less-than-successful tactics we saw included delaying communication, making up plausible excuses, forecasting at a time when no one could properly forecast, and sometimes opting out of communicating altogether.

Take the health care company we worked with, for example. Its leadership caused an uproar when they sent an all-staff email in early 2021 reporting a potential return to the office for June of that year. But leaders didn't anticipate the extent of their misstep. They knew how the first year of the pandemic had fueled anxiety on the team, so they wanted to give people a guide post. It felt responsible—and even considerate—to let them know what they were thinking far in advance. Alas, they failed to communicate what people actually needed: clarity, details, and reasoning.

Since there were no criteria for the back-to-office guesstimate other than "oh, it's what we should do!", it felt like they let the (what came across as an arbitrary) date drive the plan more than team safety. So the leaders' email came across as an extraordinarily cavalier move that didn't fully consider the impact on the lives of employees as well as a poor attempt at forecasting what couldn't be forecasted. It created confusion and fear and left people questioning whether the leaders cared more about seeing people at work doing work than their health and safety. And, to be fair, the team—stressed and anxious as they were—saw only what leaders did wrong instead of trying to understand the work behind the messaging. This tension between what employees needed and how leaders attempted to manage (or sometimes disregard) those needs was, and still is, a major communication hurdle.

Communication during crisis management is a whole topic unto itself. But missteps in how the pandemic was handled within companies, and examples of leaders who handled it well, reveal some basic tenets of effective, impactful communication, whether you're in the midst of a (hopefully) once-in-a-lifetime global pandemic or not. At the heart of it all is a keen awareness of others (listening), individualizing the approach when possible (the Platinum Rule), and remaining ever-mindful of how your message is being received (empathic communication).

✦ NOW WHAT?

Communication—as a theme, a concept, a skill—is not a to-do that can just be crossed off a list. Language is an ever-evolving thing, as are the ways that people interact with each other. The next generations will continue to enter the workforce, tools will be introduced that shift how we conduct our work, and new societal expectations will urge us to reconsider and revise outdated norms. We encourage people to think about communication as a practice that evolves and improves as the world changes. It's a gift when you think about it; as the world evolves, so do we.

And here's a pro tip: As communication norms evolve, try to see the humor in them. The laughing-crying emoji was the word of the year in 2015. This baffled our audiences then. Now, Gen Z mocks us Millennials for using it. The more accepted emoji for laughter (by the youths anyway) is now the skull, as in "I laughed so hard I'm dead." Five years from now (or—let's be real—by the time this book goes to print), it'll be something different again. Better to roll with the changes than try to fight them.

There are, however, some foundations that inform strong, effective communication in the here and now that will likely serve us well into the future, no matter how innovative or unexpected our new methods of communication may become.

THE INDIVIDUAL (COMMUNICATION 101: THE BASICS)

No one can have an "awesome" environment, relationship, or anything at work without going back to the basics. In our experience, the following three techniques represent the most impactful ways an individual can strengthen their communication game from the bottom up.

ACTIVE LISTENING

Listening—truly listening—is the first step in leveling up communication. This is one of those things that might feel obvious but is often overlooked. At work, we are often focused on ourselves and how we can best relay our messages clearly. And we think faster than people speak, so it actually takes effort to really listen (and not just to pretend to listen by smiling and nodding). But to meaningfully connect and build a culture of fluid, multidirectional communication, we need to upskill how we receive and interpret messages from others.

Active listening is a skill that takes away the passivity (the second-class status, if you will) of listening. When we actively listen, we turn it into an activity that requires effort and action. We show up not for ourselves and our objectives, but for the other person. To actively listen, you need to consider how you show up before, during, and after the message is communicated.

THE POWER OF EMPATHETIC COMMUNICATION

Before: Leave Judgment at the Door

Don't arrive at the conversation expecting anything in advance. Try to quiet your own biases. Show up with the mindset of someone who has come to learn. Lead with curiosity, which means suspending any expectation and participating in the conversation in as judgment-free a way as possible.

During: Listen to Understand, Not to Respond

Put aside the thoughts that can creep into your mind when you're listening to someone else, like "What am I having for lunch today?" or "Actually, I disagree with what you're saying, and here are all the reasons why." While the other person speaks, try to focus all your attention on them and not your own musings or reactions. Pay attention to body language and cues to stay grounded in the moment. Focus on taking in the message they're trying to relay with as much accuracy as possible. If you catch yourself listening to your mind more than to the person in front of you, take a deep breath and relax your gaze

on them to get into your body and back to the moment. Don't worry about your response or gathering your thoughts into a cohesive reply. Your primary goal at this stage is comprehension and understanding, not thinking about how you're going to respond.

After: Slow It Down

When it's your turn to respond, don't jump right into it. Before you speak, take a pause. Even just a breath or a beat of silence, especially if the person who's speaking has been delivering a longer or more

---

CALLOUT: For Your Consideration

Active Listening, Digital Style

Active listening is not just for when we meet in person or have a real-time conversation. It applies to digital, delayed communication as well. And oh, if we applied active listening to email encounters, how much better our work could be!

Have you ever labored over an email, formatting it, proofing it, bulleting your request, being super intentional to ensure it's clear and concise, only to receive a message that reads only "Yes" or maybe answers one of the four questions you asked? Or perhaps even answers a question that you didn't ask? When we are on the go and aren't taking time to read messages from an active listening standpoint, digital communication gets super frustrating, super fast. As you read a digital message, make sure you're reading it to understand the writer's point of view. Too many people scan these messages to find their to-do and not to understand the message that the writer intended. This is a recipe for confused, frustrating messaging and more back-and-forths than are necessary.

serious message. With that pause, consider whether you truly understood what the other person was trying to convey. If you need to, ask open-ended questions that will help you come to a better understanding. To be doubly (or triply) sure of what the other person intended, follow up with "What I heard you say is..." to confirm that you've received their message accurately. A good mindset to employ is to think about responding, not reacting. To respond appropriately, you first need to understand. Reactions are impulsive and based on gut feelings or hot takes. Responses are measured, thoughtful, and considered. Be a responder, not a reactor.

THE PLATINUM RULE

Another simple but mind-bogglingly effective skill in communication is to operate by the Platinum Rule. Most of us are familiar with the Golden Rule, which asks us to "treat others the way you wish to be treated." We learned it as wee five-year-olds from our kindergarten teachers or our parents as a valuable nugget of wisdom. This rule of communication is great in theory, but in practice it's not as successful as one would hope. Because the world is not populated by clones of the same individual. It's made up of all sorts of diverse folks with varied preferences. For example, Hannah loves voicemails. For her, it's an easy way to learn what someone may need from her without requiring scanning a long text or email. Lisa, on the other hand, hasn't checked her voicemail inbox since maybe 2010. It's a wasteland of unlistened-to messages. Maybe it's her introvert acting up in a weird way? Or, more likely, it's a sign of her preference for written communication over audio.

These differences in communication style are where the Platinum Rule can be used to great effect. **The Platinum Rule asks us to treat others how *they* wish to be treated.** It's a rule that comes in handy in all areas of life and work, and we find it extremely useful in improving communication within organizations. Like with active listening,

THE FUTURE OF WORK IS HUMAN

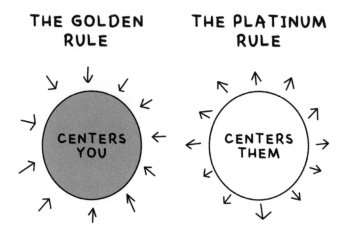

the Platinum Rule shifts the focus off oneself and onto the person who's being communicated with. To be clear, the Platinum Rule is not about bending over backward to accommodate other people's preferences. It doesn't mean turning into someone we're not to cater to the needs of everyone else. It is about flexing, moving the needle slightly to heighten the odds of getting our intended message heard.

How do we make the most of the Platinum Rule at work?

Learn About Generational Preferences

Our background is in generational studies, so we've seen the power of looking at the why behind generational identities when communicating with others at work. Where an ellipsis for a Gen Xer might signal "more info to come," for a Gen Zer (like Reece in our earlier story) it can feel more like a harbinger of doom. Sending a Slack or IM to a colleague while you're in the office together could read as a sign of disrespect to a Baby Boomer (*Why didn't he just come tell me this to my face?*), while for the Millennial it was just a convenient way to send a nonurgent message without interrupting the Boomer's workflow. This is a good time for another reminder that communication style is not singularly defined by your generation—not by any stretch of the imagination. BUT! When used as an extra layer of insight, an awareness of each generation's communication style and habits can be super helpful toward landing your message with them (and having them better understand you).

As a brief, tip-of-the-iceberg primer in that effort, we've found that, at work, generations prefer their communication in this way:

- Baby Boomers: Relational and polished
- Gen Xers: Transparent and backed up by proof
- Millennials: Informal and open to input
- Gen Zers: Specific and frequent

Take the Time to Uncover Communication Preferences

Learning about each generation's preferences is helpful. But as we said earlier, it's not the be-all and end-all. No generation is a monolith, and there are always outliers to that conversation. Not to mention that there are all sorts of ways that people like to communicate. Some, like Lisa, are highly introverted, whereas others are more toward the extroverted side of the scale. Some think off-the-cuff and like to jump right in at meetings. Others are more deliberative and prefer to slow down and write out their responses. Many organizations don't take the time to ask about these preferences, let alone make accommodations for them. Most employees don't get this granular about how their colleagues prefer to interact at work. The communication matrix in chapter 5 is a simple, straightforward tool that gets right to this point. Each organization may have slightly different prompts, but to get you started, here are some great questions to ask:

✦ Which communication platform do you prefer for day-to-day questions?

✦ What times are best for contacting you? (This question is especially valuable when working in a hybrid environment and/or asynchronous work schedule.)

✦ How do you like to receive instructions for a project or initiative?

✦ Do you have any communication pet peeves?

✦ How do you like to receive feedback?

✦ How often do you prefer to receive feedback?

PRACTICE EMPATHIC COMMUNICATION

Active listening and the Platinum Rule are the first steps toward practicing empathetic communication. They provide the groundwork for us to communicate in a truly empathic way. When empathetic communication becomes the default mode, connection and clarity become the norm. Here's how to bring all the pieces together and put empathetic communication into practice.

Be Mindful of the Impact of Your Words

It's not enough to know you meant well or didn't intend for that email to come off as passive-aggressive or rude. If it was interpreted that way, your intention doesn't really matter. The damage is done. Where possible, emotion-proof your words and be thoughtful about the tone of your message. There will be times when your intended message and the actual content of said message will be at odds. Whether you're communicating audibly or via email or text, consider your messages with an eye for how other people may interpret them. Proof it from the receiver's point of view not just to see if

CALLOUT: For Your Consideration

Using the Platinum Rule to Support Diversity, Equity, and Inclusion (DEI)

Using the Platinum Rule allows us to replace assumptions that people will like what we like, communicate how we'd want, and act as we act with true understanding. This streamlines communication but also leaves space for diversity of people and preferences at work. For example, maybe Robert actively hates being called Bob at work. In another vein, maybe a new colleague isn't comfortable talking about their personal relationships at work. Or maybe a coworker who has recently come out as nonbinary is too shy or nervous to speak up when they are misgendered. The examples are vast and vary in intensity and potential to harm the individual. Being tuned into operating by the Platinum Rule—through active listening, curiosity, and remembering the world is not made up of carbon copies of ourselves—primes us to pick up on these important differences so that we can be truly considerate and respectful of how *others* want to be treated. It reminds us that we need to sensitively solicit opinions and preferences from our teammates, especially if they come from a different background than us. That is forever our goal in operating by the Platinum Rule at work (and in life).

---

you understand, but also to estimate if the receiver will. This includes scanning for clarity and tone to ensure that the impact of your message matches the intent, and making sure you've provided all the necessary context to fully understand the point you're trying to convey.

And even after all of that proofing, there's a chance your messaging will still be misinterpreted. In fact, chances are high that this will happen. You can only do the best that you can. When a message of yours is inevitably misinterpreted, go back to active listening and work to forge a more informed communication path forward.

Let's look at an example: You're the leader of a small organization that pitches directly to clients, and these pitches take *so much* work—hours spent collaborating, creating a pitch deck, revising said deck, practicing who says what when . . . you get the idea. You almost never went along on pitches because you trust your team. But when your team is pitching a client you have a personal connection with, you tag along. This pitch was led by the newest member of the team. Your well-intentioned feedback was, "That was the best pitch I have ever seen!" Experienced, senior staff (who just trained said new person) felt that their contributions didn't matter; they'd never received singular, direct praise from the CEO. Though well-intentioned, your praise actually led to some resentment and confusion.

Picture this instead: You return to your office and say something like this to the group, "That was so good! It's so clear how powerful this team is and how great you all are at what you do. While Stacy is the newest team member here, it's like she's been here for years."

Don't Jump to Giving Solutions

When you're communicating in a way that's focused on yourself versus focused on others, it's natural to jump to solution-giving. As we've already discussed, Lisa held deep pride in being a "problem solver" until she realized that people don't always need to be offered a solution. In fact, solution-finding often makes the solution-giver feel better than the solution-receiver. Sometimes people just need to vent or work through a problem out loud. Before trying to turn into the fixer-upper (and thereby take yourself out of feeling discomfort at their discomfort), ask what this person needs from you.

Understanding what they need is key to showing up as an empathic communicator. Otherwise, you're just jumping to solutions.

Be Watchful for Those Whose Voices Aren't Being Heard

As an empathetic communicator, you want to be sure that everyone's voice is considered. And while this role is often ascribed to leaders, all levels of employees can actively participate in making communication more equitable for everyone, including those who are more introverted, whose voices—like women and Black employees—are frequently talked over, or whose ideas are co-opted by other, louder voices. When you see someone forcefully truck over a colleague who is more deliberative, you can jump in and say, "Hey, I don't think Sameera was quite done with her point. What were you saying, Sameera?" You can also practice amplification; in other words, if someone isn't being properly credited for their idea, you repeat it and cite them. This may sound something like, "I think that you captured Nicole's point really well, and I'm glad you agree that it's a great revision of our onboarding process."

Be Clear and Kind

Empathetic communication doesn't mean "being nice." When we try to be nice at work, it can lead us to gloss over or totally ignore hard and necessary conversations. Difficult feedback is shoved under the rug; and rather than saying what we mean, we'll say what we think the other person wants to hear. This might be nice, but it's not kind—and it corrodes psychological safety and team trust.

To truly be kind, you have to be clear about what you're thinking or feeling. This means, to use a phrase and practice coined by Kim Scott, being radically candid.[5] People can't guess what's going on in your head. If you're struggling at work, you need to let someone know. If a colleague has said something hurtful, you need to tell them.

Transparent, open, frequent communication—especially about the hard stuff—is a nonnegotiable for any healthy work environment. And it's not self-serving to be radically candid, but rather extremely empathic and important for other individuals and the team at large. We love the mindset we mentioned earlier of "being direct with heart." While the following acronym definitely has middle-school classroom poster vibes, it's a great way to gut-check your messaging to make sure you're communicating directly and with heart.

THINK acronym:

T: Is it TRUE?

H: Is it HELPFUL?

I: Is it INSPIRING?

N: Is it NECESSARY?

K: Is it KIND?

Take Callie, who told us about a radical candor moment. Her colleague Carlos asked her to help out with a sales call last-minute in hopes of landing a new client. He was nervous about it going well, and he thought that Callie's expertise would not only help win over the client but also calm his anxiety. Eager to support her teammate in a pinch, Callie fielded the call with limited background on the specifics but ready to ask questions and learn (and, of course, armed with her expertise on their offering).

As things turned out, Callie wasn't given the space to participate or even ask questions for almost the entire call. And when she did finally jump in, she figured out pretty quickly that her company wouldn't be the right fit for the client's project. When the call ended, Carlos called her to ask how she thought it went. Callie took a deep breath and said, "For me, the call didn't go the way I hoped (*true*). I typically like to ask more questions upfront to learn about the client in the beginning and to make sure I know how and what to pitch to

CALLOUT: BEWARE!

The Dangers of Toxic Positivity

There's nothing wrong with an organization where positivity and positive attitudes are the norm. However, if positivity feels more like a mandate than a mindset, people will find themselves in the unhealthy realm of toxic positivity. "Good vibes only" and "everything happens for a reason" are common word art slogans that people wield in service of toxic positivity. It's cringey at best, and damaging at worst.

Toxic positivity is actually a form of gaslighting. When people are told "everything will turn out okay," rather than having their real hurt or frustration acknowledged, they're pretty much being told that their feelings aren't valid. When leaders ask colleagues and employees to show up *only* as their positive, sparkly-vibe self, they're asking people to show up inauthentically at least part of the time. That's not to say we should allow people to be rude at work or openly flaunt a bad attitude. We can allow for a healthy spectrum of emotions (rage is obviously not an emotion to let fly freely at work) and still be present in a professional way. A span of emotions is, after all, a natural part of being human. But in the end, well-intentioned or not, toxic positivity does more harm than good and sacrifices the validity of other people's emotions.

them (*helpful*). I know our product is awesome; I just want to be sure it's what people need! (*inspiring*) The next time I join you on these calls, can we chat first, even if just for a minute or two, and strategize how we want the conversation to flow? (*necessary*) I want to be sure I'm doing right by you and our clients. (*kind*)" This primed Callie and Carlos to work together more effectively while preserving their interpersonal relationship. Callie didn't bury the experience and let resentment grow while ineffective meetings continued to happen. She addressed the problem head-on, in a direct but kind manner.

THE MANAGERIAL (GREAT COMMUNICATORS MAKE FOR GREAT LEADERS)

As it goes for most things within an organization, those in positions of leadership bear an extra responsibility to communicate exceptionally well. While we'll caveat this with "People will do as you do, not as you say," if you are a leader, your messaging still means a lot. Truly great leaders have mastered the art of communication and are not only clear and transparent in how they communicate, but also compassionate and understanding of others.

Here are a few things we ask managers to keep in mind as they try to embrace the empathetic communication approach in their management styles.

> **BE MINDFUL ABOUT HOW STRONGLY YOUR VOICE IS AMPLIFIED—BOTH WHAT IS SAID AND HOW IT'S COMMUNICATED**

What Is Said

The volume (figuratively speaking) of what managers say tends to be much louder than what an employee says. That means management needs to be extra thoughtful about what they do and don't say. That one offhand comment made in a moment of frustration can stick in a direct report's head for years to come—or even be the reason they leave the organization. Take Emily, a Gen Z intern whose boss made a joke about her being "the silent girl" in big meetings, since she was hesitant and shy about jumping right in. Rather than encouraging Emily to speak up, this shut her down even more, making her dread those larger meetings and constantly worry about how others were perceiving her.

Managers are humans, so of course there will be times when an overly blunt or not-well-thought-out comment will escape. But having an awareness of the outsized impact of managerial communication is key as managers and leaders move through their day-to-day.

CALLOUT: Story Time

"I Need an Attitude Adjustment"

One of our clients, Justin, is extremely self-aware about how his attitude affects his employees. He knows that when he's in a place of stress or frustration, he can come off as really harsh. When he's in that headspace, he actively calls it out to be clear that he's not angry or frustrated with his team and takes a breather when he notices it's impacting how he's behaving and communicating. He'll tell his staff, "Hey, I'm gonna take a quick lap around the building because I need an attitude adjustment," and returns after he's feeling more grounded. This lets his employees know it's not them, it's him—and that it's normal to have days or moments when you're just a bit off. Call it out, make the adjustment, and come back when you feel you can participate and communicate in a way that doesn't shut down others in the room (or on Zoom).

How It's Communicated

Good communication is about way more than just the words being shared. There's so much that can be read between the lines. This means that managers need to tone-proof their messaging and how they express themselves in workspaces. A typically talkative manager who sits through a meeting with arms crossed and an angry face can instill fear in his employees. Employees will be reading between those lines, whether the intent was there or not.

TAILOR FEEDBACK BASED ON THE DIRECT REPORT'S REACTIVITY

Feedback is a whole topic unto itself, but there's one empathetic communication-related, Platinum-Rule-specific point we want to cover here: Please be aware of how important it is to tailor your feedback approach depending on the employee receiving it.

Our former boss, Debra, uses a steering wheel analogy (bear with us) to describe how she adjusts feedback for different employees. Some car models will have light, reactive steering wheels. They need but the slightest whisper of a touch for the car to move in that new

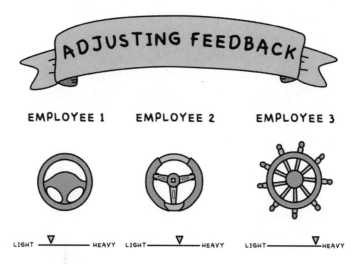

direction. Others (like sports cars) have heavy, almost hard-to-maneuver steering wheels. You really have to put in some elbow grease to get it to move.

Employees, and how they receive feedback, can be similar. There is no value judgment on either one. (There are pros and cons to both ends of that spectrum.) One employee may only require one comment, for example, about their lack of attention to detail on a project, and they'll doggedly do everything possible to avoid making that mistake again. Another might require ten instances of the same piece of feedback before they internalize the message.

If we don't take this under consideration when we're giving feedback, then we could potentially push the person who's very receptive to feedback too far and/or make them feel insecure about what they can or can't do. Also, remember that some people might not know how they want to receive feedback. Others will be on a journey of learning what's best for them. It's up to leaders to keep adjusting how hard and how often they need to steer the feedback wheel.

FOSTER A HEALTHY PUSHBACK ENVIRONMENT

It's often the case that managers think everything is good with their people, only to later find that discontent has been growing behind closed doors and in quiet side conversations. Even when the manager is a great communicator and open to feedback, they may find themselves working with employees who come from a culture where speaking up, pushing back, asking questions, and pointing out potential flaws was punished. A manager's work toward fostering a healthy pushback culture or environment is never done. You have to constantly tend to this effort and make people feel safe to bring things up.

To examine whether you're actively supporting a healthy pushback culture, consider the following:

- What daily actions do you take to encourage a pushback environment?

- Have there been negative consequences for employees who questioned leadership? What actions did you take (or not take) in response to that employee's feedback?

- Reflect on how you react to pushback. What are your verbal and nonverbal cues? Ask a trusted peer for their take on your response. (Sometimes our self-reflections don't capture the full picture.)

- Have you given your employees a clear way and/or system by which to disagree with you? With each other? How do you regularly reference it and encourage people to make use of the system?

- How do you praise those who respectfully push back on an idea or point out flaws?

THE ORGANIZATION (GREAT COMMUNICATION MAKES FOR GREAT COMPANIES)

Organizations are not humans, obviously. So it may feel weird to talk about how organizations can be more empathetic in their communication. But! There are a few considerations, organizationally, to keep in mind when trying to create a culture of clear, empathetic communication.

INVEST IN COMMUNICATION TRAINING AT ALL LEVELS

We'll say it again: It's a mistake to assume that communication is something that just comes naturally to everyone. Especially when it's empathetic. Make it a practice to, from an organization-wide perspective, invest in communications training at all levels. From finessing emails and phone etiquette, to learning how to best interact with

CALLOUT: THE REAL WORLD – A CASE STUDY

Fostering Pushback for the Long Term

One health care organization we worked with realized that they had a huge problem with people not feeling okay about speaking up to leaders, especially surgeons, when they noticed something was amiss. One employee even voiced "I honestly don't think people would feel comfortable saying anything even if they realized the surgeon was operating on a patient's wrong leg." Scary!

So leadership at this organization made moves to counteract this phenomenon by investing in a "caring reliably" initiative to address the problem. They conducted training with every employee, teaching communication tools like SBAR (Situation-Background-Assessment-Recommendation)[6] to equip them with a reliable process to raise a question or thought when things aren't going well and how to respond when an issue or challenge was brought up by someone else. Using printed versions of tools like SBAR on the back of everyone's name badges served as easily available reminders. So if there were ever questions or hesitancy about how to push back, they could simply turn their badges around and reference the phrasing on the badge.

Critically, all of the leadership actively supported and backed this training so that it became a part of their corporate culture. But it took four years for this initiative to really take root. Which may have you, dear reader, reacting like, "WHAT?! FOUR YEARS?! Are you kidding?" Yes, massive cultural shifts like this take time—and frequent retraining. But they're well worth the effort, and you have to start somewhere.

team members, time spent brushing up on these skills is never time ill spent.

FIND WAYS TO CAPTURE AND DISSEMINATE THE UNWRITTEN RULES

Companies with a culture of empathetic communication make a concerted effort to ensure that information is easily accessible to those who need it. This means that any unwritten rules need to be captured explicitly and accessed easily. *Do we have unwritten rules around expected responsiveness? Is there company jargon that isn't immediately obvious to newcomers? When meeting with clients or customers, what behaviors are okay? And which ones aren't? Are classy jeans okay to wear to the office?* Are exclamation points welcomed or ridiculed? All these things and more should be explicitly captured and widely shared. This will also make the culture more accessible for neurodivergent employees and those from other cultural backgrounds.

DON'T SIMPLY COLLECT EMPLOYEE FEEDBACK—ADDRESS IT (AND, BETTER YET, ACT ON IT)

Communication, and feedback specifically, is useless if it's not digested and acted upon. A common complaint during the pandemic years was that while organizations spent a good deal of time and effort collecting employee feedback, it was either left ignored or unaddressed or the company never acted to implement the changes employees had asked for. One study found that nearly half of the people they surveyed felt that the feedback they provided to their organizations didn't lead to any real change.[7] Some have speculated that the lack of action on feedback may have been a driver behind The Great Recession.[8] Whether specific actions in response to feedback are possible or not, it's critical to make sure that, organizationally, employee feedback is openly addressed in an honest, transparent fashion. Share what's possible in terms of acting upon that feedback, and what isn't.

If you can, share the results of your surveys! Don't try to obfuscate negative feedback; that's an excellent way to sow seeds of distrust and poison the culture. Many employees from all sorts of organizations and industries have shared eerily similar responses to their organizations' pulse surveys that sound something like, "They never share the full survey results. We know there's negative stuff in there, but they hide it like we're not adults or can't handle it. They're obviously curating what is shared, and it makes me suspicious about what else they're hiding."

Rather than keeping the negative feedback to the inner sanctums of the board room, face the challenges head-on. Address what may change in the near future and what might not be an option at present, and always do your best to share the why. Most importantly, show employees that their feedback is being heard with an intent to act upon it in some way. Otherwise, this ever-important feedback loop of communication will eventually peter out.

Entire lives could be devoted to the quest of learning the art of good communication. We have seen time and again with our clients that effective communication is the backbone of successful organizations. As with most things worth doing, it's a skill that requires time and intention. And because language is a living, breathing thing that's always evolving, our communication skillset must also evolve. Which is precisely why we devoted this entire chapter toward that effort.

✦ THE GIST ✦

PRE-PORTAL STANDARD

Historically, there has been little effort toward helping people communicate effectively at work. In many (most?) instances, it's assumed that effective communication will just innately be baked into every employee. But communication is a skill like any other that needs to be developed with care.

PORTAL LESSONS

With a shift to more virtual and hybrid styles of work, as well as an en-masse adoption of tools like Zoom and Slack, opportunities for miscommunication and frustration are rife. We can no longer ignore that excellent communication is essential to maintaining a healthy organization, and we must all be intentional about crafting and utilizing those skills daily.

NOW WHAT? STEPPING THROUGH THE PORTAL

Individuals can improve their communication game right away by practicing:

- ✦ Active listening – leave judgment at the door, listen to understand not respond, and slow down your reactions to truly soak in the message being delivered.

- ✦ The Platinum Rule – learn to communicate with others the way they wish to be communicated with.

- ✦ Empathic communication – consider the impact (not just intent) of what you say, try not to jump to conclusions, watch out for those whose voices aren't being heard, and always aim to be clear and kind.

THE POWER OF EMPATHETIC COMMUNICATION

Leaders need to be particularly in tune with the subtext of communication, and understand the nuances behind:

- ✦ What is said – your voice carries extra weight, so be extra mindful about what you do and don't say.

- ✦ How it is said – tone proof your messages to consider how employees might read between the lines.

- ✦ To whom it is said – tailor feedback based on the receiver.

- ✦ By whom it is said – encourage a multidirectional feedback loop so it's not just leaders delivering information and giving feedback/praise.

CHAPTER 4

Our Burnout Emergency

✦ *"The grind never stops. Work hard, play hard. You'll have to work your ass off, but it'll be worth it." Is this really true? And if so, at what cost?*

Welcome to the U.S. workplace, where if you work really hard, you can achieve your professional dreams! Well, at least, that's the pervasive messaging in today's work culture. Not included in that messaging is the simple truth that working all the hours does not by any means guarantee success. And the messaging certainly doesn't include the toll of chronic stress and the numerous sacrifices required to live by the "hustle and grind" mentality, which in the end leaves people feeling like a shell of a human.

In our survey, we asked people to describe the American workplace in three words. The top results were telling: competitive, overworked, stressed.

Burnout, it would seem, is the small-print (but large-impact) side effect of embracing #hustleculture to achieve the American dream, of which professional success is a huge component.

When in the company of U.S. workers, we can usually swap tales of when we realized, "Whoa, this is what burnout feels like." Hannah has a few of her own. It's not surprising if you know her; she's always had a habit of saying yes to everything because it gave her a sense of pride to succeed while stretched between many responsibilities. Earlier in her career, she attempted to juggle leadership, traveling to speak at conferences six to ten times a month, and writing a book (not this one).

Needless to say, it was all a bit much. After a while, the passion she used to feel for her work was replaced with dread and apathy. The work travel that had initially thrilled her started inducing regular anxiety attacks. The enthusiasm she had previously put toward listening to and empowering colleagues turned into brief, efficient, and mostly transactional exchanges. Sometimes it even became sharp, like when after seeing a small typo on a meeting agenda, she snapped, "What is this? Did you mean *finnacle* or *financial*?!" It was such an un-Hannah-like response that the whole room was completely caught off guard.

On one trip, deep into her burnout (and scarily sleep-deprived), Hannah landed in Atlanta for a speaking engagement. Upon arrival at her hotel, she received an unexpected text from the client reading, "We'll see you for dinner in an hour!" Hannah was unaware of the plan to meet. So she hurriedly changed out of ragged athleisure to business professional, then hyperventilated on the way to the restaurant, panicking that she wouldn't have enough time to finish work (so many apologies to that Lyft driver!). She managed to emotionally pull herself together for the dinner and present the next day to an ultimately happy client. (Adrenaline was her friend.) Then, with body and mind fatigued, she walked zombie-like through the Atlanta airport and spotted a sign for a plane to Amsterdam. She started (slowly but determinedly) walking to the travel desk to ask if she could get on the plane but stopped two paces away. In that moment, escape from all responsibility was a hell of a lot more appealing than flying home to Minneapolis, where more work awaited her.

That's what happens when we're operating on empty and accustomed to a vibration of busy without room for emotion. It takes a major toll. Hannah didn't cry for five months. (And Hannah cries at dog commercials. Crying is her way of processing. Not crying was a huge red flag.) The burnout was all-consuming, and that relentless pace of work was leading to subpar, joyless work—and, if we're being honest, a subpar, joyless life.

Organizations have strived to solve the burnout crisis because it lowers employee well-being and productivity. Individuals have been seeking burnout solutions because of the high personal cost. And while it's been a focus of conversation for a long time now, the pandemic put the topic front and center. People tasked with taking care of work, themselves, and their families—all with little accommodation from employers for the challenge and uncertainty of the time—felt their energy become totally depleted. Collectively, we saw burnout negatively affect so many around us and said, "No more! Burnout should not be

CALLOUT: To Be Clear

Stress Neither Begins Nor Ends with Work

This chapter speaks specifically about how to prevent workplace burnout, and we acknowledge that stress comes from plenty of other areas in life. Tackling workplace burnout may powerfully impact lives, *but* it is not the only source of people's extreme exhaustion and stress. We recommend that everyone take it upon themselves to identify other areas of burnout in life and address them accordingly, with compassion.

the norm. Feeling exhausted, stressed, depressed, and apathetic at work should not be the norm. The idea that it is the only way to succeed and thrive is a lie."

We now have this opportunity to create a future of work that is—dare we say—burnout-free (or at very least, burnout-light). But first, we have to identify the root causes of why burnout exists in the first place, then work to eradicate those causes. Spoiler alert: It's going to take more than a few mental health webinars.

✦ PRE-PORTAL

Workplace burnout has been on the rise for years. The World Health Organization (WHO) included it in the International Classification of Diseases (ICD-11) in 2018.[1] And yet too few leaders and organizations paid attention to the urgency of the warning signs. Many of those cautionary symptoms can be seen in how people experience acute and chronic stress, which can make the differentiation between stress and burnout slightly muddled.

So let's be clear about what burnout is and what it isn't. Burnout is the point of stress that, when you're in it, can be hard to name. It can feel like a deep cavern you're trying to escape but can barely find your footing to climb out of (and you might not even have the energy to find it in the first place). In the medical realm, burnout is defined not as a medical condition but as an occupational phenomenon. As the WHO put it:

> Burnout is a syndrome conceptualized as resulting from chronic workplace stress that has not been successfully managed. It is characterized by three dimensions:
>
> • feelings of energy depletion or exhaustion;

- increased mental distance from one's job, or feelings of negativism or cynicism related to one's job; and

- reduced professional efficacy.[2]

In less medical speak, burnout is when people feel emotionally exhausted, detached, and disconnected from work and have low belief in their capability to do hard things. It is more than acute stress, chronic stress, or a general apathy for our work. In the spirit of listicles, on the next two pages is a chart to differentiate the stages that lead to workplace burnout (though, of course, this isn't always linear and may actually operate more like a feedback loop).*

Learn more from the Burnout Stages chart on the following pages →

NOTE: We are not doctors, and the following is not meant to be medical advice.

ACUTE STRESS

SYMPTOMS	Rushing heart rate, digestion issues, irritability, anxiety, jaw and back pain. Think about what happens to your body in the fight-or-flight response.
WHEN IT HAPPENS	Specific on-the-spot moments, like giving a presentation or finishing a project.
THE COST	Short-term moments of discomfort that may include tummy aches, poor sleep, and an elevated heart rate. May cause you to be more prone to mistakes or struggle to unwind.
WHAT'S REALLY HAPPENING	Acute stress can be in reaction to a serious, traumatic event. It can also be eustress, the positive kind of stress that spurs you into action.

CHRONIC STRESS	BURNOUT
Short tempered, constantly worrying, overwhelmed, taking on too much, more prone to sickness like cold and flu, withdrawing from friends and family, higher intake of alcohol and/or tobacco.	Inescapable exhaustion, apathy, mental distance from job, general professional cynicism, withdrawal, hopelessness, trouble concentrating, and work absenteeism.
After repeated similar situational moments of stress. Basically, it's the continuation of a pattern of many demands but little control.	When chronic stress at work is prolonged and hasn't been managed properly.
Heart disease, Type 2 diabetes, high blood pressure, depression, high cholesterol, insomnia.	General lack of motivation and zest in all areas of life. Constantly feeling numb, detached, and disengaged from work.
Chronic stress and the almost-constant exposure to cortisol and other stress hormones means that almost every body process is negatively impacted.[3]	You have fewer hormones to manage the stress. Burnout differentiates from depression because the symptoms are significantly more work-related.[4]

In most workday experiences, here's what this can look like:

Acute Stress Monster: Let's say that you have a new Chief Human Resources Officer (CHRO) who is starting in your organization. You have never met them before, and your first introduction coincides with a presentation to the entire Human Resources (HR) team. When it's time for you to present your material, you are both making a first impression with the new boss and presenting in front of a group of people. Naturally, you were up late preparing, tossed and turned all night for fear of not waking up in time, could barely eat breakfast because your stomach was so upset, and felt like your palms were at a steady condensation level all morning. The stress monster keeps you up all night, whispers messages of doubt into your ear, and twists your gut into knots. After the presentation, the monster starts to retreat.

Chronic Stress Monster: Turns out your new CHRO is ambitious—and demanding. No matter what you do, you feel like it isn't enough because the drive is to go farther, faster, stronger! Every attempt you make to organize your calendar and maximize productivity seems to fail because you keep taking on more to prove yourself; and then when you succeed, you have more work to do (yay?). Busy is your norm. You go from meeting to phone call to home, all while feeling like you're running without awareness of when a break might come. Most moments of rest are saturated with guilt. How could you possibly take a day off when there's so much to do?! The stress and busyness are so predictable, they've become routine. Every day you're operating at 100 miles per hour. You get sick a few more times that year than usual; and when you hear stories about people who go to the ER, certain they're having a heart attack only to discover it's a panic attack, you think, *I can relate. I've felt that way, too.* The stress monster is your constant companion, urging you to keep picking up the pace while your whole body crumbles bit by bit.

Burnout Stress Monster: You're over it. What exactly? All things work. The unceasing pace, the never-ending demands, the high expectations, and the feeling that every task, every project, every request is urgent. The motivation you once felt has escaped you. The passion for your work has all but disappeared because there just isn't time to feel passionate when you have all that work to do. Your performance is dipping; and where you may normally have felt fear, any sense of worry is outweighed by apathy. Maybe you're grieving the previous version of you who was enthusiastic and upbeat, excited to tackle new challenges, and eager to put in the extra work. These days, the only times you feel somewhat normal is when you have time with yourself. Small incidents spark irritation, and simple tasks feel like moving a giant boulder. The stress monster has taken over your life. It drags you from place to place, and you're so deeply tired and over it that all you can do is submit and let it pull you along, dragging your feet behind it.

Before the pandemic years, there were some attempts to address the stress struggle. But the sense of urgency was ... well, lacking (aside from certain industries, like health care). And that created a pretty heavy toll, both on people and on organizations. Employers spent between $125 to $190 billion per year in burnout-related health care costs.[5]

Many businesses did see it as a pressing issue, but one that needed to be addressed on the individual level with self-management tools. As a result, those who were experiencing the associated negative symptoms spoke about it in private conversations or did their best to hide it, for fear of losing their jobs.

Then the pandemic hit—and exhausted, overworked, emotionally spent employees started dropping out of the workforce en masse. Organizations woke up, and managing (or, better yet, preventing) burnout by truly addressing the larger, overarching causes became an absolute top priority requiring immediate attention.

✦ THE PORTAL

During 2020 alone, the number of people who were feeling burnout reached 73 percent by May[6], while another report found a 33 percent increase in burnout signs over that year[7]. In our conversations, 65 percent agreed they had felt burnout in 2020, with the majority strongly agreeing. That year marked a significant change on the burnout discussion front. Workers everywhere talked of Zoom fatigue, work overwhelm, and hitting the pandemic wall. More than ever before, leaders began seeking tangible ways to help their employees because they collectively felt the impact of a team operating on empty.

The burnout epidemic resulted in the following:

A DECLINE IN . . .	AN INCREASE IN . . .
• Creativity	• Turnover
• Empathy	• Irritation
• Productivity	• Resentment
• Well-being	• Withdrawal
• Clear communication	• Safety accidents
• Motivation	• Finger-pointing
• Teamwork	• Individualism

OUR BURNOUT EMERGENCY

If one person is experiencing burnout, chances are high that they're in good company. When we operate from that place—making more mistakes, tapped of creativity, and easily frustrated with one another—it makes for a not-so-great work environment and may perpetuate a culture of burnout.

You know you're in a workplace culture of burnout when you see the following:

- People don't take vacations, work while they're on time off, or make you feel guilty for taking a vacation in the first place.

- Employees boast about not taking any sick days (especially pre-pandemic).

- People are expected to go to work, even in torrential weather. (GCC is headquartered in Minneapolis, where it's not uncommon for snow to triple or quadruple commute times. And yet people are still expected to show up.)

- Everyone jokes about being tired all the time or working extra hours.

- You are expected to return to work soon after a big life event.

- You can't remember the last time you weren't exhausted at work, and you're not alone.

- Late night, early morning, or holiday emails are the norm and are to be returned quickly.

- Emotions are expected to be in check, and speaking openly about them is against workplace norms.

- It's common to make personal sacrifices for professional gain.

- You feel an entire lack of control over your work circumstances.

CALLOUT: IT'S TRENDING

Revenge Bedtime Procrastination

Picture this: You're totally zonked after a string of long workdays. Your eyelids droop from weeks of sleep deprivation, and you can't wait to catch some z's. But when you finally get into bed, you realize it's the first time all day that you've had any time to yourself. Maybe you brought your phone with you (as 66 percent of us do[8]). Or maybe you were answering a few emails in bed, so your laptop is handy. Why not watch some Netflix? Or scroll through Twitter? Or TikTok? Or doomscroll? Just for a few minutes? Then a few minutes become a few hours, and pretty soon it's 2:00 a.m. Your eyes are bloodshot, and you know you're going to be destroyed the whole next day. Still, you eke out another thirty minutes to watch videos of dogs befriending chickens on YouTube before finally shutting it all down and getting some rest.

This is revenge bedtime procrastination. The term is actually a translation of a Chinese phrase, "報復性熬夜," or "报复性熬夜," popularized by journalist Daphne K. Lee's Twitter when she described it as "a phenomenon in which people who don't have much control over their daytime life refuse to sleep early in order to regain some sense of freedom during late night hours."[9] People are squeezing in leisure time at the expense of much-needed hours of sleep. And for them, it feels like it's worth it, even though in the long term it's detrimental to their health—and their ability to produce quality work! Frequent practitioners of revenge bedtime procrastination are probably in the toasty land of burnout.

There were a few common, solution-oriented approaches to the burnout crisis during the pandemic years. Eighty-seven percent of companies surveyed agreed that it was "very or extremely" critical that managers support employee well-being, **but only a quarter do much about it**.[10] Those who did do something tended to take a limited (rather than holistic) approach to promoting well-being and solving the burnout puzzle. We saw organizations host mental health and stress management webinars. Some tried to take it a step further and offered days or weeks off in the name of mental health and unplugging, as mentioned in chapter 1.

Many burnout resources encouraged gratitude journaling, meditation, and accomplishing what you can with the energy you have. While these tools are useful (Lisa is a particular fan of a well-formatted journal), they send a message that curing a crispy burnout culture is on the individual. But one human cannot be expected to handle all of their job stress if support is absent from their peers, leadership, or the organization itself.

Let's take Cactus Bank as an example (fake name, true story). Cactus Bank was overwhelmed for a lengthy spell due to low-interest mortgage rates, SBA loans and apps, stimulus payments, and shifting to WFH, all while going through a merger. When we spoke to the leaders, they were concerned and resigned to the reality that these material challenges just wouldn't change in the near future. They needed people to rally emotionally and tried offering some of the Band-Aid resources mentioned above. The individuals we spoke with voiced their appreciation for these tools as well as a longing for what would actually decrease their exhaustion: lightened workloads. They needed more from the organization than empathy or instructional tools. They needed action.

Validation, webinars, resources for the individual, even days off—these are all great! But they're simply not enough for long-term burnout prevention. To create a burnout-free workplace of the future, we have to keep the conversation going and take a long-term systemic approach that doesn't place the onus of curing burnout on the individual alone.

✦ NOW WHAT?

Everyone plays a role in combating burnout. Remember that pyramid from the introduction? Consider the impact at each level. Previous approaches have focused too much on the individual at the bottom of the pyramid. While they can certainly make some changes within their day-to-day and their sphere of influence, the bulk of the focus should be at the top layer (the organization) and the middle tier (leadership). These two layers of influence will make the biggest difference toward establishing a culture that actively pushes back on overwork and instead supports overall employee calm and well-being.

Top: The organization. If an organization is not doing the work to prevent burnout, then all efforts underneath will be far less effective.

Middle: Leadership. In a traditional hierarchical organization, leaders act as a buffer between organizational standards and the people they lead. They must be doing the work from both sides to help everyone prevent the burn.

Bottom: The individual. You do have the power to help yourself with burnout, and you can advocate for peers who are also feeling it. But it is never, ever all on you to prevent your own burnout.

PREVENTING BURNOUT WITH MINDSET SHIFTS

Before digging into the tactical ways to address work burnout, we have to seriously rethink the mindsets that are holding us back. Unless we make efforts to shift these mindsets, then none of the tactical solutions will lead to lasting change. For organizations and leaders, this is a critical first step. Individuals can employ all the personal burnout prevention tactics they want, but until organizations shift, employees will still be feeling the pressure to conform to old norms.

We suggest starting with the examination of what your work environment considers "old guard" or "just the way that things are" using the Three R's Method:

- **Review** the norms in your work environment. This could be what you believe, what you've been told to believe, or what the workplace culture believes to be true. (In this step, it is *imperative* that you speak with people at all levels in the organization. Don't just focus on the top talent.) Are those norms still relevant? Are they preventing burnout or contributing to it?

- **Redefine** the norms that no longer serve you.

- **Reinvent** what the workplace can be. What new norms or beliefs can you introduce in support of a more balanced working environment?

To assist in this journey of the 3 R's, here is one norm to consider: "The definition of success = more is more."

REVIEWING THE NORM

Traditional American workplace code would have everyone believe that success equals a combination of the following: money, power, rapid growth, high responsibility, and a boast-worthy title in the hierarchy. The success ladder looks so appealing because of the promise of what lies at the top. In reality, few make it to the top of that ladder, and droves of people are forever on the climb. Privilege is a large indicator of who gets the prize at the apex. Many (or most?) people find themselves floundering, fighting back voices of imposter syndrome telling them they aren't enough, which drives them into overwork to prove their worth. This traditional workplace view of success needs a new definition.

Ask yourself, and then ask your peers and colleagues[*]:

- Broadly speaking, what does it mean to be successful at work?
- On a specific level, what does it mean to be successful in this organization?
- On a personal level, how do you define success for yourself?
- Does your organization support your quest for success?
- What does your organization expect you to sacrifice for success?

REDEFINING THE NORM: WHAT DOES SUCCESS ACTUALLY MEAN?

Taking in all the information above, redefine what it means to be successful, accomplished, or labeled a "rock star." When you redefine this on a personal level, it can shift how you set boundaries, make career decisions, and value yourself. For organizations and leaders, this means opening your mind to new (and multiple) definitions of success. Share a draft of this changed definition with people at all

---

[*] *If you are not a leader, answering these questions and then bringing them to your manager could start a conversation about what you need to succeed at work and how that could change for the better.*

levels until it is refined into what success looks like for the future of the company. Then make this change crystal clear to folks in the organization itself by explaining what kind of work is celebrated and what is not. For example, maybe before you, people who edited the pitch deck on weekends were granted more opportunities. Now, that person would be candidly told that weekend work is not a measure of dedication and that they can save the work until Monday.

As a team member, you can work with people around you to propose a modified definition of success to leaders, with an assurance—and proof—that goals will still be met. We know that not every organization will be open to this feedback, but the process of redefining it for yourself can be empowering.

> **REINVENTING THE NORM: HOW WILL YOU SUPPORT AND CELEBRATE THIS NEW DEFINITION OF SUCCESS?**

Individuals, congratulate yourselves when you reach success on your terms. If your goal is to scan an email you're writing once instead of three times and you act on this new goal, pat yourself on the back. Others might not see it as progress, but that doesn't matter as long as you do see it. Take time to acknowledge your growth.

For leaders and organizations looking to make this change, put that redefined norm into practice. Adjust the markers for success on your reviews. Give feedback and show appreciation based on those revised norms. Make it so that everyone is accountable to help each other achieve those new definitions of success. It's up to you to ensure that you're taking these new mindsets, putting them into action, and encouraging employees to embrace the corresponding behaviors, too.

Shifting mindsets is the foundation for creating sustainable change. It's hard but important work that we're all capable of doing. And speaking of shifts, we're going to highlight a few "old hat" ways of working that fuel the fires of burnout and, in our opinion, desperately need some rethinking.

WHY IS EXPLOSIVE GROWTH (SOMETIMES AT ANY COST) SUCH A POPULAR BUSINESS PRIORITY?

Ted, who works in publishing, explained that during the pandemic, his employer yielded higher profits, reader engagement, and overall business growth. In response, his leadership said, "Let's keep the momentum going!" They hired more people, launched ambitious and risky new projects, and forecasted bigger numbers to hit. Ted had not had a raise for a year, was required to work in the office, and was dealing with outdated equipment. He looked at these changes and said, "Really? We've all been drowning, we're getting snappy with each other, and colleagues are starting to gossip. Can't we just keep going at a steady pace for now and not always need to strive for more?"

This example illustrates a common cost of exponential growth: burnout. And yet that kind of quick, unsustainable scalability and all its rewards (e.g., higher revenue, greater impact) create a sweet, addicting taste of the growth-at-all-costs cookies. Just one cookie, and you're feeling good and sugar-high. Eat a whole sleeve of them (or experience a whole year of unsustainable growth), and you're slammed by uncontrollable stomach pain.

Rather than chase the addiction to growth, the solution is simple—or at least straightforward, though it reads as radical to most: To effectively manage burnout, lessen the workload when possible. Lower expectations when possible. Sacrifice profit (just a bit) when possible. Choose not to scale for a little while.

When we propose this idea of lessening workloads to audiences, we often hear, "Well, that's just not an option for us." And sure, the situation will be different depending on the organization. We also know that growth, scaling, and profits are so highly valued in the American

CALLOUT: Toolbox

How to React When a Lighter Workload Isn't an Option

During the pandemic years, certain industries had no option but to continue to increase people's work to-do lists. Health care workers, for example, did everything in their power to save lives with limited support and resources, all while making countless personal sacrifices. Lessening the workload wasn't an option for them. In these instances, it's worth acknowledging the challenges of the moment and trying to understand how to create systems, resources, and workplace cultures so that if ever an uncontrollable chaotic event occurs in the future, better plans are in place. It's where we encourage asking these questions:

- How can we acknowledge the challenges and accomplishments of how we reacted in this time?

- How will we manage the continuing trauma response that may occur?

- How can we do better in the future, knowing what we know now?

- What microsteps can we take in the short term to, at the very least, relieve the pressure?

---

workplace culture that they can cloud reasoning, even when people's well-being is at stake.

And listen, we do get it. Certain industries are affected by circumstances outside of their control, and an increase in their employee workloads might not always be preventable. Which is fine when that's a temporary state. But lack of control paired with increasing job demands is the definition of stress at work that can ultimately lead to increased rates of heart attack and hypertension[11]—and, for an even bleaker truth, it has been shown to lead to a shorter lifespan[12]. Chronic stress and burnout that linger for an extended period are quite literally unsustainable for the human being and the human body. A workplace that operates in that mode of "overworked and understaffed" for the majority of the time is one that's doomed to burn their people out and, with time, reap the attrition rewards they've sown.

If you are making organization-wide decisions or are in a leadership position, and circumstances are primed for the burn, do everything in your power to make reasonable shifts in expectations. While you may be sacrificing profits and productivity in the short term, you are creating conditions for retention, happiness, and a more effective team in the long term. Which would you rather have?

Regardless of your role, reconsider how you view business (or professional) growth. As an organization, you can adopt a core value that speaks to burnout prevention. HawkSoft, a management systems company, has the core value of "Work to live, don't live to work." And they've been listed as a best place to work since 2015. (Maybe the two are related.) As a leader, consider an antiburnout personal core value and take action based on its meaning. If you notice that people are showing signs of burnout, close the office for a few days. Tell people to take time off, and make sure your fellow leaders respect PTO. Hold honest, actionable conversations to address why so many people are burning out in the first place. Appreciate freely, and get specific with individualized praise (without glorifying overwork). Strive to make sure your people feel seen, heard, and valued—which in and of itself can prevent burnout.

And finally, to all of us individuals: We have to stop complimenting others' burnout-inducing behaviors (e.g., "Wow, you were up until midnight working on that project! Dang, that's amazing!!"). Instead,

OUR BURNOUT EMERGENCY

be more active about setting and enforcing your boundaries. Burnout is, unfortunately, contagious. But boundary-setting can be too.

WHY IS THERE SO MUCH PRESSURE TO BE PRODUCTIVE?

The US is famous—well, infamous—for its "live to work" mindset. There is this cultural messaging that being successful means being hyperproductive all the time, delivering results no matter what.

Productivity propaganda is everywhere. It's seen in the "Do or do not—there is no try" slogan written on the walls of company lobbies. It's seen in the phone cases that read, "The grind never stops." This messaging clouds our minds with a voice that tells us, "If you aren't tired, you aren't working hard enough." It's the discomfort we feel if we're successful but not drowning in tasks. It's the lazy label placed on colleagues when they have time in the day that they're not working. It's the way team players are celebrated because they're the ones who always say "YES!" regardless of the personal toll. This toxic celebration of productivity has made the American workplace revere (knowingly or not) overwork and overwhelm. It's made us all want to wear busy as a badge of honor.

That's not the only badge of honor for the super productive folks in the office.

The result is a workforce of people who are either pushing themselves too hard to produce more and grow faster, putting in longer hours, or finding themselves stuck in the "not enough" trap, where everything they do feels like it falls short. This is a dangerous loop that predictably veers to burnout.

When the pandemic hit and millions of people started working from home, it didn't take long for headlines to read, "Productivity is the highest that it has ever been." The shift to remote work was evidence that yes, people really can work from home—and, as a bonus, it makes

THE FUTURE OF WORK IS HUMAN

them even more productive! However, this deserves a big cautionary flag: Many people were more productive because they were terrified of losing their jobs and felt the need to repeatedly prove their worth. Or they struggled to set boundaries between work and home because life and work became so intermingled, and colleagues and bosses were contacting them 24/7. Or maybe they were just trying to distract themselves from all the chaos, so they threw themselves into their work.

While some organization execs may conclude that "WFH equals higher productivity, so let's keep doing it," this ignores the danger of people burning out from that higher rate of productivity. What's additionally worrying is that because people are often only "seen" during Zoom calls (especially in remote-only workplaces), they can better hide all the signs that they're struggling. As Margaret, a security analyst at a financial services firm, told us, "In the office, you can walk by colleagues' desks and see if they're panicking or stressed out. When you're working remotely, you can't see that." In any workforce of the future with a virtual or hybrid model, this is a concern for us. Which isn't to say that WFH isn't a good fit for many organizations. (It is! We love it!) But it requires extra diligence about proactively preventing overwork.

CALLOUT: TO BE CLEAR

A Time and Place for Hard Work

We often talk to people who take pride in the energy and tenacity they put into their work. These folks have a dream and work their ass off to achieve it because they know what they're pursuing is important. To this, we say: YES! Go for it! Just because we strongly believe burnout should be eliminated does *not* mean that folks shouldn't work hard, do more than is expected of them, and take pride in following their personal passion and drive. It's always a return to *why* that hard work is happening in the first place and how those personal expectations are (or aren't) being projected onto others.

Also, be mindful that you don't overdo it. Sometimes the most passionate people (or especially the most passionate people) lead themselves into burnout because of their devotion. If you care about longevity, be as disciplined in your rest as you are in your work.

We all need to recognize our role in promoting productivity propaganda, and do our best to *not* adorn ourselves with the busy flair. Consider this: Are you consuming and contributing to this productivity narrative? And if so, ask yourself these questions:

✦ What busy badges do I wear?

✦ Do I take real vacations (i.e., log off completely during vacays—no cheating!)?

✦ Do I think less of people whose goals are not directly related to career growth?

- Do I enjoy moments of true rest? Moments when I, quite literally, do nothing? Guilt-free?

- Do I place more value in the results or the number of hours worked to get to those results?

With that last question, be wary of praise for people doing more just because it's more. For example, back in Hannah's high school days, when the teacher assigned a five- to seven-page paper, Hannah would write an eight-page paper. Not necessarily because she had more to say (and we can guarantee there was some repetitive content in there), but because she thought the teachers would then see her as someone who goes above and beyond. When she got into the workforce, managers saw Hannah as a real team player because she'd stay late or send messages on weekends. Don't be those managers or coworkers. Be the teacher who grades a four-page paper higher because it so succinctly captured what needed to be said. Be the manager who watches out for and advocates against overwork.

If you'd like to continue rethinking work, here are some other themes worthy of the Three R's exercise:

- What "working hard" looks like

- What defines "top talent"

- Expectations for career progression

- The purpose of productivity

- And so many more

CALLOUT: For Your Consideration

Tackling Bias, Discrimination, and Racism at Work

Discrimination, harassment, and racism at work all contribute to burnout. Stress is not experienced the same by everyone; groups that face discrimination based on their identities have an added layer of stress. Women are more likely to experience burnout than men for a variety of reasons, including the burden of balancing work and home duties, less decision-making power[13], and the ongoing and very real challenge of getting their voices heard.

One report by Catalyst in 2018 explored the emotional tax that BIPOC individuals feel at work and found that 58 percent of Asian, Black, and Latinx employees are on "guard" while working.[14] This emotional tax can become emotional labor when folks are managing their emotions while trying not to ruffle the feathers of people around them (while also just trying to do their job!). It can lead to "representation burnout," described by Martha Tesema as "that feeling of exhaustion that comes from being the only person of a particular identity in an environment."[15] In response to a viral piece about Millennial burnout, author Tiana Clark wrote "This Is What Black Burnout Feels Like," in which she writes, "for millennials of color, not only do we have to combat endless emails and Slack notifications, but we also get strapped with having to prove our humanity."[16] Not to mention the small but damaging moments that contribute to burnout, such as experiencing microaggressions and being on the receiving end of others' conscious and implicit bias.

CALLOUT: FOR YOUR CONSIDERATION (CONTINUED)

During the early pandemic years, patterns of burnout for women and BIPOC individuals continued to rise (unsurprisingly). Women were more likely to report physical symptoms of anxiety and stress than men and were spending more time on childcare, elder care, and housework than their male counterparts, averaging twenty more hours. Black and Latina women were on average spending even more hours than white women on the same work.[17]

Add to these draining tasks the inescapable trauma of the pandemic years. This includes loss of loved ones to COVID-19, navigating devastating coverage of the latest police brutality incident (like the murders of George Floyd, Breonna Taylor, and Daunte Wright, to name a few), and the contentious presidential election and its aftermath. Sadly, these events led to organizations placing even more demands on BIPOC employees, often in the form of ill-conceived DEI and Employee Resource Group initiatives.

As organizations, leaders, and individuals, we have to do better. We must face these realities head-on and take sustainable action to counter how bias negatively impacts the work environment. In 2020, more people recognized the urgent need to tackle not only diversity but also inclusion at work. And yet, according to a 2021 Gallup poll, only 42 percent of managers say they strongly agree that they are prepared to talk about race at work (and managers account for 70 percent of the reason people feel engaged at work!).[18]

CALLOUT: For Your Consideration (Continued)

One step here, if it hasn't already been taken, is investment of time, money, and attention to understand the experiences people are having in your own work environment, and where differences lie. Sharon Steed, founder of Communilogue, says that "The first step is learning through listening: Leaders need to initiate one-on-one conversations with employees about their experiences[...] make sure each individual understands that their opinions matter and will in no way affect their employment. Ask them: Do they feel included? Heard? Like they belong? Listen to their stories without judgment, and try to internalize their struggle." Stephanie Creary, Assistant Professor at Wharton, and DEI and workplace relationships expert, has outlined a "MERIT" framework to emphasize the importance of not just doing the DEI work, but valuing it . This research-backed approach cannot be summarized in mere sentences here; we encourage you to read further and take steps now if you haven't already begun to.

The urgency of this work continues. It is not a checklist or program to complete and walk away from. It's an ongoing effort. While we don't have the answers for how to do this, there are many brilliant individuals who do, and they're just a Google search away. If you don't know where to start, look to the work of experts we reference.

PREVENTING BURNOUT WITH TACTICAL METHODS

In tandem with mindset shifts, there must be directed efforts to prevent burnout. In the more tangible sense, ongoing prevention tactics will hopefully one day make for a work world where burnout culture is not the norm.

The essential component of a culture that prevents burnout: boundaries. They provide a clear structure to help individuals understand when to say yes and when to say no (and allow us to feel guilt-free when saying either). They also tell others in plain terms what's expected and what's not. When boundaries are blurry, even the act of trying to figure out what's okay and what's not can contribute to higher levels of exhaustion. Clarity is queen (or quing, or king).

For boundaries to be effective at work, they need to come from all three of the layers addressed earlier (organization, leadership, and the individual).

PREVENTING BURNOUT AS THE ORGANIZATION

Think about this: a company that prides itself on its calm nature, where chronic stress and burnout are a rarity. Reads like fiction, right? Sadly, these environments are shockingly difficult to find. Which is unfortunate, because organizational structure is essential for creating workplaces that support and promote boundaries at all levels.

It might not happen overnight (correction: it *will not* happen overnight). But here are a few ideas to get you started.

How Organizations Can Set Boundaries with Mindsets

- ✦ Overwork is not celebrated (but balance is).
- ✦ "Good enough" is an accepted state of being done.

- Overall employee well-being is supported.
- Effectiveness is valued more than productivity.
- No is a badge of honor.

    The age-old customer-centric motto of "just say yes" can be damaging if boundaries are crossed in the process. When no is celebrated because it protects the business, its people, and its customers (because interacting with an uber-stressed human is not so pleasant), everyone wins.

How Organizations Can Set Boundaries Through Action and Policies

- Embrace "camera off" meetings and encourage "meeting-free" Fridays.
- Set structured email hours (i.e., emails are only sent within certain hours of the day).
- Establish an "Unplug for Vacation" policy:

    One small business we worked with actually logged employees out of their servers and changed the password so that there wouldn't be any "oh, I'm just going to pop in and answer an email" behaviors while employees were on vacation.

- Create a PTO system that people actually use:

    Unlimited PTO, while it may sound nice, can quickly turn a work culture into one of vacation shaming because some people take six weeks off while others take two. This disparate approach to PTO can quickly lead to resentment and shaming. Might it not send a stronger message to give all employees, regardless of their level of experience, six weeks of PTO rather than unlimited, along with policies that encourage them to use every last day of time off?

PREVENTING BURNOUT AS A LEADER

The role of a leader is not easy. Especially in times of crisis, leaders bear the responsibility of communicating transparently, managing projections, and shouldering their team's stressors while tending to overall emotional culture and employee morale. Despite all this weight that leaders carry (or perhaps because of it), they'll always need to set the precedent for what boundaries look like in practice.

If you're a leader, how you show up for yourself is what others will model. You need to determine what your energy vampires are and create a solid salt (or garlic) line between you and that vamp. And stick to those boundaries! In so doing, you'll give others permission to do the same. If you find yourself in a boundaryless culture, remember that while you might not be able to change your organization's expectations, you can set the example of starting something new that works. A microculture, of sorts. What if, for example, your team sets strict boundaries around work times that everyone honors? What if that makes them even more effective, creative, and motivated than those teams that are putting in work around the clock?

This setting of boundaries as leaders, starting with the self, can be really hard. During our interviews, we heard many examples of "what not to do." When we spoke to Karen, a middle manager at an advertising firm, she told us about one time when her leader's offhand comment actually eroded the boundary she tried to set for herself. Karen had been preparing to take time off for the holidays and sent a message to her boss that read, "I'm logging out completely for Christmas. If there's an emergency, you can reach me through WhatsApp. But otherwise, I plan to be out!" Her boss's response was, "Oh wow, that's brave. Good for you. I'll be available in case anything comes up." This response made Karen feel uncomfortable and uneasy about taking a

CALLOUT: RETHINK THE NORM

Redefining Leadership

"It's lonely at the top" is something most leaders have said or felt at least once in their careers. Leading, as defined by hierarchical corporate America, can be all too exhausting, lonely, and stressful. Leaders often tell us about the necessary sacrifices that come with holding their positions: time, extracurriculars, soccer games, and anniversary parties with family and friends. Many talented employees who would make for incredible leaders choose not to go down that path because of those very costs—it too predictably leads to a lower overall quality of life. The solution isn't to find more people willing to make those life sacrifices to take on leadership roles. It's to change the way we view leadership.

Imagine a world where leaders aren't inherently expected to work ten to twenty more hours than everyone else, or make all the big company decisions. One where they aren't paid five to fifty times more than their employees because the work is shared more evenly across roles. (And really, is one person worth paying fifty times more than another? No.) If leaders are less stressed and burdened by responsibility, might they have more capacity to take care of their people? Or more space for innovation? Would those who've been hesitant to consider taking on leadership roles but would make great leaders step up to the plate? Would we finally see diversity at the top, including single parents, BIPOC individuals, and people with disabilities? The expectations for leadership output can change (and should).

work-free vacation. It's also an indication that the leader might not have had clear boundaries for herself and that she doesn't see it or expect it from others. Remember back in chapter 3, when we talked about the importance of your tone, especially if you're in a leadership position? This is a great example of why!

How Leaders Can Set Boundaries for Themselves and Their Employees

- ✦ Regularly take your allotted vacation time (and don't work while you're out!).

- ✦ Only send (or schedule send) emails during predetermined work hours.

- ✦ Change workload expectations as needed. For example, if a global pandemic tears through the world, maybe readjust team goals for the year to make accommodations for the fact that people might be struggling.

- ✦ Prioritize boundaries around mental health over organizational health.

- ✦ Keep the communication lines open around leader capacity (in terms of workload and time available) and employee capacity.

PREVENTING BURNOUT AS AN INDIVIDUAL

If you, like many employees, want to show up for your team, work hard, and contribute to something greater, it can be very hard to set boundaries. We speak with so many people who are scared of setting boundaries for fear that they won't be seen as a team player—or, alternately, that the boundaries they set won't be respected.

If you're one of those people, we are here for you. Setting boundaries is hard. While much of the burnout prevention will come from the organizational culture and the approach your leadership takes, you do have some agency to define and set your boundaries (however incremental they might be). When you set boundaries to protect your energy and time, you provide clarity to others while giving permission to do the same. If you're someone who's traditionally struggled to say no and set boundaries, you can create change in your daily routine by getting clear on where and when you're willing to bend.

How You Can Set Boundaries

Make some lists (who doesn't like a good list?):

- ✦ What are you actually responsible for (your workload, living your core values)? What are you not responsible for (others' feelings, others' workloads)?

- ✦ What are your negotiables (additional meetings are fine, moving around the schedule)?

- ✦ What are your nonnegotiables (having dinner with your family, getting eight hours of sleep)?

- ✦ What do you need from others? How can you advocate for yourself?

Define examples of when you will say yes and when you will say no:

- ✦ To get you started, your "YES!" list may include things like these:

    - Opportunities that help develop your skill set, so long as they aren't adding significantly to your hourly workload

    - Delegation, even when it makes you feel uncomfortable that others might not complete the task the same way you would

- ✦ Your "No!" list might include things like these:
  - When asked to work over the weekends, unless it's a rare exception for something like an urgent team deadline (that said, if "urgent" deadlines are happening every weekend, it's time for your team to revise the definition of urgent)
  - Requests to be available for quick questions or emails while taking PTO
- ✦ Wear the "no" badges of honor

A CULTURE OF WORK-LIFE HARMONY

Work-life balance has long been a heralded goal in the American workplace and, in some ways, the answer to a stressed workforce. "Just find some balance!" the work-o-sphere preached to all us stressed people. But balance felt like a fantasy, a calm state of being while juggling a full life and busy work seemed next to possible. The next iteration of this concept was work-life integration, blending work with home so that they coexist and intermingle. But that also wasn't it. Home and work became too enmeshed, too muddied; and both areas suffered. In our opinion, the more practical, attainable, healthy attitude toward reconciling these two parts of our human experience is work-life harmony.

Work-Life Harmony: The state of finding peace and ease between work and life, acknowledging that they can be complementary forces.

CALLOUT: Story Time

When Boundary-Setting Is Innate

Some people are more comfortable with setting boundaries. For Lisa, it's a common practice. She's the one who will be so clear with her boundaries that it could throw you off. She'll champion you to set your own and model how to do so with grace. But for Hannah, setting boundaries can be a painful and vulnerable thing. When she sets or honors her boundaries, she may do so with a shaky voice and a sweaty upper lip.

Know that what boundary-setting looks (and feels) like will be different for everyone. If you're more like Lisa and setting boundaries comes naturally to you, empathize with those who find it challenging and set the model for how it's done. If you're more like Hannah and boundary-setting is hard, learn from those who do it well and follow their example. And know that it's okay that it's harder for you. Think of setting boundaries as a practice that gets easier with time.

Creating this culture of harmony requires finding what disrupts the calm and managing those stressors. As leaders and individuals, we have to support ourselves and each other to create a culture where stress management is the norm and harmony between work and home is the goal. If you are a leader, it's up to you to create an environment where people can speak up about their stressors without fear of reprimand. Be the culture that invites employees to take a walk or podcast break during the day. Go out of your way to make flexibility a hallmark of your culture by embracing people who leave early for personal obligations or name mental health as a reason to take a day off. Think about enriching employee lives at work not just for the sake of productivity and the work product, but also for their overall well-being.

For individuals, part of embracing work-life harmony means learning how to properly manage stressors so that you don't carry the burdens of work back home with you. It's about learning how to take the time to sit with and examine the negative emotions and patterns that are leading to stress.

Here's what won't work: Telling yourself, "Stop being stressed!" or "Sarah can handle it, so why can't I handle it? What's wrong with me?!" If you really think about it, trying to force yourself to feel differently because you're telling yourself to do so is a bit like waving around a wand and expecting the spell to work.

Here's what you can do instead: Sit with the feelings and process them. (We know—ugh, not so fun.) Emily and Amelia Nagoski wrote a whole book about how to appropriately process stress called *Burnout: The Secret to Unlocking the Stress Cycle*. In it, they explain that emotional exhaustion is the main component that contributes to negative impacts on health and work. They write that "emotions are tunnels. If you go all the way through them, you get to the light at the end. Exhaustion happens when we get stuck in an emotion."[19] So, in short, to beat the exhaustion, you have to get through that stuck place in the tunnel.

A way to get started is to figure out where that emotion is held in your body. The most effective way to do this? Move your body. Yes, this advice is everywhere, and for good reason—because it works.

Our bodies hold on to every emotion. So if you are very stressed and feeling lethargic, angry, frustrated, or numb, MOVE. This doesn't have to be marathon training, and movement varies for people in different bodies. Some ideas include practicing yoga, doing modified desk squats with your chair, or trying progressive muscle relaxation by tensing and then relaxing muscles in your body starting at your feet. Take a walk, even if it's just a lap around your company building (something Lisa and Hannah used to do frequently at their previous jobs!). Go into a bathroom stall and jump around. (Will it make you feel silly? Probably. Do it anyway.) Rachael, an advertising producer, used to run the creepy back stairs in her building while reciting "This is just a job" to keep herself going.

You can take this movement a step further by reflecting afterward. Ellie Roscher, a writer and yoga instructor who deeply believes in the power of pairing movement with reflective writing, shared these words of wisdom with Hannah during a conversation:

> Take a few minutes after moving to write. Don't overthink it. You don't have to craft beautiful sentences or worry about grammar. You can even write on a scratch piece of paper, crumple it up and recycle it immediately. The point is to get what is stuck in your body out of your body. Getting the thoughts looping in your brain out on paper, creating geographical distance, can loosen their hold and lessen their power. A brief reflective writing session after moving your body releases and sloughs off that top layer of stress and emotion so that you can live and work from a deeper sense of self, reacting less and responding more. Pairing movement and writing as a regular

practice can bring a sense of ease in your body and mind, benefiting you and those around you.

Moving, while often the most effective thing to do, is not the only thing to get you unstuck. Spend some time with people who fill you up. Laugh. Hug someone (or an animal) you love. Create art. Cry in private to release hormones (this is Hannah's go-to).[20]

And here's a bonus step: Be SO kind to yourself. When feelings pop up in your brain and you start judging them, you are telling your mind and body to plant your feet in the emotion. The processing stops. Self-judgment is a dangerous game, so try to win that game by letting the judgment go. Instead of saying to yourself, "I'm so tired, and I'm so annoyed at myself that I'm so tired," say, "I'm so tired. And that's okay." And then take a deep breath.

Work and life can coexist without one draining all energy from the other. When we focus on the harmony between the two, we can create space for both—and reap the benefits.

ADVOCATE FOR ONE ANOTHER

Working while stressed and on the verge of becoming an extinguished ember can feel incredibly lonely. In an attempt to manage impressions, it's common to try and keep your struggle under wraps for fear of looking weak or incompetent. Whatever the reasons may be—a difficult boss, work culture, or personal woes—suffering in stressed silence can quickly lead to isolation and exhaustion. The good news is that a bit of kindness and care can stop the burnout cycle if enough people step up for themselves and one another.

If you are the stressed someone, and you have at least one peer you can share your problems with, do so. Perhaps it's just to say it out loud. (It's shocking what a release it can be to simply have someone listen and say, "That does sound stressful." 'Tis also affirming.) It's in sharing that people can relate and find what stressors they have in common.

When the stressors are more known, you can stand up for one another. Take on some extra tasks if someone else is having a hard day. Confront leadership when their demands are too high. Respect and honor one another's boundaries. Maria, a CRNA at a Minneapolis hospital who was on the front lines of COVID-19 patient care, recognized how the extreme stress and burnout were affecting her peers. As someone who was feeling more capable of managing her own mental and physical stress at that time, she decided to share some resources. Maria created a Wellness Wednesday email with her peers, sharing nutritious recipes, affirmations, journaling prompts, and meditations to ease the strain she saw in others. This simple gesture garnered so many positive responses from her peers that the email spread beyond that group to other departments.

Maria's example is one to follow. It's about coming from a place of care, appreciation, and acknowledgment to honor one another's stresses no matter the role, responsibility, and expertise in an organization. Adam, a billing coordinator at a nonprofit organization, loves his job and appreciates his leader. To him, it makes sense to take it upon himself to help his leader prevent burnout. "I know that all it takes to turn a great job into a horrible one is a change in leadership. And if [my boss] burns out and leaves, I'll miss having a good job. It's a mutually beneficial thing. Please don't burn out. Let's support each other." It is never on just one person's shoulders to help another prevent burnout if the environment is toxic or a leader is too demanding—and if it's in your emotional bandwidth, do what you can.

We have a long way to go in the American workplace when it comes to burnout. And it's going to take time, especially when most of us who want to change the narrative that "working equals burnout" are, in fact, extremely stressed! Channel some grace, because if you are recovering from burnout, it will take months—potentially even years—to recalibrate. It took years of practice for Hannah to overcome her bout with extreme burnout and adopt a mindset of calm over one of hustle. It still requires daily reminders to herself and her circles of support that work can be successful and life can be happy. But the key is to fiercely protect your energy and be honest about your limitations. Our sustainability as a collective depends on taking steps to change the narrative that burnout is the norm. Let's start now, doing what we can for ourselves and for others.

✦ THE GIST ✦

PRE-PORTAL STANDARD

With "busy" being a pretty ubiquitous badge of honor, burnout is one of the biggest threats facing employees and organizations today.

PORTAL LESSONS

During the pandemic, that busy standard became completely untenable. Massive spikes in rates of burnout forced us all to reconsider how we work and take necessary steps to redefine work ethic and expectations: lowering workloads, hiring more staff for the same work, adding holistic wellbeing resources, and changing messaging about what it means to be a great employee.

NOW WHAT? STEPPING THROUGH THE PORTAL

To prevent burnout, take these steps:

- ✦ Update your mindset, especially around work norms, growth, and effort.
- ✦ Tackle bias, discrimination, and racism at work.
- ✦ Set and honor boundaries, especially at the organizational level; and make sure that leaders are modeling good boundaries.
- ✦ Encourage a practice of work-life harmony.
- ✦ Advocate for one another.

CHAPTER 5

FLEXIBILITY OR BUST

✦ *"WFH is impossible! We could never do that!" The pandemic proved otherwise. Now what?*

For years, people have wanted the flexibility to do at least some of their work from home. Leaders hesitated to grant that request for fear that employees would do any combination of the following:

- Slack off
- Fill their time with nonwork tasks (e.g., housework, errands, childcare, exercise)
- Be unreachable
- Start feeling less connected to the team
- And the list goes on....

Clearly, there was a wee bit of resistance. Then the pandemic hit; and across the country, those who previously thought WFH was impossible were forced to make it work. All of a sudden, people were like, "Wait. So WFH *is* actually possible? Was all that energy and resistance from before unnecessary? Perhaps even a little exaggerated? Employees actually can get work done from home? Whoa."

When organizations successfully made accommodations on the fly to keep business going in the middle of a pandemic, it demonstrated an invaluable and unforgettable lesson: Despite what some might have us believe, we can indeed think and act outside of previously accepted workplace norms. Things actually can work out (sometimes for the better), even when everything about our lived work experience thus far tells us otherwise. Whoa, indeed.

Now that we've seen the light, people are wondering, "Wait. What does remote work look like moving forward? How do we keep WFH for those who want it? Are there trade-offs in moving to WFH that were hidden by the immediate crisis of the pandemic? Do we really need people in the office? How often? What about the throngs of folks who dislike working virtually and prefer to be in the office? Do we consider extroverts versus introverts? How do we allow people to work in a way that works best for them *and* the company? How do we keep a team connected and successful if they're not working in the same place at the same time?"

All great questions. And we want to add one more.

In our research, we went straight to the source—employees themselves—and asked what they missed most about working in an office. The answers landed in a range that looks something like the illustration on the following page.

The people. The connections. The humans at work were most missed. The number of people shocked about this outcome? Zero.

WHAT DO YOU MISS FROM THE OFFICE?

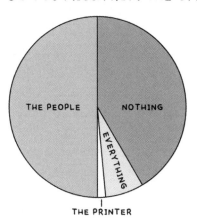

So clearly, as we envision a WFH world, connecting with other humans must be a top consideration. If we want to create a workforce of the future that's conducive to happier employees and a healthy bottom line, we have to consider a redesign that combines the best of the office environment and the best of the virtual environment. We need to be realistic about the potential trade-offs in an all-remote environment while fostering flexibility and choice. When we can do that, perhaps we'll be surprised by how well virtual and hybrid work . . . well, works.

✦ PRE-PORTAL

The office, as it was originally conceived, held a specific purpose: It was quite literally where work got done. As Wi-Fi, laptops, and smartphones became more readily available, many office workers wondered, "Can I go off-site occasionally? Somewhere with fewer distractions? Fewer interruptions? Closer to home? Farther from Glenn, the guy two desks over whose work behaviors drain my batteries?"

Some organizations and leaders responded with "Yes, of course!" and offered various WFH policies, pilot programs, or entirely remote positions. Other companies saw the benefits of remote work and decided against ever having an office altogether. And then there's the majority of organizations—those that hesitated, resisted, or just plainly said, "Nice idea, but no."

There were many reasons to say nope to WFH. But of course it wasn't yay or nay. There was a scale of acceptance, and organizations fell into different categories of remote-work enthusiasts (or not so much):

- **The "We're Just Not That Kind of Company" Organization**: This is the organization that believed their success was defined by people doing work together, all in one space and place. Adopting WFH policies would have disrupted the entire culture that was years—decades, even—in the making.

- **The "As It Makes Sense" Organization**: These companies may have seen the merits of WFH but staunchly believed it really only made sense for *some* roles or on *some* occasions. Maybe they tried WFH in bits and pieces; and if it worked, they folded it into their policies. But if it didn't work, it was right back to the office. Experiment over.

- **The "Hybrid Is the Norm, So Let's Hot-Desk!" Organization**: Okay, these organizations might not all have had hot desks, but they infused flexibility into their culture. It was not uncommon for people to spend Mondays at home or to leave in the afternoon for some quiet work time away from the office.

- **The "All Remote, All the Time" Organization**: This is the group that viewed WFH as the future of work and, wanting to ride that wave of the future, they embraced it enthusiastically. These folks proactively found creative ways to communicate, collaborate, and build culture across time zones, schedules, and work styles.

FLEXIBILITY OR BUST

It wasn't just organizations that had varying opinions and stances on virtual or hybrid work. Employees also brought their fair share of opinions to the table:

The WFH Enthusiast: The employees who always wished to work outside the office their entire career or have already found that dream job. They thrive away from office environments (and maybe people!).

WFH By Choice: The employees who always wanted the convenience and flexibility to work from home at least once or twice a week. It would give them the chance to carve out space they needed free from distraction, interruption, or inconvenience.

WFH By Default: The employees whose role was initially defined as a WFH position, but it wasn't their first choice. If they had their druthers, they would spend more time in the office.

The Office By Default: The employees for whom working in an office is all they've ever known. To consistently work from another environment would be jarring, uncomfortable, and maybe not conducive to good work.

The Office By Choice: The employees who preferred to work in an office because their home or home life didn't foster a productive (or, in some cases, safe) working environment.

The Office Enthusiast: The employees who love the office and many of the perks of being there. One may assume these are extroverts, but there are introverts in this category, too. To these people, being in the office means happiness, success, and drive.

Essentially, the concept of WFH felt complicated and messy pre-portal. Opinions about it were all over the map; and even though some organizations dipped their toe into the WFH pool, the how felt nebulous at best. It's still complicated, but we've been pushed into the pool now. Sink or swim, baby!

✦ THE PORTAL

In a matter of days and weeks, all those fears and hesitations about WFH didn't matter because a pandemic paid them no mind. Leaders rushed to move everyone out of the office, making mistakes and finding solutions along the way. It wasn't easy. And, after a roller coaster of pivots to cater to a new working norm, organizations gathered information (statistical and anecdotal) about what worked and what didn't.

There is some consensus between leaders, organizations, and individuals, as we'll show below.

THE NOT-SO-GOOD

The high-level feedback on what didn't work so well with WFH includes:

- It's very easy to feel lonely and disconnected from teams. Also, connection equals support, creativity, and innovation.

- WFH is not for everyone, and assumptions that all benefit equally from WFH are a mistake.

- Boundaries are fundamental to a healthy WFH environment, and lines can easily be crossed when it's a ten-second walk from the bedroom to the laptop.

Here's what people said to us:

- "I miss face-to-face interactions to build stronger relationships, joke around, help out, and create stronger networks of support."
- "Boundaries between my home and work are so lacking. It's like I can't turn off."
- "I worry new employees don't feel a part of the organization when onboarded remotely."

 And here's what the research says:

- The average workday lengthened by 48.5 minutes.[1]
- Loneliness and isolation are the largest reported concerns of those working remotely.[2]
- For younger and up-and-coming workers, full-time WFH may lead to reduced networks and opportunities to advance.[3]
- Struggling to unplug is the biggest challenge for remote workers.[4]

THE GOOD

While there was some not-so-good about the shift to remote, there were also a lot of celebrations for the new way of working. Some of the positives we found about the move to WFH, from a high-level perspective:

- More time spent with kids, partners, and family because of less time spent on extraneous work activities and treks back and forth to the office.

- The capability to hire people from anywhere to do the job.

- An awareness of new ways of structuring work that provided flexibility and accommodations for different employee needs.

 Here's what people said to us:

- "No commute—and more sleep!"

- "I love that I can go to work in my pj's."

- "I appreciate the flexibility. It's easier to take mental breaks, go for walks, or start a load of laundry."

 Finally, here's what the research says:

- People with commutes have lower life satisfaction and happiness than people with no commutes at all.[5] So no commute equals a thumbs-up.

- Organizations save around $11,000 per employee each year[6], so money can be allocated elsewhere. Also, people personally save about $4,000 per year.[7]

- It led to increased autonomy, with people doing 50 percent more activities through personal choice and half as many because someone else asked them to.[8]

- It also led to way higher productivity (34 percent higher according to employees, 52 percent according to employers).[9]

✦ NOW WHAT?

In the wake of a decline in COVID-19 rates and an increase in vaccinations, a leader approached Hannah, saying, "I feel like my staff are struggling, and being in person will really help them out. How do we get people back to the office now?"

CALLOUT: Beware!

On The Rush to Be Office-Free

Organizations made some sweeping proclamations at the beginning of the pandemic: "Productivity is high, so we're staying remote for years!" "Stop the building of new offices! We're never going back." After the pleasant surprise that productivity remained so high (or even increased in some cases), they decided to make moves to permanently transform their work environments. But it's possible that some of those choices were made rashly. Perhaps rates of productivity rose during the pandemic not only because of the lack of office distractions, but also because employees were scared of losing their jobs.

Rushed decisions based on preliminary positive findings have been made in the workplace before. Look no further than the hurry to create open-office environments before ensuring that it was what teams really wanted in the first place. So the overall lesson to learn here? A crisis creates an opportunity for change, and seizing that moment is important. It's also critical to seize that moment with care, thoughtfulness, and a whole lot of listening so that the positive shifts remain.

Hmm, she thought. "What makes you believe the office will help them?" she asked.

He paused, considered, and responded, "Well, I guess it's the only way I know what to do as a leader. And I think it's what I would want."

Remember that whole piece around Platinum Rule of communication versus the Golden Rule in chapter 3? It's applicable here too! While this leader thought he was acting in everyone's best interest, he was actually acting based on what worked for him.

Chances are high that you, like many, have been trying to make WFH work. We need to consistently make time to reflect on what works and what doesn't. If we don't, we risk operating in the mindset of this well-intentioned but misguided leader and can end up creating an environment that works for some, not most.

So the question becomes, "Okay, how do we do this?" Keep the mindset that working in the hybrid/virtual model will never look like working in an office; and because this is such new territory for so many companies, we have to be in a learning and iteration space of mind. Be curious, ask questions, solicit feedback, observe carefully, and give yourself and others a heavy dose of grace. We're all figuring this out together.

THE THREE R'S REVIEW

Let's use the Three R's Review from chapter 4 to evaluate WFH workplace culture.

1) REVIEW THE WFH WORKPLACE CULTURE

This process requires collaboration between leaders and individuals. Pay special attention to who is answering the questions, keeping in mind that the majority response is not always reflective of what should be done. For example, disabled people have been asking for remote flexibility for years because it gives them more access to career and financial opportunities. Obviously (or at least it should be obvious), accommodations should absolutely be upheld for disabled people even if their asks are outnumbered by able-bodied people within the organization.

When you collect information from employees, you can summarize the learnings by defining the good and the not-so-good for both working in the office and working virtually.

	THE GOOD	THE BAD	THE UGLY
Office			
WFH			
Hybrid			

2) REDEFINE THE WFH WORKPLACE CULTURE

Completing an exercise like the above should ground you in what needs a refresh. And like most big changes, the redefinition process may feel like a combination of uncomfortable, exhausting, and exhilarating.

To redefine your workplace culture with the remote workspace in mind, embrace evolution and open yourself up to the opportunity of starting over. Shed what you know, and stay curious about new modes of thinking. We often get so trapped by what we believe to be true that we hold ourselves back from innovation and creativity. Policies and procedures that worked well in a mostly office-based environment likely won't translate to a mostly remote space. That's where the power of the team truly lies. Workplace evolution shouldn't be decided in a room with a few key players unless you want a bumpy journey where every ridge results in declining trust.

This practice of "revise and redefine" is one to return to time and again. You may be reading this one year into a new WFH policy. Is it working? Or can it improve?

3) REINVENT THE WFH WORKPLACE CULTURE

Once you have the definition as an aim, get to work! Operate within your sphere of influence to enact change, whether you are six months or three years into a hybrid work environment.

Regardless of what kind of workplace culture you're trying to create, the reality of remote working that became the norm during the COVID-19 pandemic has forever changed the world of work. Building a workplace culture where the best of remote and office

---

CALLOUT: A Space for Grace

Holding Space for Feelings About Change

Accepting that work won't look the same way is no small task. If you are grieving the loss of always being in person, that's okay. If you are upset that you have to go back to the office at all, that's okay, too. If you are annoyed that it takes so much effort to create a work environment that works for everyone no matter where they show up physically, that's okay as well. All of these feelings are valid and worthy of acknowledgment. Then when you know those feelings, name them—and don't suppress them. You can (well, we all can) start from a place of truth, candor, and transparency as we continue the process of reinventing what work can look like for the future.

intertwine will take time. Maybe *lots* of time. The temptation to go back to the comfortable and familiar way of working in an office will be difficult to resist. And yet we must resist that pull to what we once knew so that we can create a better work environment for everyone.

Here we are, a work world of people operating from different places at various times to get things done, move companies onward, and create an impact where they can. And yet, to make employees, revenues, and markets happy, we have to maintain that forward momentum. To embrace the practices and mindsets it takes to maintain a remote work world that really works, we have to tackle its greatest challenges head-on.

REMOTE/HYBRID WORK CHALLENGE #1: LACK OF TRUST

Pre-pandemic, most people did not work from home. And when we look at the myriad of reasons why, the running theme was lack of trust from leaders *and* employees. Let's start with leadership.

Some people (leaders, yes, but also some coworkers) didn't trust or believe that work was getting done if they weren't physically seeing others doing their work. There was a general feeling that if people weren't in a place where manager surveillance was possible, they couldn't be trusted to do their work and do it well. Eesh.

As more people started to work remotely, the lack of trust didn't necessarily go away. In the most extreme cases, we saw organizations implement policies and rules about WFH expectations because they feared productivity loss. Some organizations purchased AI software to monitor employee work habits, while others dinged people if they were away from their desk for too long.[10] Maybe this was a familiar WFH setup for you: diligently keeping track of your hours, standing up on camera to prove you were wearing professional attire and not just a business blazer on top and sweatshorts on the bottom, or being on camera in every meeting even if that very meeting used to be a phone call.

Mid-pandemic, while feeling the likely permanence of working from home, Dexter, a tech operations manager, shared with us, "I think [employers] see that remote work might be a possibility; and because it's a possibility, they want to control as many factors as possible. My thought process and viewpoint is maybe you need to hire people who function and don't need to be babysat, and then just go from there."

We agree. Here's how you can dial up that trust.

ADMIT TO YOURSELF WHEN YOU LACK TRUST

If we've been operating in one way for a long time and it has been mostly successful, it can be hard to envision a world that runs differently and is even more successful. If we're full of doubt, we can look for everything that goes wrong to prove our hypothesis that something won't work. But this can also make us lower our trust in our peers—and that can, in turn, rob joy from people who work both in an office and from home. If we can admit we doubt that people are working to their full potential at home, then we can do some digging to shift our mindset.

OUTLINE EXPECTATIONS

To better operate from a state of trust, clearly outline expectations for the following:

- **Results**: Set reasonable deadlines (emphasis on reasonable), and measure work based on the quality of the output and the thoughtfulness of the process.
- **Behaviors**: Align these with core values, and ensure you clarify what is not tolerated. For example, harassment and bullying of

any kind will not be rewarded or accepted regardless of productivity or successful outcome and will result in immediate suspension and potential termination.

+ **Autonomy**: If you trust others to get their work done, then others should, too. Demonstrate your trust, advocate for it in others, and call out distrust when you see it.

TREAT WFH AS AN INVESTMENT, NOT AS A MONEY SAVER

Yes, more employees working from home means that company overhead decreases. Also, more employees working from home means that companies need to reinvest some or all of that saved money. We get that there's a temptation to feel frustration here. We've heard leaders share concerns like, "We've spent all this money on the office, and now we have to invest in remote workers, too? When does it end?!" That is a natural feeling. But think of the cost of unhappy employees leaving because they were not supported by the organization.

Even more, as hybrid becomes the norm, job seekers are looking for employers who will financially support their remote setup. James, a graphics editor, recently applied for a remote job and received an offer. He knew that to be successful, he would need an improved home setup (his current role was office-bound) and that being around people was necessary for his productivity. So he asked for a minor increase in salary to cover the cost of a coworking space, or at the very least a new desk to handle multiple monitors. In response to his ask, the recruiter said, "No. Everyone has to be flexible with the restraints of working from home." James didn't accept the job.

Investing money could mean directing resources to the following[*]:

+ **Internet Costs**: This can cause some of the greatest challenges for employees working remotely, so it's in a company's best interest to offset the cost of high-speed Internet access.

- **Office Equipment**: Just as you would pay for a desk, ergonomic chair, multicolored folders, and flawlessly smooth pens in an office, consider what you need to supply for individuals on your team.

- **Digital Collaboration Tools**: If you whiteboarded in the office, then whiteboard virtually! Budget for these tools.

- **Connection Opportunities**: You can't gather people into Conference Room A for a birthday party, but that doesn't mean you should forgo those celebrations. They definitely matter. Budget for sending people a slice of the birthday person's favorite strawberry banana cheesecake that you would have otherwise provided in person. Budget for a gamification app to gather people in a fun way. Or, if your workforce is spread around the country (or even the globe), allocate a line item for all-company attendance at the annual in-person team meeting.

- **Coworking Space**: Some people don't want to work in the office but also prefer not to work from home. Consider a coworking space or coffee shop stipend for those who may want an alternate place to create (away from potential distractions at home). This can also be a potential solution for folks who may need the occasional place to work collaboratively with their team.

The counterperspective here, of course, is that employees might not trust their leaders and peers to watch out for them in a remote world. Proximity bias is very real, so you may relate to the hybrid workers who question if their career progression will look the same as office employees or harbor concern that their leaders will pass over them for promotions.

If you are one of those employees who reasonably questions the odds of career success while working remotely, try constructively talking about your concerns. Whether they are teammates or leaders, find people who will listen and either provide space or share constructive feedback. When more people share challenges, a culture of accountability develops naturally where you watch out for one another's success and champion each other in meetings, messages, and emails.

CALLOUT: BEWARE!

Don't Be a Lazy Leader

Remember when Facebook first became popular, and organizations everywhere wrote social media policies dictating whether people could log into Facebook (or other social accounts) at work? And then said organizations realized that Facebook wasn't a huge issue, and they could trust their employees to get their work done (even if they were checking status updates a couple of times a day)? It makes us think of wise words shared with us by Lani, a business owner and strategic consultant: "Lazy leaders rely on policies and rules." This is so true. When leaders face something new that they don't understand, like Facebook or remote working, it makes sense that they make decisions out of fear. It's easier to write rules about, say, work hours rather than listen to people and create expectations that everyone can get behind. If you're a leader, don't let fear dictate your actions.

REMOTE/HYBRID WORK CHALLENGE #2: BLURRED BOUNDARIES

The boundary between work and home softened when smartphones entered the picture and we could bring work around in our pockets. Now, those blurred lines are almost indistinguishable. With the reality that work happens in the same square footage as your home, there is this expectation that responding to one more email or quickly hopping onto a call should be easy, so why not just do it? Clocked out for the day? Okay, . . . but one more small task won't hurt. This assumption fails to recognize that answering a quick email means stealing time and energy from everything else that matters to you, like family time, friend hangs, volunteering, self-care, and even sleep. In your daily work, that tiny task can knock you out of focus, where it can take as much as twenty-three minutes and fifteen seconds to return to your original task.[11]

The message we all need to hear is that work is not more important than anything else going on in our lives. Our time is sacred and should be treated as such. Working remotely shouldn't mean that we're available at all times, even if that assumption is for when we work from home two days a week. It should mean that we are available when we can be available.

In practice, we suggest the following:

REMEMBER THAT "ALWAYS VIRTUAL" DOESN'T EQUAL "ALWAYS AVAILABLE"

It is so easy to tell ourselves the story that people can answer a quick question because they're right next to their computers. Just as it is helpful to have uninterrupted time to focus on work, it's even more helpful to have uninterrupted time to focus on life. And that's not only helpful. It's also necessary for having a life of calm, happiness, and fulfillment.

SET BOUNDARIES NOW, NOT LATER

All levels, and all roles, need boundaries so that the conversation about them is less like, "LOL, I could never delete my email app from my phone!" and more like, "I see that boundary. Cool." So here's what to do:

- **Agree to a Window of Shared Working Hours as a Team.** This can look like a two-hour chunk of time determined by a majority consensus where everyone is available and online. Other than that, work is asynchronous. This agreement gives enough structure so that people know when and how they can show up for each other while giving flexibility for the rest of the day.

- **Honor Sign-on and Sign-off Times.** Set a time that everyone is expected to shut down their computer. It's up to your discretion if you work past those hours, but at least the expectation won't be there! Oh, and ensure that folks plan to send emails during working hours. If you are a leader, remember that you set the example.

REMOTE/HYBRID WORK CHALLENGE #3: POOR COMMUNICATION

Communication at work is always tough because, as humans, it can be challenging to clearly communicate. We don't listen well, we're patterned for negativity bias, and distractions can easily pull our focus away from who's talking. In a virtual or hybrid environment, communication can be even more difficult. Work is asynchronous, nonverbal cues are limited (if not nonexistent), and there may be even more distractions than when you're in the office (e.g., kids asking for lunch, dogs barking at every living creature outside the window, loud construction work). So what's the solution for improved remote work communication? Not to be redundant, but the best thing to do is to talk about it. A lot. And capture those conversations. Here is what this looks like in action.

OPERATE FROM AN OVERCOMMUNICATION MINDSET

Whether we work remotely three hours a week or forty, we spend a lot of time in white space where clarity is lacking. We may have

CALLOUT: TOOLBOX

Physical Boundaries Are a Necessity

The beauty of WFH is that you can walk to your office in minutes, perhaps seconds. That is also its downfall. While working remotely, it can feel like there's no visual or physical escape from work itself. Days of the week turn into Blursdays, where work seeps into every element of life. To reestablish ownership over your time when your workspace and home space are the same (even if only for a few days or hours out of the week), it can be really helpful to create your physical boundaries. Treat these as cues for your brain to go in and out of work mode. Here are some examples:

- Designate a specific mug or glass used only for work.

- If you can, work in a separate area of your home. If you're working in a shared space, try to put all of your work things in a spot or bag at the end of the work day.

- Start and end your work days with rituals. For example, a ritual can look like this before focused work time:

    - Light a candle.
    - Put your phone in its "home."
    - Delete all other open tabs in your Internet browser.
    - Start a timer.
    - Take three deep breaths.

moments of connection during a regular Zoom meeting, but between that call and the next, it's so easy to fill our heads with untrue narratives. These narratives may be about how we're doing ("I'm failing, and everyone hates me!"), what we could be doing better ("None of my projects are good enough."), how your colleagues are feeling ("I bet they wish that Vivica was on their team, not me."), or what is needed for the client pitch next week ("That deck needs, like, five revisions!"). It's also very easy to miss information. Five people could be in a hybrid meeting, but then the three employees in the office discuss an idea together later that day that leads to a whole other way forward. All of those small conversations need to be documented. To avoid the miscommunication hazard zone where everyone is talking and no one is listening, or where some know a lot and others know a little, stay in the overcommunication headspace.

GET REALLY, REALLY CLEAR ABOUT COMMUNICATION IN YOUR WORK ENVIRONMENT

Rather than making assumptions, get super explicit about preferences and expectations. Discuss what works for people individually and how that supports everyone collectively. Here are a few ways to do this:

- **Have a Process for Taking Great Notes at Every Group Meeting.** Don't make one person be the notetaker. Hannah prides herself on taking great notes during meetings, but that has often meant in previous roles in life that she was less of a meeting participant and more of a meeting scribe. But note-taking is a skill that everyone can—and should—develop, especially in these WFH days. A way to make this successful is to assign a notetaker and then make sure that the assignment rotates.

COMMUNICATION MATRIX

EMPLOYEE	LISA X. WALDEN	HANNAH L. UBL	
BEST TIMES TO REACH	10AM – 6PM	8AM – 3:30PM	
UNAVAILABLE TIMES	7PM – 9AM	5PM – 8AM	
BEST WAY TO REACH	TEXT, SLACK, EMAIL	TEXT, EMAIL	
URGENT REQUESTS	TEXT	CALL	
EMERGENCIES	CALL	CALL	
SPECIAL REQUESTS	NO VOICEMAIL. TEXT PLEASE	INCLUDE DEADLINES WITH REQUEST	

+ **Craft a Communication Matrix.** It's very common to believe that people want to communicate the way you prefer. It's the Golden Rule playing over and over again in our subconscious. And yet it's often true that others will have quite different communication preferences. (Oh look, it's the Platinum Rule, rearing its head again!) So take a beat to find out what those are. A straightforward, tactical strategy is to collect information about those preferences into a matrix for your team. Despite the fancy name, this is just a simple spreadsheet, but having the information captured and readily accessible by any team member makes it so much easier to communicate fluently despite varying styles. These columns can, of course, be customized to be more representative of what is most useful at your organization.

+ **Create Communication Codes.** Think of these as your communication core values. GitLab, an all-remote organization, has an entire set of communication values to guide communication in their environment. It creates clarity to address and prevent misunderstandings. Of course, those will still happen, but a code to refer back to sure can help. It also serves as a way to reinforce culture daily while promoting a style of communication that is filtered through the values that guide the work GitLab does. A couple of our favorite examples from their communication guidelines include the following:

- No ego (i.e., Don't defend a point to win an argument or double down on a mistake).[12]

- It's impossible to know everything (i.e., You can't know how your words are interpreted without asking).[13]

- Say "thanks" (i.e., Take every opportunity to share praise, which creates a climate where feedback is viewed as a gift rather than an attack).

REMOTE/HYBRID WORK CHALLENGE #4: VIDEO FATIGUE

Video calls are one of the reasons we can make remote work effective in this decade when, only thirty years ago, it would have felt impossible. Meetings, gatherings, and one-on-ones may feel easier when that camera is turned on. It also invites people into coworkers' homes and lives to the point that it's now no longer embarrassing to have your children run in mid-meeting or your cat accidentally type some gibberish into the chat box. And while there is so much good that the Zoom enthusiasm has brought, there's definitely the danger that it becomes too much of a good thing and people feel the video fatigue. So here are some considerations to make the most of video conferencing.

YOU NEED A ZOOM-HAPPY (NOT ZOOM-HEAVY) CULTURE

Think of the concept of "less is more." ("But wait!" you might push back. "Enforcing video meetings boosts connection, lets us collaborate more effectively, and shows how actively engaged we are!") When you overuse video, it can become more of a hassle than a help. Sure, face-to-face interactions may be important when having tough (but empathetic!) conversations. But when video is the standard for everything, its value is diminished.

In addition, there is an extra cognitive load in trying to read facial expressions over a screen.[14] There's also a strain on our eyes and bodies from sitting in front of a screen all day. And if you haven't figured out how to hide the thumbnail of your face on your screen, there's the added stress of seeing yourself on camera for hours upon hours a day—which, for many folks, is no fun as they pick themselves apart, thinking things like, *OMG, what is wrong with my chin? That's what it looks like?! Or, How did I get this old? Look at my wrinkles. Look at 'em! Ugh, how depressing. What if I just stretched my skin to create that smooth look? Is there an app for that?* This overwhelming self-criticism increased so much during the coronavirus pandemic that there was a "Zoom Boom" in cosmetic procedures![15]

During the pandemic, people were in more meetings than ever before.[16] Which begs the question: Were all those Zoom meetings even necessary? Or overkill? Our guess is the latter. If you really want virtual video meetings to help connect versus exhaust, to boost engagement instead of disengage, then don't just institute a "whenever we connect virtually, we connect via video!" policy. Instead, meet less often on camera and more often on the phone (or via email). And when you do host video meetings, be clear about the why, explicit about the objectives, and mindful of time (aiming for short and sweet). And offer grace to those who might not want to turn the camera on that day, for their own reasons.

WRITE SOME ZORMS

Zorms, or "Zoom norms," are a standard set of expectations for when you log onto a video call. They offer clarity and can help eliminate the guesswork as well as feelings of guilt if a case arises where an employee really needs to opt out of video. Here are a couple of examples of Zorms we're particularly fond of:

+ **Zorm Example #1: Everyone is allowed to be "not camera-ready" at times.** Whether it's because they've had no time to shower due to a pressing deadline or some family responsibilities, or they're simply having a bad mental health day, this Zorm gives people some freedom to choose when to turn on their camera.

  When it isn't those times, many people ask us, "How do we get people to turn on their cameras?" The answer is, there is no great answer. If you are opting out of using your webcam for the day, ask yourself why. There may be moments when turning on your camera means that you are showing up for other people on the call to listen, engage, and be "with them," so to speak. And there may be days where the camera needs to be off. As long as you're in a culture of compassion, empathy, and understanding, this shouldn't be as big of an issue as it's become for so many organizations.

+ **Zorm Example #2: Default to a virtual background.** Showcasing your fancy bookshelf (or competency library, as they've been cheekily renamed) might look nice. But what about people who don't have that option? Some employees may be dialing in from their crowded kitchen table, while others are in their Arizona vacation homes, with cacti and the sunset in the background. This Zorm asks people to be self-aware of the impression of their space. Research has shown that "our conscious or unconscious assessment of that physical space can affect how we view an individual's status and in turn, their competency."[17] Discrepancies in settings can be distracting while also highlighting inequities. So, one great option and easy solution? Default to a virtual background.

A critical step in creating these standards is seeking input from people at all levels in all roles and then reaching the best agreement possible. For leaders, this means that writing rules for your teams is not going to work in the long run! You need buy-in; and it's guaranteed that you, as a leader, have things that only your team can reveal! So start simple. When do you think "camera on" is necessary? How do you decide when a phone call, email, or video call is the right course of action? What would make video calls easier for you? When you talk to your friends about work video calls, what do you complain about? Or talk about? Or wish was different?

Working from home (or from another location) in the most productive, positive way will take time. Even if you're reading this book five years from its publication date, we expect that improvements can still be made to WFH norms. Keep that growth and improvement mindset. And remember that, for some people, the shift to remote work led to more balance, freedom, and opportunities. It led to the opposite for others. Giving all employees an option as a foundation will set up your office for the better so that people can have the freedom to choose what kind of working situation will be best for them.

CALLOUT: THE REAL WORLD – A CASE STUDY!

IBM's Work from Home Pledge

When the pandemic began and droves of employees started working from home, IBM leaders turned to their people to crowdsource the best way to create a remote work culture that was built on grace, effectiveness, and flexibility. It started with listening to the struggles people were experiencing in the new WFH world, then with drafting guidelines about what it looked like to work from home and what to expect of your peers. A team of people within IBM—Paul Papas, Monica Logan, Nancy Kramer, and Molly Vannucci—developed personas to align with the guidelines. Then the guidelines went around for feedback.

In response, it became a voluntary pledge instead of a guide. The pledge included lines like, "I Pledge to be Family Sensitive," "I pledge to support flexibility for personal needs," and "I pledge to frequently check in on people." Then it went to the employee Slack channel, where thousands responded positively and signed on. Ultimately, CEO Arvind Krishna also signed the pledge and posted about it on LinkedIn, inspiring other companies to follow suit. If you don't yet have a pledge of your own, we recommend taking the steps to write one, using IBM's process as an example.

✦ THE GIST ✦

PRE-PORTAL STANDARD

For a long while employees have asked for flexibility from their employers, be it through options for remote work, flexible scheduling, or seasonal shifts. Unfortunately, most were met with the frustrating refrain of "it will never work for our company/industry. Sorry."

PORTAL LESSONS

Forced to figure something out by lockdowns and other pandemic-related restrictions, even the most recalcitrant organizations found a way to make it work. Employees experienced the benefits of flexible employment (while also experiencing some unexpected challenges) and have come to expect flexibility as an option.

NOW WHAT? STEPPING THROUGH THE PORTAL

When adapting to the more flexible workplace model, consider the following:

- ✦ Allow for your hybrid model to evolve. It will never be perfect, but it will keep improving if you work at it.

Leaders, remember:

- ✦ Working from home is an investment, not a money saver.
- ✦ Role-model boundaries by schedule-sending messages and honoring sign-on and sign-off times.
- ✦ Establish norms and expectations for hybrid working, but first ask your team what they want and need.

Individuals, remember:

- ✦ Use rituals to begin and end your day.
- ✦ Operate from an overcommunication mindset.
- ✦ Spend time during your week building relationships with peers and leaders.

CHAPTER 6

CARING FOR CAREGIVERS

✦ *You can be a good caregiver, or you can be good at your job. But you can't be both. Or so they would have us believe...*

If nothing else has come through in this book, we hope you are realizing that because employees are #humansnotrobots, business-wide policies need to account for the messy reality that is *real human life*. In no area is this more obvious than when it comes to caregiving: the overwhelming, draining, fulfilling, painful, loving act of making sure that other beings survive and thrive.

Caregiving takes many forms; and while we'll focus this chapter on caregiving in the parenting sense, we want to acknowledge upfront that it looks different for everyone. From our interviews, we know that the struggles of caregiving can look like the following (in no particular order):

- Driving aging parents to appointments and managing their care
- Balancing full-time WFH schedules and "Zoom school"
- Rushing a pet to the hospital in the middle of the night
- Attempting self-care (and feeling guilt while doing so)
- Dedicating time every day to care for a disabled loved one
- Moving to your childhood home to care for parents or grandparents
- Being a single working mother for the first time, without any access to support

Caregiving is a sometimes chaotic and draining, often sporadic, and always adventurous (in some way or another!) mode of living. It was the dog that always insisted on sleeping on your best suit right before an important meeting, or the reason why dry shampoo replaced morning showers as you try to get yourself and your kids out the door in the morning. But before the pandemic, this chaos mostly stayed at home, hidden from your colleagues. With the pandemic years, these realities of caregiving were thrown mercilessly against the tides of video chat backgrounds, when people could no longer pretend that work and life don't intersect.

✦ PRE-PORTAL

Even before the pandemic brought our worlds of work and home together through WFH life, most US businesses weren't doing a great job of structurally supporting their workers. From the small things (like a lack of flexible work hours to handle the realities of school pickups and drop-offs) to the huge (a system-wide dearth of paid leave policies for families welcoming new members), the picture for American families wasn't great. It was—and remains—incredibly common for workers, especially women, to feel they were being put on a "mommy" track (i.e., being given the opportunity to pursue a career with balance at the cost of progression in title and pay) for daring to prioritize family responsibilities, parental leave, or even basic work-life balance.

Many families—the lucky ones—relied on a patchwork of relatives, daycare, and sweat to make it through the workday. No matter how creative you try to be, this gets pricey very quickly. In the United States, as a whole, the average cost to provide center-based childcare for an infant is $1,230.00 per month. (In some big cities, that cost rises astronomically.)[1] That's a huge amount of economic and logistical pressure on families with caregiving responsibilities. And that pressure leads many families to make the difficult but often more cost-conscious choice of sacrificing one parent's career so that they can play the role of the full-time caregiver.

THE LEAKY PIPELINE (OR THE LACK-OF-SUPPORT PROBLEM)

The impact of a work environment not built to support caregivers hits everyone hard, but women and low-income families traditionally feel the pain most intensely. Call it the "leaky pipeline," if you will. Study after study shows that traditional pathways to professional success tend to lose women and people of color along the way.

How does this work? Take, for example, PhD recipients and their likelihood to acquire tenure afterward. One study of female PhD recipients in science found that marriage and family formation are the primary reasons for the "leak" between getting a PhD and acquiring a tenured role.[2]

While not every part of the leaky pipeline can be connected to problems in caregiving, we know it's a common reason why people leave the workforce. In 2019, one in three workers with caregiving duties said that they had quit a job because of those duties.[3] While this problem is far from new, we have yet to see a sweeping, comprehensive set of policies that support caregivers at work. Instead, they're left to try and figure it out mostly on their own, making small sacrifices every day for work or family. Take the kids to swim class, or attend the end-of-day project recap? Stay for breakfast for the first time in a couple of weeks and get behind on work tasks, or quick morning kisses goodbye and a head start on the day? Risk disappointing the team and your employer or those you're caring for at home? Absentee parent, or absentee

CALLOUT: Just the Facts

Caregiving Around The World: Does It Have to Be This Way?

It may come as no surprise that the US has one of the lowest rates of governmental and policy support for working parents, including zero weeks of mandated paid family leave (though there's some talk of new and promising changes, which will hopefully have come to pass by the printing of this book!). According to a recent Pew Research Center study, the US ranks last in terms of parental leave out of forty-one nations (Estonia leads the pack, with eighty-six weeks paid).[4]

In Sweden[5], for example, at the time we were writing this book, new parents get 480 days fully paid if they are single parents, with co-parenting arrangements getting ninety days each plus the remaining 390 days to split between them. The government also supports daycare (with public options) and long-term work flexibility (with a policy that allows for working 70 percent of your hours until the child is eight years old).

This flexibility has long-term effects. A recent study by the Institute for Women's Policy Research estimates that paid family leave policies lead to 20 percent fewer women leaving the workforce.[6]

employee? It's no surprise that often the most logical choice is to simply drop out of the workforce entirely.

This reality can be even worse for retail workers, restaurant staff, and other lower-income job holders. Many of these roles aren't eligible for Family and Medical Leave Act (FMLA) protections, and they also traditionally provide less schedule flexibility than white-collar jobs. Horror stories abound of people who were forced back to work mere weeks or even days after giving birth, unable to get leave when family members fell ill, or faced the difficult and potentially dangerous choice of leaving children unsupervised while going to work.

The impact of no true, robust support system for caregivers adds up to all sorts of losses, which affect both employers and individuals: loss of time, loss of talent, loss of opportunity, loss of diversity, loss of choice, and loss of the chance for caregiving and work to coexist peacefully without burning people out or forcing them to make the unfair decision of "Do I stay, or do I go?"

✦ THE PORTAL

In March 2020, whatever support systems people had been relying on disappeared almost overnight countrywide. Daycares and public schools closed. Nannies and babysitters represented a potential risk to a family's health. Nursing homes and elder living facilities shut their doors to visitors, forcing families to move loved ones in with them or accept FaceTime-only visits for the unforeseeable future. Even the ever-reliable fallback of begging family members for help meant potentially risking exposure to an unknown virus threat. The scaffolding of the caregiving network had effectively collapsed.

The impact was immediate. Sometimes, it showed up in almost LOL-inducing ways: dogs howling loudly during phone calls, kids making their expertly ill-timed demands like "I need ice cream!" mid-Zoom meeting, bosses holed up in their child's nursery that's strewn with onesies and baby wipes while trying to find a slightly less chaotic space for one-on-ones. There was even that one news story from early 2022 about a group of moms in Boston who were so exhausted and fed up with their lot that they gathered on a football field to release a primal scream.

The collapse of the caregiving network took a more serious toll on some. Many people switched to part-time hours or quit working altogether when the stacked challenges of caregiving, work, and lack of time to grieve lost loved ones felt damn near insurmountable. Ugh.

THE SHE-CESSION

The impact wasn't felt uniformly across the workforce. Article after article highlighted the outsized burden that childcare and family caregiving responsibilities took on women.[7] Some of the noteworthy headlines included "Enough Already: How The Pandemic Is Breaking Women,"[8] "The Pandemic's Toll on Women's Careers,"[9] and "America's Mothers Are in Crisis."[10] Job losses were disproportionately held by women. Their unemployment rate jumped by more than 12 percentage points between February and April in 2020[11], with the losses for lower-income women and those without college degrees even more staggering. What's more, one out of four women who lost their job cited childcare as the reason for losing their job. We heard words like *she-cession* make the rounds, and experts warned us that women's participation in the job market was hitting all-time lows.

CAREGIVER OVERLOAD

For parents who kept their jobs, a new problem cropped up: acting as a full-time caretaker, a full-time teacher, and a full-time employee, all without the option of adding hours or manpower to their days. Anecdotally, we heard many women speak about feeling that their jobs were less important than those of their husbands. Women were

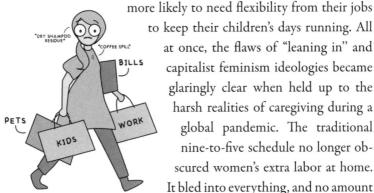

more likely to need flexibility from their jobs to keep their children's days running. All at once, the flaws of "leaning in" and capitalist feminism ideologies became glaringly clear when held up to the harsh realities of caregiving during a global pandemic. The traditional nine-to-five schedule no longer obscured women's extra labor at home. It bled into everything, and no amount of "you can do it!" could counter the incredible drain that playing the roles of mom and professional had become (or, let's be honest, had always been).

In response, some businesses scrambled to try and solve this long-standing problem that, almost overnight, became elevated to a workforce staffing emergency. There were those who took a hard look at their policies and how they might be actively damaging to the caregiving contingent of their staff. They jumped to offer childcare stipends and much-needed flexibility (while embracing a culture of grace and compassion for caregiving colleagues along with it). Disappointingly, there were also those who took the approach we'll call "waiting out the storm." They acted on the assumption that after a few weeks of turmoil, things would eventually settle down and return to "normal." So rather than approaching the problem holistically, they made those short-term Band-Aid accommodations, like temporarily assigning work to someone else or allowing a "flexible" schedule that resulted in caregivers regularly working until 2:00 a.m. (Not the best Band-Aid solutions.) Even worse, some expected the same amount of productivity and output on WFH day one!

One employee we spoke to raved about an employer that immediately changed sick policies, implemented flexible work hours, and allowed employees to prioritize their family's well-being. Others spoke of inconsistent expectations, resentment from other burned out colleagues, and a feeling of failure both at home and at work. Trista, an AV production director, told us, "It's like I have to pick between being a good mom and being a good employee. But I honestly just feel like I'm failing at both."

The flood of responsibilities and almost superhuman effort it took to shoulder the burden served as a stark call to action. It revealed the urgency of rethinking and reimagining the intersection of work and caregiving.

✦ NOW WHAT?

How can we use this disruption to fuel a tide of change in our workplaces? What does really caring for caregivers mean? And why should we do it?

CALLOUT: TO BE CLEAR

Caregiving as a Survival Mechanism

Caregiving-friendly policies aren't just beneficial to the employee. They're also beneficial organization-wide in both the short and long term. We'll get more into the long-term benefits later. But in the short term, caregiving can help balance people out. When properly supported, caregiving can be a centering, grounding act. During the pandemic, many previously petless employees found that their new fluffy friend gave them a reason to look forward to waking up in their quarantine space every day. Workplaces that supported employees in developing and maintaining caregiving relationships frequently benefited from happier employees.

THE BUSINESS CASE FOR CARING

This isn't just about "self-care" or "being nice." Companies miss out when they fail to provide a proper support system for caregivers. On the flip side, there's so much good that can come from supporting caregivers, including retaining employees with years of experience and pretty valuable skills (e.g., deep focus under pressure, excellent time management, and honed problem-solving capabilities). Caregivers in a work environment are often generous with compassion and thoughtfulness for others. Lots of offices have the regressive (and unfortunately named) "office mom" who remembers everyone's birthdays and makes sure that the holiday party stocks gluten-free options. Direct caregiving skills like these have a beneficial impact on overall culture.

On top of all the good we miss out on, lack of caregiving support can cut off the next generation of thinkers, forcing them into an impossible choice between having the work life they want and the home life they've dreamed of. Tammy, one of our interviewees, captured this when she said, "My mindset shifted the moment I had my daughter. You see higher-ups not having that work-life balance. I told myself that I was okay not really rising past my current level to get into a leadership position. I've found my sweet spot where I'm comfortable. I have the responsibility I want, and I get to spend time with my daughter."

In this way, the next great CEO might get lost in the shuffle because they were forced to take a step back, rather than activating their own brilliance against a flexible work schedule that worked for everyone. The health care system might miss out on the doctor whose background in her low-income neighborhood helps her better treat patients. A company may never get the chance to hire that HR director whose empathic open-door policy leads to greater office harmony. The time and skills (and money) put into training people are being lost, as well as the institutional knowledge that comes from longtime employees. As a whole, the business world is missing out on top employees who could thrive with better work-life balance or a culture with greater caregiving support.

It's also important to reiterate that the impact is disproportionately on women and lower-income individuals. As businesses look inside themselves to see what they're missing and how they can better recruit and retain diverse employees, this is a major, pressing business problem. Collectively, we're missing out on a massive, essential pool of talent. By supporting employees during their caregiving years instead of losing huge numbers to the leaky pipeline, we give them the potential to grow into true leadership positions—an investment that will undoubtedly pay great dividends (for business and our society alike) when the next generation of leadership begins to take over.

Every single person we interviewed, regardless of gender, expressed a desire to be set up for success at work while having an opportunity for success with their home responsibilities. The will is there. They just need their employers and organizations to meet them halfway. But how?

The solution to the caregiving conundrum is not simple, and it's certainly not going to look the same in every organization and every situation. Since this is the type of problem that needs to be approached mainly from an organizational and managerial level, we'll start there. Then we'll address how caregivers can advocate for themselves.

CARING FOR CAREGIVERS AS AN ORGANIZATION

BOLDLY RETHINK "THE WAY THINGS HAVE ALWAYS BEEN DONE"

Companies, as a whole, are not known for being quick to embrace change. When it comes to caring for caregivers at work, we've needed a revolution for a very long (no, too long) time, and the portal is a golden opportunity to act boldly.

Now is the time to take an almost ruthless edit of your policies and rethink them with care. If you haven't done so already and it's within your power, we recommend adding a "Caring for Caregivers Revision" project to next quarter's list of priorities.

Melissa, a leader at a PR firm, told us that she's always thinking of this. When she received feedback from colleagues that their parental leave policies were outdated, she started to seek advice from her peers. "I thought our policy was generous!" she said. "But clearly I was out of the loop. We have to listen and reconsider our offerings if people are telling us they don't feel valued. That's on us as leaders to listen and make a change."

Below we'll outline some of the areas and ways you can take a cold, hard look at assumptions that often underlie institutional policies. How can you revise and rewrite them to be more welcoming and supportive for caregivers now as well as those of the future?

- **Look at Your Leave Policies**. If your parental leave policy allows three months for women recovering from birth and only two weeks for men, what is the long-term impact of that on women's growth and retention at the organization? Also, are you unintentionally (and perhaps unconsciously) creating a condition whereby young male candidates for roles are more appealing than female candidates, because men won't be eligible for three months of leave if they decide to start or add to their family? It's worth considering these unintended consequences.

- **Flex That Schedule**. Take a critical eye to how scheduling, email hours, meeting-free days, leave policies, and more can support caregiving and promote a shift from a burnout-heavy culture to a more balanced one. And if, as a manager, you would allow a parent to leave at 4:00 p.m. to pick up their children but don't provide the same flexibility for a single man trying to help his mother get to doctor's appointments, what impediments are you putting in the way of success? Really think about your organization's needs and whether providing more flexibility for your team can allow everyone to be more successful.

+ **Create and Enforce Boundaries**. The same strategies that reduce organizational burnout can, of course, help caregivers, too. Having a flexible schedule doesn't mean always "on." Having clear boundaries—and respecting your employees' clear boundaries—helps people separate working from home and caregiving. Start gently pushing back when you see a peer or colleague online after hours, using strong but empathic language. Or start scheduling emails to go out during work hours—even if you are working flexibly at other times—to help reinforce these boundaries.

+ **Where Possible, Think Programmatically**. With big organizations in particular, consider programs that allow you to directly provide caregiving support (e.g., day care partnerships, college savings plans, access to Education Saving Accounts). Nothing shows that an organization means it like putting organizational time and resources against these kinds of programs!

+ **Nurture the Next Generation**. Think about the way that flexibility and generosity sometimes get concentrated at the top levels, with an assumption that younger people without caregiving responsibilities will pick up the slack. How are you supporting the next generation, no matter what needs and requirements they may come in with? Are you making accommodations for young people who might be caring for ailing parents or siblings? How can you make sure that your policies aren't getting in the way of equity and retention goals?

There are a lot of workplace policies that get carried over from generation to generation without a deep look at the assumptions underlying them and whether those assumptions still apply in the modern workplace. The pandemic helped shake up our assumptions about all kinds of things—caregiving included—and now it's time for institutions and managers to bravely take action on creating a working environment where caregivers can actually succeed.

Here's a big caveat, though: Effective and equitable caregiving support policies don't prioritize parents over everyone else. Instead, they take multiple perspectives into account. Policies that simply shift work from parents and onto single and child-free coworkers can breed long-term resentment and ultimately hurt a woman's capability to advance in the workplace. Deloitte, for example, boasts up to sixteen weeks of what they call "family leave":

> At Deloitte, our family-friendly culture isn't just about maternity leave. Our inclusive approach and expanded paid family leave program recognize changing family dynamics and evolving needs that emerge at different phases of life and career. Deloitte's paid family leave program gives our eligible professionals up to sixteen weeks of paid leave, which can be used for happy occasions—to bond with family after the arrival of a child—or for challenging ones, like the illness or incapacity of a spouse, partner, sibling, parent, or grandparent.[12]

CALLOUT: Toolbox

Keepin' Up with the Employee Handbook

An employee handbook is often the first "statement of values" that a new employee gets about a company. It's also the first place a potential caregiver goes to figure out what their employer provides in terms of support. It's essential, therefore, that organizations regularly review their employee handbook to make sure it reflects the company's actual values. Look particularly at the leave policies. Obviously, parental leave is a must-have, but also review the way a company encourages or discourages things like using FMLA to care for a sick relative, or the way it writes bereavement policies. These say more about a company's values than any mission statement.

CARING FOR CAREGIVERS AS A MANAGER

MANAGERS, THE CAREGIVING POLICY CONCIERGE

Like we said at the beginning of this chapter, supporting caregivers is complicated and requires complex analysis. That analysis can't just be done at an organizational level, especially at bigger organizations. HR and managers absolutely have to work together to take into account individual employee needs. Consider a study where 88 percent of the surveyed employers offer some type of caregiving resources, and 71 percent of workers are unaware of these offerings.[13] Good, informed management and management practices will be key to leveraging a more caregiver-friendly work environment.

This doesn't look like assuming you understand employees' needs. Think of the example of the manager who, while their star employee is on parental leave, decides to reassign their major clients to someone else to help them "smooth their transition back to working full-time and spend more time with their new baby." Suddenly, she goes from gaining experience with top-of-the-line clients to working on projects more suited for junior associates. This kind of "benevolent sexism" is a pervasive problem on its own and could be the focus of a whole chapter. But suffice it to say that you want to avoid perpetuating harm while operating with the best of intentions. Overall, both legally and ethically, managers need to be extremely careful not to make assumptions about what a specific employee may need in terms of support.

This looks like staying aware of your expectations and adjusting them when necessary. Ranae, a manager at a small nonprofit, described working with her editor, who was suddenly balancing providing full-time childcare and working from home. "It was sometimes frustrating, because I felt the pull to expect her to return to full productivity two, three, four months after the pandemic started. But every time her rambunctious two-year-old wandered into the frame wearing a diaper and a face full of scrambled eggs, I realized that I needed to adjust my expectations and work with my organization to adjust theirs."

One way organizations can take a careful (and intentional) approach is to adopt and implement standard training for managers on how to support employees so that at-home responsibilities are not in constant friction with at-work ones. Knowing that this is a company priority can empower its managers to operate in good faith and, hand in hand with HR, help to figure out what's in the best interest for both the business and employees.

Managers, be A students in these trainings and do your homework. Become as familiar as you can with your organization's policies so that you don't have to constantly tell caregivers you need to "look into" expectations or exceptions for them (otherwise, you risk having caregivers feel like they're a burden or "other"). Consider it your responsibility to learn not only what people need, but also what resources are available to caregivers in your organization. Be the messenger of those resources and policies to your entire team, and know who they can go to if they have further questions. So often there may be available help that's underutilized; be sure that isn't the case for your caregiving colleagues.

CALLOUT: Toolbox

A Checklist Against Creating an Unfriendly Workplace for Caregivers

Managers, check yourselves to see if you're doing any of the following, which can contribute to an unfriendly work environment for caregivers:

- Being rigid with start and end times

- Allowing flexibility for some types of caregiving, but not others

- Expressing frustration when people prioritize their family's needs

- Bragging about your hustle or how you missed your kids' recitals because of a big project

- Assuming your employees' needs and assigning them work based on what you think they need, rather than asking them for input

- Planning team events that aren't caregiver-friendly

- Penalizing team members for speaking honestly about their workloads and life responsibilities

LISTEN, LISTEN AGAIN, AND THEN LISTEN SOME MORE

When it comes to assessing caregiving employees' unique needs, constantly listening and showing up with curiosity is truly the best way for managers to get the necessary intel to actually help. During the pandemic, this sometimes looked like weekly touch-bases on how WFH was going or mental health check-ins from HR. Moving forward, it's important to foster a safe environment where people can share how they're struggling with confidence that leaders will prioritize flexibility and want to put in the work to find a win-win solution. Importantly, caregivers need to know that they won't be penalized or measured against their non-caregiving peers whose potential for output may, for a time, be greater than theirs.

When working to find a solution around whatever issue or challenge arises, walk into those conversations assuming good intentions. A chronically late employee, for example, may be trying to get a child to daycare. An employee whose output has decreased may be spending evenings with their parent in the hospital. Do your best not to jump to conclusions, and let employees share as much or as little as they feel comfortable. Work with HR if these conversations wander into protected class issues, such as chronic illness or religious accommodation needs. The goal isn't to have one conversation where you solve all issues; it's to foster a culture where these conversations happen naturally and safely.

CARING FOR CAREGIVERS WHEN YOU ARE A CAREGIVER

First of all, acknowledge that this is *hard*. Cecilia, the mother of an eight-year-old and a manager of a team of ten, reflected to us that caregiving—especially during a global pandemic—is simply one of the hardest things you can do. The people who struggled through it are nothing short of amazing.

Second, know that it doesn't have to be this bad. We believe that the pandemic years will usher in a kinder, more supportive era for caregivers at work. There are myriad ways that organizations and even national governments can shift to better support caregivers, and we've seen just how critical this support is to not only have a functioning workplace but also a functioning society. Which all sounds great from a long-game perspective, but the average overwhelmed parent just needs to make it to next Tuesday. Even that small goal can feel like an insurmountable feat.

Cecilia described trying to make distance learning work while feeling like she was "adulting for everyone at home and at work." This led her to the harrowing feeling that getting COVID-19 might be easier than dealing with the joint pressures of being a mom and an employee at the same time, all the time. People are humans, not robots, of course. But one thing we have in common with our computerized brethren is that there's a finite amount of resources powering our processors.

And yet, when anyone is in a caregiving role, it can be hard (or sometimes impossible) to ask for more resources, say no to a request, or just plain stop. The danger is that if this constant giving goes on too long, the caregiver's energy will be entirely drained and they will hit rock bottom and burn out. As the list below outlines, This caregiver burnout frequently looks like GUILT:

- **Giving** everything you have to both home and work
- **Unforgivingly** looking at your shortcomings and failings
- **Inflexibility** for you so that everyone else gets flexibility
- **Losing** sleep, mental health, and self-worth
- **Treading** water, feeling like you're just barely staying afloat

We don't have the cure for this GUILT, but take a good look at chapter

4 on burnout, because a lot of those strategies apply here. It's so important to focus on the things you can change over the things you can't and to let yourself feel the feelings. Sometimes you have no control over your workload. You may have no control over your organization's policies (although, if you are in a position of power, #AdvocateDontWait). You have no control over the cost of childcare (or, you know, the fact that there might be a sudden global pandemic getting in the way of childcare). *This just SUCKS*. And acknowledging that and letting yourself sit in that truth can help cut off the train of self-recrimination.

Where possible, be vocal about what you need. Many organizations are afraid to ask too much about their employees' personal lives for fear of wandering into problematic, protected class territory. So there's actually a key opportunity for you to advocate for yourself, like defining your schedule needs and questioning leave policies.

Being vocal can start with getting clear on what you need. Try running through an exercise like the one below before you bring your needs forward:

CAREGIVER STRESS EXERCISE

On a scale of 1 (low) to 10 (high), rate your:

- Stress level
- Exhaustion
- Inability to focus
- Feelings of guilt

Reflect on caregiving support at work that could change those ratings:

- What exists currently? Are you making use of it?

- ✦ What doesn't exist that you would utilize?

What help do you need from:

- ✦ Colleagues
- ✦ Leaders
- ✦ Your organization
- ✦ Yourself

Finally, remember that one of the hardest parts of caregiving is pulling yourself out of a guilt mindset to one that honors every part of what you do and who you are. What this looks like is shifting from a mindset of *apologizing* to one of *optimizing*. Rachael, a strategic consultant we worked with in writing this book, started an MBA program while parenting a one-year-old. She told us, "I feel like all my classmates have infinite time—time to work, plan, and, most importantly, time to really think big—whereas I am cramming it all in between naps and sleep-deprived nights. But whenever I am tempted to think of my caregiving responsibilities, experience or age, and scheduling constraints as a downside to working with me, I remember that I bring a wellspring of empathy, patience, and strength that make me a more valuable employee and leader today than when I was a carefree twenty-three-year-old."

If you're also finding this big mindset shift difficult, start small and choose where you can optimize instead of apologize. The chart on the next page shows some of the most common examples we see:

CARING FOR CAREGIVERS

APOLOGIZING

OPTIMIZING

Saying no makes me "less than" others.	Boundaries make me more effective.
I should be able to do it all.	Caregiving is hard, and giving myself grace sets an example for others.
Self-care is a luxury I can't afford.	Self-care is nonnegotiable.
Joy is for home, work is for work.	Joy exists both inside and outside the workplace, and I deserve both like everyone else.

These exercises and conversations will hopefully get you more of the caregiving support that you need. But more than anything, try to leave GUILT behind and have the same compassion for yourself as you do for your coworkers.

─────────── ✦ **THE GIST** ✦ ───────────

PRE-PORTAL STANDARD

Poor workplace support for caregiving workers meant a huge segment of talent constantly felt overworked, overburdened, and at their wits' end.

PORTAL LESSONS

For employees who were also caregivers, the pandemic made an already challenging task (managing work and home life) almost impossible. It served as a bold call to action, requiring us to reshape the work world to make accommodations for this critical talent pool.

NOW WHAT? STEPPING THROUGH THE PORTAL

For a caregiver-friendly workplace:

- ✦ Remember that caregiving takes many forms beyond the traditional idea of parenting.
- ✦ Here's how we can all support caregivers:
    - **Organizations**: Boldly rethink your policies.
    - **Managers**: Listen constantly and carefully to caregivers' needs and know the ins and outs of available support within your organization.
    - **Caregivers**: Give yourself grace and get clear on how to self-advocate.

CHAPTER 7

A Culture of Connection

✦ *Connection can be an easy thing to take for granted, but we're nothing without it.*

Think back to some of the best jobs that you have ever had—the ones where you may have woken up excited to go to work (or, at the very least, ended the day with energy). The kind of job that made you respond to the question "How are you?" with a genuine "Oh, I'm great!" When you think of these "happy job" times, consider why it was so great and (for the sake of this chapter) who was there to make the experience superior to all the others.

Hannah has been extremely fortunate to work in jobs that she has enjoyed, even loved. (Some were doozies, but that's for another time.) One job that stands out for her is when she worked as a barista. Sure, there are memories of spilling milk and customers who angrily threw down their cappuccinos, barking, "Hey, I wanted this *bone-dry*."

Rude. But overall, she remembers the colleagues who laughed with her as they counted the amount of milk spilled in a week. (Yes, she's a huge clutz.) She remembers the hugs from fellow baristas after the mean cappuccino man left the store and the time everyone made DIY holiday-themed costumes when they had to work on Christmas Eve. (Seriously, all stores should be closed everywhere on these days. Sales be damned.) The people Hannah worked with were what made her barista years one of her best-ever work experiences.

Hannah's experience is far from unique. Always, always, it was—and is—the people who make the work worth doing. When we have quality connections at work, we're happier and therefore more productive, collaborative, and less stressed.[1] It's sound logic, really. Human beings are social creatures; and at work, solid bonds can be the difference between a job that's wonderful and a job that's horrid.

This is why so many of us experienced that hollow feeling of isolation during the pandemic years. With the absence of regular office chatter and gatherings, combined with the inability to meet socially with friends and loved ones, a lot of us felt like we could relate to that lone tree on a hill of prairie grass.

But these feelings marked merely a continuation, not a beginning, of an oft-discussed issue: the "loneliness epidemic." Yes, it is just as uplifting as it sounds. (*sigh*)

The rather disheartening research tells us that more than 60 percent of Americans report feeling lonely, left out, poorly understood, and lacking companionship.[2] And when social connection is our most basic need behind food and shelter, the absence of it can be physically and psychologically painful.[3] So, essentially, loneliness in life . . . is not good. Like, *really* not good. And when we feel lonely in the place where we spend a third of our days, ... well, that's not good for us, either.

It's easy to react to these findings with some version of, "Just get to know your colleagues! Have coffee with them!" But we can't just set up a video call with Stacy the new intern, spend fifteen minutes talking about favorite bands and ice cream flavors, and be super chummy forever. Connection isn't that simple. Some of us might feel a bit awkward and ask too many questions during the first meeting. (Hannah raises her hand here.) Others may fear expressing who they really are, and still others may be protecting themselves from bias or even microaggressions. And while we may be hardwired to seek bonds at work, the modern workplace—in many ways—can divide us. Meaningful connection requires confronting the connection roadblocks with thoughtfulness, allocation of company resources, and a collective desire to lead (regardless of level) with care and support. A lot of this chapter will focus on the ways that organizations and the leaders who guide them can get out of the way and actively facilitate opportunities to connect.

✦ PRE-PORTAL

Before diving any further into this topic, we want to be clear about our definition of connection at work. This kind of connection is not necessarily one where employees are BFFs who provide each other a shoulder in the darkest of times. It can be, but it doesn't have to be. The strong connection we mean is one where there is deep respect, curiosity, and compassion that ultimately leads to engaged, happy, healthy workplaces.

Pre-pandemic, these working relationships absolutely existed, but there was also a whole lot of disconnection. A reported 40 percent of Americans felt physically and emotionally isolated in the workplace.[4] And if we dig into those numbers more, we find that some people experienced that loneliness more acutely. Fifty-five percent of Gen Z reported feeling disconnected from others at work, while just 27 percent of Baby Boomers agreed.[5] Hispanic and Black workers agreed in higher numbers that they felt abandoned by coworkers when under pressure at work (37 percent and 30 percent, respectively, versus 25 percent of white people).[6]

The costs of weak connections at work are steep. Employees who are lonely are less approachable and less productive[7]; and if we're all working alongside each other but feeling alone in the process, team morale will decline. When team morale is low, the entire company culture is negatively impacted. We spoke with Stefan, who told us that he started on a team where he instantly felt like an outsider. One particular afternoon, he went for a walk with a colleague and when he returned to the office, not one person met his eyes or started a conversation. While he acknowledged that they may have been busy or just needed some alone time, he couldn't help feeling awkward and alone. "I kind of felt scared to speak up in meetings even, like I didn't know how to be a part of the team." When people feel like Stefan did, they may withdraw from others, feeling like they won't belong no matter what they do. But then we're missing their input, presence, and influence on a whole group of colleagues.

In another vein of the cost of missed connection, consider Claudia, a director of learning and development, who shared a story with us about a time she decided to leave her office job and start consulting. After a year on her own, she said that the absence of colleagues throughout the day made her less motivated, and the moments that typically brought her daily joy—taking her dog for a walk, cooking dinner with her partner, volunteering—weren't as fulfilling because she still felt drained from her lonely work day. Eventually, she recognized how this resulted in a net negative for her life as a whole, and she found her way back to an office. Maybe you can relate to Claudia. Or, maybe you're thinking, *I feel like the opposite of that*. But investment in different kinds of work relationships has too many net positives to ignore.

As we saw in Hannah's barista example, connection can act as a great retention tool. Which means that in low-connection environments, we may lose great people and are more likely to become aimless, dragged down by our loneliness, and less inclined to feel the support and community we need to thrive.

Whew, what a heartwarming picture. Take a break, call a friend while hugging a Squishmallow (Google it if you're unaware of their splendor), and nourish some connection. Then, let's think about a better future.

✦ THE PORTAL

The year 2020 shocked our conception of connection at work. The shock wasn't subtle. Nor was it gradual. In a moment, millions of people were directed to work from home. And stayed doing so for months. And months. And . . . months.

With all the pros this brought (see chapter 5), the limitation of connecting solely via video left a gaping hole in many people's connection-craving hearts. In our survey, over half of respondents used words like *camaraderie, community, socialization,* and "the ability to make friends" to describe what they missed about the office. For some, this loss of connection was devastating. For others, it widened a divide between themselves and their colleagues that had been growing for years.

And yet, the more remote work world encouraged connection. Jason Fried of Basecamp has called offices "interruption factories," and that is spot-on. In a virtual environment, without constant interruption, we can save our social energy for extended exchanges on the afternoon check-in or even be grateful for when they show up in the first place.

Jeff, a video producer we spoke to, told us that he admittedly used to get annoyed by the constant chatter throughout the day. But now, since the connection moments are scarce, he values them exponentially more. When we did connect virtually and muscled through the challenges of "You're still on mute" while trying to talk about the new season of *Ted*

Lasso, our "I've been remote for years" colleagues cracked a knowing smile. They had been long familiar with tech challenges while trying to build rapport, concerns that witty comments would go unheard (and unappreciated), and the biting anxiety that finding a work community may be impossible. But now, people were all facing those tech challenges simultaneously.

There are positives to connecting in a virtual work world. Then there's the other side . . . and it's not all rosy. Specifically, we're talking about how we're taking less time to build relationships because it's so easy to prioritize work (since it's right there in front of us all the time, and small talk via a two-by-three box on a screen is almost physically painful). Heather, a senior consultant, shared with us her supreme embarrassment when she learned of a colleague taking time off to get married. (She didn't know her coworker was engaged.) "It made me realize how lost I was in my work. And when I extended my apologies to [my coworker], she laughed! With all the stress of the past years, and never seeing each other, . . . well, we were in the same state of clueless."

Chats about life happenings tend to decline when people are lost in the onslaught of instant messages, emails, and video calls. Work can get transactional very, very quickly. It's almost too easy to feel out of the loop about someone's life—and about work. And that's when the anxiety sets in: "Do they know what I'm working on? Do they like me? Am I a helpful teammate? Are they talking to their dog off-screen or muttering a frustration about me under their breath?" Paranoia about what coworkers think about us is, not so shockingly, normal in a remote world.[8] In addition to that understandable state of worry, people can wonder if their colleagues—or, even worse, their leaders and managers—aren't thinking about them at all. Proximity bias tells us that people can be overlooked for promotions or pay raises simply because they're not physically close to decision-makers, which can stunt careers and growth (not to mention leave people behind who deserve to be pushed ahead). BIPOC folks who are underrepresented in their organization can face a shrinking network of integral BIPOC support while working from home, which they would more spontaneously grow in the office.[9]

And keep in mind that many (maybe most?) work relationships manifest in different ways. Consulting firm and research house Gallup is well-known for touting how best friendships at work make people more engaged. But *forcing* a BFF culture is super difficult to do, if not impossible . . . and odd. Peer-to-peer connections operate more on this spectrum (which is not in "value" order):

- **Nonexistent**: You don't know this person. Maybe you see their name on group emails every so often or recognize their face on a Zoom or in the hallway. Otherwise, you would consider them a stranger.

- **Work Acquaintance**: You swap emails and may work on projects together with separate roles, but the relationship is essentially transactional. All work, nothing personal. If you see them in public, you'll wave and continue walking.

- **Friendly Work Acquaintance**: You work together and share personal details about life. You banter in watercooler chats. You wouldn't go get dinner together on a Friday, but overall you feel supported by them and they by you. A public run-in includes some genuine small talk.

- **Work Friends**: If you think of leaving your current job, these folks are the biggest reason you hesitate to do so. You look forward to after-work happy hours together and maybe even have some workplace inside jokes with them. You work well together and might not be hanging out all the time outside of work, but it wouldn't be awkward if you did.

- **Close Friends**: You have a strong personal relationship outside of work with these folks, like they would attend your wedding or maybe even become a godparent to one of your kids.

The bottom line is, we have to look at the benefits and the flaws of the modern work environment—whether that be remote, hybrid, or in-person—to create cultures of connection where no one gets left behind.

✦ NOW WHAT?

Moving forward, we carry the knowledge (made so clear by the connection dearth during the pandemic) of how vital working relationships and connections can be in our professional lives. Now, we have the added task of figuring out how to move forward in a world where in-person work may no longer be the standard. As many companies maintain their pandemic virtual work status or shift to a hybrid model, they will need to reassess how to build and establish these ever-important workplace connections, and we all can pay serious attention to how we contribute to a relationship-focused environment. There are some barriers in the way, but they're nothing that can't be overcome.

CONNECTION BARRIER: COMPETITION OVER CONNECTION

The American workplace legacy is one of competition where there are winners and losers. And this pervasive message lives on: To get to the next level, achieve rewards, or take the lead on the next project, we must set ourselves apart from our peers. That desire (and pressure) to win influences the way we interact with each other. We may begin drawing a strict line between our personal and professional selves, demand perfection in ourselves or others (hey, chapter 2!), or withhold vocalizing vulnerabilities to manage impressions. We may begin feeling that any setback is a failure, so we hide it to show ourselves as still being on top. Basically, it's easy to become that player on the team who hogs

A CULTURE OF CONNECTION

the ball and scores points but entirely neglects their team's assistance, capabilities, or desires. The win becomes entirely about the individual.

Not to be all Millennial about it, but there is no *I* in the word *team*. And yes, there may be an *I* in *win*, but when that win is more important than the team—especially in a work setting—it can lead to a culture of finger-pointing, hoarding information, and relationships for opportunity instead of relationships for camaraderie, collaboration, and support. You may make the win in the short run, but in the long run you are diminishing the capacity of your team to keep winning. Leaders and individuals, you need to be intentional about fostering a team mindset.

ELIMINATING THE BARRIER: TAKE A TEAM APPROACH

When coworkers don't see their colleagues as adversaries, they can reach an entirely new level of relationship where it's less about who's MVP and more about how they all fly together, like ducks. This isn't just a *Mighty Ducks* reference (though it definitely is that), but it illustrates a larger point. One study tracked coworkers over twenty years and studied how relationships at work impacted their health. They found that coworkers' support—not work environment or poor behavior from their boss—had the greatest impact on their health.[10] So, leaders, take note.

Here's how leaders can diffuse the competitive approach:

+ **Lead with an Abundance Mindset**. Competitive thinking usually drives people to think in scarcity mode where there's only so much promotion, praise, and money to go around. People then operate in a way to make sure that they will, no matter what, receive the coveted rewards. Abundance thinking allows people to operate from a mindset of "there is always enough." And even when certain resources are in short supply (like allocations for raises, promotion opportunities, time with leadership), there's a way to frame these as outside of the norm, especially if you can tie a plan to how those norms will break in the future. When people believe there's enough to go around, it inherently makes people more supportive and generous.

+ **Celebrate Team Successes**. This starts with teams having shared goals (along with individual benchmarks). When your team meets their goal, celebrate *together*. One small business owner gave her team of twelve travel stipends; everyone could adventure and then relay stories when they returned, knowing that their vacay was possible in part to their team member's successes. Another leader of a midsize organization told us that at the end of a project, they celebrate by giving everyone a day off. Once they get back together, everyone shares how someone helped them on the project. It's a balance of rest and gratitude.

For *individuals*, we want to hold space for the reality that there's a limit to how much you can achieve without buy-in from your leadership and organization. But you are also not powerless. You can help cultivate a team culture between yourself and your colleagues. One solid way to do this is to call out achievements when you see them. If Thelma, your teammate of five years, gets a win and it sparks a jealous twinge within

CALLOUT: TO BE CLEAR

The Difference Between Competitiveness and Overcompetitiveness

Competitiveness is not inherently bad! Overcompetitiveness is. There is a delicate line between ambition and drive (good!), and ambition and drive *at all costs* (bad). This is the line to be wary of.

One of the biggest tolls of the "at all costs" competitive spirit is that the opportunity to develop workplace relationships is sacrificed due to an "everyone for themselves" modus operandi. For those of you out there with a strong competitive drive (*cough, cough* Lisa is among your ranks), as long as it doesn't negatively interfere with your working relationships or lead to behaviors like neglecting to delegate or incessant (often vocal) criticism of others, then you're good! Maintain that fierce ambition, and bring others along with you on your quest for success.

Lisa and Hannah complement each other well in this aspect. Lisa, as competitive as she is, has a knack for wanting to outdo her previous capabilities and efforts—which is why so much of her output is exemplary! But that drive for excellence can sometimes lead to top-level work at too high a cost, which is when Hannah jumps in with, "Is this time and effort worth it?" Or, "Can we lower the expectation slightly, put in a bit less effort, and still produce something great?"

you, acknowledge how your competitive side might be getting in the way and turn the moment into one of appreciation. Write a thank-you note with specific reasons for your gratitude. Recruit team members to sign a congratulatory note when Ron the intern gets promoted to a full-time gig. Focusing genuinely on others' successes will do more for connection, relationships, and personal well-being than holding back support or saying it through clenched teeth.

CONNECTION BARRIER: CLIQUES

The jocks, the nerds, the "it" girls who only wear pink on Wednesdays—most of us are familiar with the stereotypical high school cliques. An entire genre of teen movies has done an impeccable (if not sometimes exaggerated) job of illustrating how exclusive and obnoxious these inner circles can be. This common teenage trope doesn't really go away as people grow up. In the workplace, cliques have formed most notoriously as "the old boys club." Or they're the group of new hires who never feel a part of the current team and form their own Slack channel. Or it's the team of middle managers who bond over the opposition to big organizational change. Or it's a group of work friends who turn a listening session into a complaint dump where, instead of working through the problem and moving forward, they stay stuck in the

emotions of what's making them frustrated in the first place and forgo potential to see things differently.[11]

Anyone who has ever been outside of the group or the "popular" crew (and we're guessing most people have) knows how painful it can feel to be excluded. And it happens at work all the time. There's this natural tendency for people to gather at work with people who look, think, and act like them. In times of stress, this is especially common. So, naturally, when huge changes happen at work (say, navigating another revised hybrid model), people cling to what and who they know. During the pandemic, this meant that some people felt more connected, while others felt even more alienated than they did before.

CALLOUT: BEWARE!

Silos, the Not-So-Distant Cousin of Cliques

Silos form often by happenstance of organizational structure. They might not represent a group that excludes people like cliques do, but they can create a "that's not my job" mentality at work. Usually, people working in silos become distanced and disconnected from what colleagues in other departments are experiencing. In some companies, that can even create a distaste for a certain department. This siloing leads to a culture of disconnect that hurts organizations. Less innovation, dampened creativity, and dwindling empathy result from sticking to one workspace, place, or team. The opposite occurs when silos are broken down and employees work across departments, with information and communication flowing freely. It's up to leadership to make sure that the formal structures they employ don't encourage the formation of silos.

ELIMINATING THE BARRIER: CREATE A CULTURE OF BELONGING

A study of good workplaces nearly always means we stumble upon good ol' Jack Welch, former CEO of General Electric (GE), and an innovative approach he took to work before it was popular. One of those creative ideas that influenced the future of work? The concept of a "boundaryless organization." In 1992 (when Boyz II Men's "End of the Road" topped the charts and Gen X-ers were the kids at work), he shared his vision to "knock down the walls that separate us from each other . . . and recognize no distinctions between domestic and foreign operations, and ignore or erase group labels such as 'management,' 'salaried,' or 'hourly,' which get in the way of people working together."[12] He made this vision a reality via the GE Work-Out process, "a series of structured and facilitated forums, bringing people together across levels, functions, and geographies to solve problems and make decisions in real time."[13] So, basically, Mr. Welch put in the work to break down cliques and silos to solve problems as a team. Organizations still use this kind of collaborative decision-making today; and in doing so, they take a crucial step toward fostering belonging.

By definition, "[belonging] is centered on gaining acceptance, attention, and support from members of the group as well as providing the same attention to other members."[14] Many DEI experts (reminder: we aren't) emphasize the importance of belonging in diversity, equity, and inclusion work. Feeling that our voices, perspectives, and bodies belong is essential to human existence and a healthy workplace culture. It can lead to a 6 percent increase in job performance and a 75 percent decrease in employee sick days.[15] The work needed to create and maintain this kind of culture is constant.

Here is how leaders can foster belonging:

✦ **Introduce a "No Gossip" Pledge.** In many ways, gossip is an attempt to gain control and power when one feels like they have none, or a response to a lack of communication or clarity from leadership. It also quickly erodes trust, even among the very people sharing the gossip. If people are asked to sign a "no gossip" pledge, as psychotherapist and TEDx speaker Glenn Rolfsen proposes, they can hold each other accountable to it and, in turn, transform a culture of "us against them" into "us." He asked more than 250 CEOs to run this exercise in their organizations; and it led to happier employees, higher engagement, and—of course—more productivity.

Here's how it works. Ask your team these questions:

- Do you believe backbiting (or gossip) takes place here?

- How do you define it?

- Would you like to work in a place without that behavior?

Likely, most will raise their hands to the third question. Then, on a shared document, write "No backbiting takes place here" and ask everyone to sign. This is the pledge. Then for six months, meet weekly and ask, "How are we doing with gossip?" One leader we worked with said that her version of mitigating gossip is to walk around and ask, "What's the rumor? What are you hearing?"

✦ **With New Hires, Have an Intentional "Get to Know You" Process.** It's very common for new hires to feel like outsiders. That's a normal step in the process of getting integrated into an organization. In one study by Cigna, new employees who had been working less than six months had loneliness scores more than six points higher than those who had held their positions for over a decade.[16] The more attempts there are to include someone in the culture and authentically connect with them right away, the sooner they'll feel like a part of the fold. Ask them a mix of serious and fun questions on day one, then continue asking questions at later dates. One month in, ask what more they need from you, how the experience has been so far, and if any of their goals have changed. Make it a practice to continue getting to know someone beyond the work equivalent of the "first date" stage.

And this practice extends beyond new hires! Reboarding, or re-onboarding, is becoming a more common practice to retain people. A good reboarding program includes reacquainting people with the company mission, value, and vision and connecting a person's work to it. It also will include a stay interview, asking people what they need to be more successful and gauging how they are personally and professionally. We all benefit when leaders take the time to learn about who we are now and what we need to thrive.

+ **Be Intentional about Responding to Cliques.** It can be tempting as a leader to think that employee relationships are "none of your business." But the way that your team treats the other folks they work with? Very much so your business. Introduce antibullying training, make sure that people aren't being left out of business meetings, and provide ample coaching and opportunity for engagement across levels and departments. As we've said, not everyone has to be BFFs, but it's up to you to continually enforce that everyone in your office deserves a culture of respect and inclusion.

Team culture can live or die on the **individual** level, and committing yourself to building the culture you want at work can be a deeply empowering process. It can start simple: get to know your coworkers (especially the new ones), and do so on your terms. Have a meeting with new hires to learn about them and for them to learn about you. Make it about work and make it clear you're interested in them as a person without getting too personal.

We once spoke with Beatriz, a champion networker who said that she aims to have five fifteen- to thirty-minute coffee chats with people a month to get to know them better, learn about their experiences, and build a relationship. She said it helps her know people on a deeper level and equips her with a networked mind. Specifically, she knows the right time to bring people into projects to prevent errors or improve the outcome. All because of some coffee meetings.

And while we are thinking through "chatting over coffee," reflect on your role in gossiping over those brews. It can start so innocuously: letting off some steam around the watercooler, bonding over a coworker's weird quirk, wanting to fit in with new colleagues. But this gossiping can quickly become a habit, so take the "no gossip" pledge and ask others to join you!

Hannah remembers starting in a job where she often heard whispers from one person's cube. When she walked by, it stopped. Quickly, it became clear that office gossip served as a tool to bond, albeit an unhealthy one. They consistently tried to draw Hannah into the latest round of "Have you heard?" While she desperately wanted to join in the work camaraderie, she felt uncomfortable. It's a small example of how a gossip train starts and grows via the longing to be included. It's important that we stop and notice when we want to be a part of the gossip, then question why. We need to hold ourselves accountable for stopping the conversation, interjecting with another perspective, or walking away. Operate with kindness first.

CONNECTION BARRIER: LACK OF INTENTIONALITY

If you have ever planned any kind of event, then you know that it requires so many factors to go well: the guest list, schedule, food, activities, and timing. If you have ever planned a work event, then you know the same considerations need to be taken into account. And that's hard, especially at companies without dedicated staff whose job is to plan these events.

The pandemic years made it even harder. We can all relate to the people who scheduled regular virtual happy hours and trivia games, only to cancel them altogether when people stopped showing up, either because we were the person attempting to create fun or the one who ceased attending the events. Then we started trickling back to the office, dusting off our rusty social skills and asking ourselves, "OMG, seriously, what do I do with my hands?" Cue a host of awkward meetings and stilted conversations. Turns out all moments of connection, regardless of where and when they happen, require a dose of intention. And it's not as effortless as everyone has always thought.

> **ELIMINATING THE BARRIER: THINK OF CONNECTION BUILDING AS AN ART**

While working in an office might make it seem like connection is simple or something folks do without thinking, creating a culture

A CULTURE OF CONNECTION

of connection requires some serious creative skills. Whether it's a conference people are attending or a teammate's lunchtime birthday cake cutting, there are times when these events feel easy and enjoyable. And there are times when these events last thirty minutes but feel like they drag on for four hours.

Here is how leaders can rethink their approach to planned connection:

✦ **Have a Clear Reason or Goal for the Gathering.** Priya Parker, author of *The Art of Gathering*, says the first question she asks her clients is, "What are you trying to solve? Or, what is the purpose of this gathering?"[18] Is the company happy hour (in person or virtual) to celebrate the end of a long, difficult project? Is it to get to know each other better? Is it because people have asked for it? Before sending out calendar invites, get really clear on why the gathering is happening in the first place. No one wants to attend a meeting of forced fun, and sometimes an event just for the sake of an event can feel that way.

One leader we spoke to, Paige, said they wanted people to connect about anything but work, so they host "no work" lunches. Paige will order food from a restaurant voted on by the team and set the expectation that everyone set a one-hour out-of-office message. Then they have one hour, uninterrupted by work, to connect. They said that not only does it help the team get to know each other, but it also helps them as a leader to connect and take a breath. Notice how Paige is incredibly *intentional* about this connection and how they help remove the potential barriers to their team's participation. Not only is that smart management, but it also shows your team how seriously you take this!

✦ **Incorporate Some Play.** No, this does not *only* mean team ropes courses. Some people hate those (Hannah), others love them (Lisa), and still others may have personal physical or mental barriers to completing them. Play in some capacity, however, does lead to resilience and camaraderie. This can take many forms. Bruce, a hospital CEO, said that he used brevity and play to lighten an incredibly heavy workplace atmosphere. The most successful event he hosted was a leadership dunk tank, where staff had the opportunity to test their throwing skills and hit the target to dunk their VPs. Ben, a game shop owner, played *World of Warcraft* once a week with his team to keep spirits high and entertain his team with his truly beginner WOW skills.

Play can also take the form of group rituals, which, when common on your team, boost morale and a sense of meaning at work.[19] Lisa and Hannah once worked for an organization that rang a bell every time someone closed a sale. It was a call to celebrate whenever they heard the tinny *ding, ding, ding*! If someone preemptively rang the bell, they had to reverse the curse and wear a hat, spin around three times, and ring the bell once. These kinds of rituals, however you include them, foster a playful environment that increases overall well-being. It's essential to know your teammates, though; what works at one company won't work everywhere.

✦ **Plan for In-Person Connection Once a Year, No Matter What**. When people can safely gather, get an in-person annual meeting on the calendar pronto. Before those meetings, creatively plan for mostly-remote employees to have additional time with mostly-office employees. This can be as simple as seating them next to each other at an outing, including sessions that require group conversation, or simply playing the role of a host and bringing people together based on what you know about them. ("James, did you know that Louise also loves to play Dungeons and Dragons in her spare time?") And the connection begins!

+ **Offer Variety.** People have distinct interests. Bonding with others who have that shared interest *and* learning from folks whose interests are different are spectacular ways to bring people together in any organization. Intention lies in ensuring that events, meetings, and trainings span a wide range of topics. This is also a great opportunity for employees to turn to and learn from one another. Some tech companies have created open calendars for people to sign up to teach a class, and anyone can join. These classes can be work-related and work-tangential; someone could take a 401(k) class on Tuesday and a mushroom foraging course on Thursday.

UNiDAYS, the world's largest student affinity network, prioritizes variety to keep its 200 employees engaged across remote teams. Leaders worked with employees to create their Good Vibes Programme. The employee experience team seeks input from the team via surveys and conversations to create a program of connection that spans interests, including a mix of motivational guest speakers, tangible workshops, cocktail (and mocktail) making classes, and fitness activities. With this initiative, they kept their social culture alive.

+ **Be Aware of Disabilities, Caretaking Needs, and Other Potential Factors for the Planning of Events.** While not every event needs to appeal to every employee, people will notice if they're consistently and/or structurally left out of group activities.

+ **Outsource an Expert.** Maybe they're an event planner. Or maybe they're a friend of a friend who always hosts the best parties. Or maybe they're someone you work with every day. If resources are allocated to a gathering/events bucket, then

> someone can be brought in for the meetings (large and small) to treat them as the art form that they are.
>
> ✦ **Make These Events Optional.** And make them without consequence if people choose not to attend. But when possible, host them during working hours so that folks don't need to constantly take time away from family, friends, or other out-of-work responsibilities to be a part of your work community.

Sure, workplace events and gatherings are part of work life. However, most days are spent in the moments of day-to-day connection: meetings, emails, instant messaging, small talk before lunch, and venting about demanding clients. Having multiple touch points throughout the day is actually a positive precursor to a culture of healthy connection.

But this only truly works if these touch points are relational, where time is spent talking about more than just the task at hand. In one study, employees stated that frequent employee communication was the top way they felt more connected. This was twice as impactful as happy hours and more than three times as impactful as group video games.[20] These relational moments of connection don't have to take up a ton of time. Just a bit will often suffice.

We can all participate in day-to-day relational connection, and one of the easiest ways for an individual to do so is to use the communication tools at our fingertips. Specifically, we're talking about the instant messaging system. This tool is not just for the Millennials and Gen Zers out there (though give a shout-out to the Millennials, who pioneered its use with AOL Instant Messenger and MSN Messenger). Frequently—but not too frequent—communication on these channels keeps people in the loop, offers an opportunity to have fun chats about what's happening at work or on TikTok, and provides an easy way to conduct pulse checks (e.g., 🙂 =great, 😐 = so-so, 😴 = tired).

A CULTURE OF CONNECTION

Some use the system features to create space for relational conversations. For example, there could be the #petsandkids channel, a #memesandTikToks channel, a #todayIlearned channel, or (our personal favorite) #Icelebrateyou channel to praise and call out peers for wins big and small.

When in doubt, go back to basics. If you don't know someone very well, request a time on their calendar to learn about their work history, and current motivations and aspirations. If you schedule the meeting, prepare to lead the conversation and have some questions ready just in case a spell of awkwardness pops up. Every work relationship starts somewhere, and sometimes we have to be the ones to initiate it.

CONNECTION BARRIER: THE MUDDLED LEADER-EMPLOYEE DYNAMIC

When Hannah worked as a barista, her friend (a fellow employee) suddenly became her manager. It was . . . kinda weird. There was a new power dynamic where Hannah worried about breaking rules and getting in trouble with the boss. The side conversations and joking around that used to happen while making lattes disappeared as he spent more time, you know, managing the store. It was his job to make

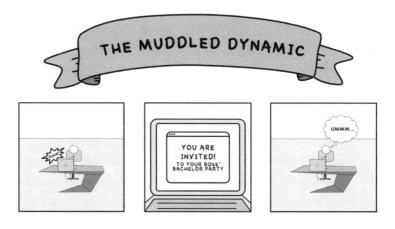

sure that Hannah was doing her job, when he used to be the person she relaxed with!

At first, Hannah balked at his sudden adherence to the rules and the serious tone that he used with her team. It was as if she didn't know who this new person was. Now, she gets it; he was trying to figure out his new role and felt discomfort holding all the responsibility when he had previously shirked it. He thought he had to shift his whole demeanor and behavior far in another direction to be successful. But after a few weeks, he dialed down his strict approach, Hannah saw him more as a leader, and they relaxed into the new dynamic.

Leaders and employees are naturally connected. A poor leader-employee connection may take on many forms, like the authoritative leader who forgets the humanness of employees, the employee who dumps every life hardship on their boss, or the leader who lives so high on the stress scale that it leaves little time to tend to the emotional culture of their team. A great leader-employee connection can look like cross-mentorship, stepping up to help each other, and leaders who know when they need to put their own needs aside and show up for their people. That said, it is really important that leaders keep in mind the power they hold over their employees. There is a boundary in these leader-employee dynamics, and it's important to draw a clear line and stick to it.

ELIMINATING THE BARRIER: GET CRYSTAL CLEAR ON EXPECTATIONS

Here is how leaders can draw the line in their dynamics with their employees:

- **Resist the Urge to Dive Too Deep into the Friends Pool with Direct Reports**. At the same time, don't completely cut yourself off by positioning yourself as "the boss." Here's another way to think of it: If you would share your thoughts in private with a friend, they shouldn't be shared with a direct report. Take Timothy, an organizational development manager, as an example. His boss often pulls him aside to act as a sounding board for what she's thinking of doing regarding employee tensions, budget shortfalls, and frustrations with her leadership—and it makes him uncomfortable. While he considers her a work friend, he feels brought into conversations and decision-making that he shouldn't be aware of because he has no influence over those matters and has to keep his knowledge of them a secret.

This is not to say that bosses and employees can't be friends! But it's a whole lot more appropriate when that friendship grows after someone leaves the organization. Hannah and Lisa both have close friendships with people they used to work with and manage. But the depth of their friendship only grew when their work worlds were separate.

+ **Be Clear About What Behaviors and Actions Are Okay as a Leader.** Then communicate with your employees about your decisions. For example, is it okay to be connected on social media? Are you okay with your direct reports debriefing their weekends in detail (e.g., "Wow, that hangover was wild!")? Do you join the team for off-hours hangouts? Think through these dynamics, and set expectations in advance.

+ **If/When It Happens, Transition into a Leadership or Managerial Role with Intentionality.** Be aware of how awkward this might be for your former coworker(s), and work extra hard to make it comfortable for them. Rebecca, an advertising producer, described the moment she recognized this transition. She was set to join a dodgeball game with her former coworkers—now her direct reports—right after employee evaluations, where she would need to let them know they weren't getting bonuses. Needless to say, she skipped dodgeball that week to give them a chance to commiserate.

For **individuals**, this is a big chance to practice knowing your boundaries and understanding that it is okay to not be "friends" with your boss in the same way you may be with your coworkers. You have the agency to set boundaries that make you most comfortable. Respect your right to privacy. Your boss is not entitled to every detail of your personal life. On the other hand, know that you are a person first and an employee second. Where safe to do so, bring your humanity to your conversations with your boss; and while you don't have to be great friends, it's absolutely okay to have a friendly relationship with your leaders.

Most companies don't refer to the place where work happens (whether virtual or not) and the people who do that work as a community. It's often referred to as a workplace, a work environment, or simply "our organization." And yet the idea of community at work, where everyone leans on one another, supports one another, and collectively works together for a shared purpose isn't just for nonprofits and coops. In many ways, our connections at work create a community that we need. The eight hours or so that we spend online or in-person with our peers is a large part of our days—and our lives. So if we can do so, and we're in a safe and respectful environment, why not invest some of those eight hours into making relationships a little bit deeper? Knowing that we have people to lean on when challenges arise and when wins necessitate celebration feels pretty comforting.

CALLOUT: A Space for Grace

It Really Is Lonely at the Top

Leaders and executives, not so surprisingly, report high rates of loneliness. Half of CEOs express feeling lonely at work,[21] and an even higher percentage say it negatively impacts their job performance. In large part, this is because leaders have no one to confide in. They also have to constantly work to appear calm even when chaos surrounds them, and there is likely ongoing pressure to manage impressions. But this loneliness is harmful, and not only for leaders. If connections are not established or nurtured between leadership and employees, then there's bound to be a disconnect on multiple fronts.

A PricewaterhouseCoopers report found that 82 percent of executives view their relationship with employees as "a committed partnership," whereas employees view it as a "marriage of convenience" or "casual acquaintanceship."[22] If executives are consistently disconnected from employees, then it's exceedingly difficult to listen to and learn from one another. Culture-wise, this is why it can be great to create a true leadership team. Provide opportunities for senior leadership to connect with one another, and strongly encourage that those relationships expand beyond the executive room.

✦ THE GIST ✦

PRE-PORTAL STANDARD

Friendships and strong connections at work have always been a great tool for retention, building strong teams, and creating a sense of overall work enjoyment. While some organizations worked to bolster these bonds at work, others employed a more transactional model that kept that culture of connection from flourishing.

PORTAL LESSONS

Meaningful relationships at work are essential for happy employees and a thriving bottom line, but the shift to a more virtual and hybrid work model introduced some novel additional barriers to connection.

NOW WHAT? STEPPING THROUGH THE PORTAL

To foster a truly connected workplace experience,

Individuals can foster connection at work by doing the following:

- ✦ Adopt a connection over competition mindset.
- ✦ Embrace a "no cliques and no gossip" pledge.
- ✦ Use communication tools to build relationships across platforms (and not simply to get work done).
- ✦ Schedule coffee chats to get to know people, especially if there are new members on your team.
- ✦ Set and stick to boundaries with everyone, especially your boss.

A CULTURE OF CONNECTION

Leaders can create an environment of connection when they:

- ✦ Lead with an abundance mindset and celebrate team successes.

- ✦ Create a culture of belonging, and welcome new hires with a very intentional "get to know you" process.

- ✦ Are super intentional about why and when you're bringing people together.

- ✦ Establish boundaries and clear expectations around employee-leader dynamics.

- ✦ Incorporate play into work.

CHAPTER 8

MEANING MATTERS

✦ *Work (and life) is better when you know WHY you're doing it in the first place.*

We ask a lot of questions at GCC because we're on a quest to understand how to help people create workplaces that don't suck. That's our North Star. We're no different from all the organizations out there spending hours in discussion to refine our why statement: Why does our company exist? And how can employees get inspired by believing in this why, too?

The why statement, mission, purpose, rallying cry, North Star—the name for this work motivator doesn't matter, but the reason we spend time on it does. When organizations have a clear North Star to guide employees, everyone can better understand their place on the work journey to build something bigger than themselves. Yes, this sounds a tad cheesy—and it's also hard to deny just how powerful it is to have a workforce that understands what gives their work meaning. One study found that those who reported "living their purpose at work" during the pandemic had four times higher levels of well-being than those who didn't and four times higher engagement.[1]

On the individual level, there are (almost) only positives when we feel like we're making a meaningful impact at work. We're more resilient and happy.[2] It makes us feel like who we are, what we do, and how we show up are valued. Which is kind of a big deal when we're spending a third of our lives working. Sherre, a small business owner, captured this sentiment well. She told us, "The hours I spend every week—and, frankly, the years I spend of my life—working need to matter. It's my responsibility to not only find that purpose myself, but also continue to connect my team's work to that. It's so motivating and meaningful to look at the impact of your work, the output, the awards, and people's feedback, and think, *I helped make that happen. My work is making a difference.*"

As impactful as it is to be organizationally and individually grounded in purpose, change and crisis send shockwaves through the system. The pandemic years provided an opportunity to pause, reflect, and re-examine how work really allows us—or prevents us—from living a meaningful life.

✦ PRE-PORTAL

There once was a time when an organization's central purpose was to make money (more or less). The individual's purpose was to do the work, earn a paycheck, and help the company make money in the process (more or less). Over the decades and generations, that money-minded purpose lost its power to attract and retain people in organizations. Salary and (actually) livable wages are still essential, but now many of us are also in search of meaningful work—and successful leaders who support and communicate a compelling mission. Retention, forever on the mind of leaders and managers, may often look like trying to solve the motivation puzzle with an attempt to incorporate purpose in the process.

If the difference between motivation and purpose feels muddled to you, we get it—because we can feel a bit unclear about it sometimes, too.

Let's talk about **motivation** first. When we talk about motivation, we are describing the day-to-day drive one has to get out of bed, finish a project, and have a tough conversation at work. This can include extrinsic and intrinsic motivations that drive you differently, dependent on the task or project at hand. **Extrinsic motivations** come from external factors, like tangible goals and rewards. We might be motivated to take a new job, for example, because it pays well. Or maybe we wake up early to prep for a meeting because we want to prove to a new boss that we can handle big projects. **Intrinsic motivations**, however, come from a place of personal fulfillment rather than external reward. This can look like taking on a new role simply because we enjoy the challenge, or spending an extra hour training a new hire because we want them to feel empowered and welcomed.

It's important to note that extrinsic motivators aren't less valuable than intrinsic ones. We need both. When you look at Maslow's hierarchy of needs, physiological, safety, and belonging needs all come *before* esteem (where one could put meaning at work). If an employer isn't providing folks with all the basic necessities to live comfortably, then intrinsic motivation will drop off.

The pandemic really laid this bare. Numerous employers struggled to find people to work in "essential" roles, and that *entirely* makes sense. Employees began to say "enough" to employers who failed to meet their basic needs. There were people who had to put themselves at risk for work during a pandemic or who had to enforce mask policies while receiving minimum wage or less. One lesson of this "worker shortage"? Pay people well and equitably, ensure everyone feels safe, and create an environment of belonging (all time-intensive, challenging, important steps). This should be done before—or at least while also—putting energy into helping people find their purpose at work. If an individual doesn't have the lower pyramid levels of needs, then they shouldn't feel pressure to find a purpose at work too.

When we do get to the conversation of **purpose**, we are pulling back the aperture to understand the why underlying all our intrinsic motivations. It's the pull or the reason we feel compelled to do our work well. Usually, it's tied to helping make something better than it was before. Some describe finding their purpose as knowing how their work fits into the bigger picture.

CALLOUT: JUST THE FACTS

The History of Purpose

For centuries, when humans lived in agrarian communities, the work purpose was life purpose. Then the industrial era came along and factory work became more of the norm, where there was work with minimal purpose. (See chapter 1 for a reminder of this history.) The past century has seen an evolution of a new kind of purpose at work. Arguably, this shift was most obvious when Millennials entered the workplace, popularizing the inspiring, challenging, and (depending on who you ask) annoying trend of asking "But *why*? Why do this work? At this time? For this company?" And while Millennials consequently earned the reputation of a cohort demanding meaning at work, they aren't the first ones who sought this sense of personal and professional fulfillment. The concept of "purpose at work" has been evolving for as long as there have been offices.

In pre-pandemic years, organizations really leaned into the idea of using purpose at work to recruit and retain employees. Leadership and company websites proudly publicized their why. All of this effort made good business sense. Studies show that when people believe that their work matters, they are four times more likely to be engaged, as well as more motivated, fulfilled, and capable of learning faster.[3] It's pretty common knowledge that when people are happy and fulfilled at work, they're happy and fulfilled in life, which is a win for the company, too. It leads to higher revenue, as evidenced by the 58 percent of organizations that put a high priority on purpose reporting a 10 percent or greater increase in revenues over three years.[4]

And it's not just revenue that benefits. So does the collective creativity of the organization. Fifty-three percent of executives who said their company has a strong sense of purpose described their organization as successful with innovation and transformation efforts, compared with the 19 percent of companies who have not thought about it at all.[5]

Phew. That's a lot of motivation to find purpose. (See what we did there?)

And it must be said that creating a work environment where people can see how their work contributes to the bigger picture was more straightforward in a shared office space. Mission statements could be prominently displayed on walls in the office lobby. Folks could see their colleague's body melt in relief when they completed part of a shared project. Positive client reviews could be celebrated in real time among the teammates who made it happen. Meetings could conclude with a conversation (and in-person cheers or celebrations) about how the work connected to the company's mission. It was just... well, easier for people to see their connection to an individual and organizational purpose throughout the day.

When the pandemic forced most office workers to work from home, suddenly the crutches in place before to create a sense of purpose disappeared. People had more time at home, separated from the persistent

CALLOUT: BEWARE!
Don't Serve the Purpose Kool-Aid

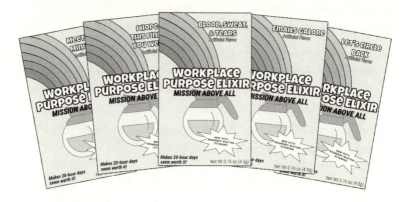

New organizations, especially in start-up culture, are almost supercharged by their purpose. In his HBR article, Ranjay Gulati described it as the soul energy of the start-up, or an "essential, intangible something."[6] Regardless if it's the energy, the motto, the purpose, or the bold mission statement, it can lead to blurred or even nonexistent boundaries.

Start-up culture is famous for a fun, lucrative, fast-paced work environment. It's also notorious for long hours, personal sacrifice, and extreme burnout. If someone feels like they're a part of something and contributing to a greater cause, it can feel like all the sacrifice is worth it . . . until it doesn't. And this happens not only in start-up culture. Organizations with a profound sense of purpose may believe that employees should prioritize that collective mission over being paid well and fairly or having an overall good place to work. The bottom line is, no matter the purpose, it's always best to keep in mind your employees' practical needs. An obsession with purpose can squeeze every last bit of energy out of people at work, which hurts everyone in the long run.

physical influence of colleagues, to think quizzically about their place in their organization and question why they were there (and working so hard) in the first place. It was easier to wonder, *Does the work I do actually matter in the grand scheme of things? Do I really believe in my company's purpose? Or was I drinking the Purple Kool-Aid?*

✦ THE PORTAL

During our research, we spoke with Erica, a project manager, who told us that when the physical space was shared, it was easy to feel aligned with the company's mission. She said that feeling connected to and supporting her coworkers felt purposeful. But when time was spent away from the space and that relational part of work diminished, she questioned if her job was especially meaningful. For many, it seemed that separation from a shared space was also a separation from meaningful impact. For others, like health care workers and other essential employees, their purpose was front and center; and they continued to see the direct impact of their work on people's lives.

Whether folks were physically in their workspace or not, everyone everywhere experienced the tumult of the pandemic years: the pandemic (of course), uprisings, the racial justice reckoning, a contentious presidential campaign and aftermath, and more. All of these moments caused a ripple—or maybe a tidal wave—of examination of the parts of our lives that may have previously been unscrutinized. In his research, Richard Alderson, founder of Careershifters, said, "A shock to the system often causes people to reassess things in their lives."[7] Shocks to the system were aplenty during the pandemic years, as were the reassessments—especially at work.

We call these "perspective stick" moments. This concept was introduced to us by Debra, who you've met in previous chapters. She described them as times when you're hit by a realization of needed change in thinking, doing, or being. Sometimes it may feel like a light tap; other times, it feels like a hard smack. Everyone senses these perspective-stick

moments differently. For some, all they need is a tickle from a feather to shift. Others need the sting from a (metaphorical) two-by-four. And when everyone is experiencing numerous two-by-fours, like so many did in 2020 and 2021, they re-examine many facets of life, including work.

"This whole year has made me rethink this job, my work, life in general, and what it means to be happy and fulfilled," said Brittany, a nonprofit director. "I've questioned a lot of that." Stephanie, an HR leader at a utility organization, similarly shared how the perspective stick changed her thinking: "There are bigger things than me... bigger things than my company. So can we stop taking ourselves so seriously and say, 'Might there be a more effective way to contribute to our world right now?'"

Brittany and Stephanie aren't alone. Other common questions sounded something like these:

- **"Does my job matter? Do I matter here?"** It's hard to imagine doing something else when caught in the unending grind of day-to-day job responsibilities. Working outside the traditional office, with countless other life stressors, made people question their impact.

- **"Is my purpose *actually* my purpose?"** Even for those who thought they understood their purpose, all these perspective-stick moments added up. All those reassessments of life and work triggered by crisis may have urged people to question and even redefine (or act to redefine) their purpose.

- **"Why have I been working this hard, so obsessed with being productive?"** The American workplace spins the narrative that being busy is good and that productivity is a measure of success, no matter what is going on in the world. But the pandemic gave people space to question if all the hours spent accomplishing tasks were really worth the sacrifice of lost family time, less joy, and increased stress.

- **"Why am I working in a job I don't like, or for a company where I don't feel valued, respected, or understood?"** Many people have accepted a work life of Sunday scaries as normal.

The pandemic years were a tipping point for many when they decided, "Enough is enough! Time for a new job."

- **"With everything going on in the world, how are my company and its leadership responding? Is this still the kind of company I see myself working at? Or do I need a change?"** How leadership responds to a crisis is very telling to employees. Folks watched as their peers and leaders responded to the impacts of the pandemic, the murders of George Floyd, Ahmaud Arbery, and Breonna Taylor with the subsequent cries for justice, the Capitol insurrection, and the lasting impacts of hundreds of thousands of lives lost from COVID-19. How an organization showed up in these moments and afterward made many people ask, "Am I in the right place?"

- **"Life is short and so much is uncertain. If I stay in this job, there needs to be some serious tweaks—or I'm out."** Routine can trap people in a daze where they focus solely on daily life and rarely raise their heads to imagine the future they want to create. Following a year of certain uncertainty and painfully high amounts of grief served as a gut check to change (if possible) the parts of life that weren't serving them well.

Of course, some have stepped back and reflected, "Wow, I am grateful for this job and the impact that I make." So rather than a period of reconsidering, the pandemic years served as confirmation that they were in the right place, doing the work they felt called to do.

Individuals weren't the only ones questioning purpose during the pandemic years. Many leaders and organizations were hit by their own perspective sticks and asked, "How do we get people to do their jobs, show up to work, and/or stay with this company?" Leading during the pandemic years taught many people how important it is to focus on well-being, burnout prevention, and—if they were paying attention—purpose. In the search for successful retention strategies, organizations and managers also questioned, "What *really* motivates our people? Is a paycheck enough? Are employee relationships as important virtually as they are in person? Is our mission statement sufficient for a tumultuous present?"

This wasn't all theoretical. For a lot of organizations, their literal purpose changed as they completely shifted their business production, whether it was clothing manufacturers sewing masks instead of T-shirts, General Motors transforming a plant to manufacture ventilators, distilleries denaturing alcohol to make hand sanitizer, or local businesses recreating their space to serve the community. Their purpose truly met the moment and invited employees into this change in purpose.

The conclusion here is not revolutionary, but it is powerful: Having a strong why is helpful—not only for the company as a whole, but also for the people doing the work.

✦ NOW WHAT?

All of the questioning, rethinking, and reimagining opened the door to a new take on purpose at work. In our quantitative and qualitative research, we saw a collective desire to shed previously held beliefs and an eagerness to adopt a new approach to work and life.

GETTING PURPOSEFUL AT THE ORGANIZATIONAL AND LEADERSHIP LEVEL

If you are in a position of influence at your organization, you can (and should) make the most of this moment to refine the purpose your company preaches and how the people at work can connect to it. Our suggestions are three-fold and best when acted on together.

HAVE A BUSINESS PURPOSE, CLEARLY DEFINE IT, AND MAKE SURE YOUR COMPANY IS LIVING IT

Okay, yes. This is obvious. But a lot of organizations don't have a purpose statement that clearly differs from their mission, vision, or values statements. Or, they've spent a lot of time writing the perfect statement, but then they completely forget about it. If the company's purpose isn't actively serving as a guide for work decisions, then it's essentially useless.

Another big mistake? Neglecting the people who are doing the work. By all means, unite people behind a meaningful purpose, which is especially prevalent in health care and nonprofit organizations. However, you must think of the *people doing the work* as much as you think about the purpose they're serving. In some situations, leaders and boards may expect the North Star to make up for neglectful or harmful treatment of employees. For nonprofits, there can be a gap between demands and employee experience. Low pay and high workload can become normalized in the pursuit of a greater good. We notice in these kinds of environments that selflessness

is rewarded above all else. Nurture the whole person, and reward self-nourishment more than selflessness.

Nathan, who works in what he describes as a mission-driven environment, told us that his day-to-day is impactful, but it's not enough to keep him motivated. "There's a time when your compassion wears thin and the mission itself isn't enough to keep you going. In those moments, I come back to *"Oh, that's right. I'm doing this work to be financially independent by age forty."* For Nathan, watching his net worth grow and retiring early with his husband to travel cross-country is far more purposeful than his work alone. So he's looked for an organization whose purpose is about improving the lives of people at work, not just the clients they serve. After changing employers, he's finally found a place with leadership who say they care and prove it in the benefits they offer, the resources they provide, and their consistent conversations about improvements.

Too often, employers make promises with their statements but fail to follow them up with action. In some cases, the purpose statement feels like lip service. Sometimes organizations know that they should have a purpose statement because consultants and marketing departments recommend that they should. (Or because they read a book that says so. *wink*) The thing is, employees can usually tell when that's the case. A true purpose feels authentic when there is action behind the words. Take the example of Patagonia, whose mission is, "We're in business to save our home planet." Over the decades, the company has experimented and innovated (many times with failure in the process) to find more sustainable and responsible practices for their products. One example is when they switched from synthetic to organic cotton, a process that took longer and cost more money. To get employees on board with the more labor-intensive supply chain practice, they brought people out to visit organic versus non-organic farms to see the positive difference in organic farming.[8] Patagonia, like any organization in the United States, is not going to be perfect, but they are a good example of a company that is constantly in action to live their mission statement.

There are many experts out there who have a process to help clearly articulate an organization's North Star. We recommend seeking out that expertise and then getting to work. To start you off, the business purpose statement should include the following:

+ A call to action

+ A compassionate angle

+ A verb, intention, and outcome or beneficiary

And while consultants can help people find answers, the best ideas are likely with the people who currently work alongside us. So listen to the people doing the work! Understand why *they* think the business exists. Then ask them to help you write (or rewrite) the purpose. This can be a great exercise to conduct every time the organization goes through large, transformational changes. Purpose statements *can* and *should* be revised if the situation, times, and employees call for it.

CONNECT EMPLOYEES' DAILY WORK TO THE GREATER PURPOSE

Every single person, and the work they do, does matter. Make it a constant practice to emphasize that connection. Employees who have worked at Johnson & Johnson over the years have shared with us how they incorporate their credo into their work. Amelia told us that on her team, at the end of every project meeting, they'd circle the work they did back to the company's credo and even call out if it didn't feel connected enough. When that was the case, they scheduled a follow-up to ensure that their work held up to the integrity of the organization's mission.

On a smaller but just as impactful scale, individuals or leaders can point out how the work done by each person contributes to something bigger than themselves. Before delivering a workshop with technicians who designed and built medical carts (think of the carts in operating rooms), an executive addressed people in the room and said, "Because of you and your work, ORs are safer and more people survive. That's no small role." Similarly, after a particularly tough quarter in 2020, Sarah, a middle manager at a recruiting firm, told us, "I was very grateful to different members of my team, so I wrote them all a letter thanking them for how they specifically impacted me that year. A lot of people told me how pleasantly surprised they were to read the words, some not even knowing that what they did was so impactful. It was a good lesson for me to extend gratitude even more." So often, we don't know how much we impact others, especially in the monotony (or chaos) of the day-to-day. Take this as a sign to reach out to someone, and tell them how they've impacted you.

Organizations have some pretty remarkable ways of encouraging this kind of peer gratitude or reward system. Take Google as an example. The company implemented a "'peer bonus" system that allows coworkers to recognize when someone does particularly great work or when their work meaningfully impacted them. They also have a "kudos" system that allows for nonmonetary awards focused on public recognition. Not only does Google facilitate these rewards, but they also bake the *idea* of peer recognition into their culture.

HELP INDIVIDUALS FIND THEIR PERSONAL WORK PURPOSE

An estimated 70 percent of people said their purpose is defined by work[9], so organizations and leaders play a large role in helping people discover that meaningful impact. Managers and leaders, start the conversation by asking yourself and others to rate on a scale of 1 (never) to 10 (always), "My purpose is front and center in my work." Everyone deserves to be asked this question, especially those who may feel forgotten in this conversation. (We see you, managers, who feel stuck between trying to show up for everyone while trying to please senior leaders.) Then ask some follow-up questions, like the following:

- ✦ When is it unclear?
- ✦ How do you know when that purpose is front and center?
- ✦ Think of some of the most meaningful work moments in your career. Describe them. What do you notice about these experiences? How do you feel? What are you doing? Who are you impacting? What from those experiences are you missing right now?

This exercise is to bring yourself and others back to their purpose center, if you will. Return to it on an annual basis, perhaps as part of a yearly review to ensure that you stay focused on your purpose.

GETTING PURPOSEFUL AT THE INDIVIDUAL LEVEL

There is no one way to integrate purpose into our work lives. What matters is discovering how those two integrate while staying true to ourselves. As you seek the place of purpose in your work, we recommend embracing the following mindsets.

> **INDIVIDUAL PURPOSE CAN BE SEPARATE FROM THE COMPANY'S PURPOSE**

It's important to understand that purpose as it relates to work broadly falls into three categories: company, work, and life. Let's explore those more.

Company Purpose

This is the supercharged version of a mission statement. A company's purpose answers the question of "Why do we exist?" Other big-picture questions that companies ask themselves include vision ("Where are we going?") and mission ("How are we getting there?") Some organizations explicitly spell out their purpose, while others combine it with vision and mission. Some popular examples include these:

- **KeepCup**: To kickstart the demise of the disposable cup.
- **TED**: To spread ideas.
- **HubSpot**: Helping millions grow better.
- **ING**: Empowering people to stay a step ahead in life and in business.

Work Purpose

This is the individual impact a person wants to have in their work. In best-case scenarios, our work purpose is connected to the company's purpose. Of course, that may not always be the case. If someone's work purpose is to create a product that saves lives and they work in a medical device manufacturing company, there's a good chance their work purpose aligns with the organization's. There are other cases where it's less clear. If a person's work purpose is to help people grow but they have an individual contributor role where they aren't interacting with or impacting other people, then their work purpose might not be aligned with the company's.

Life Purpose

This is what fuels us day in and day out. It's that motivation to create the life that we desire in alignment with our core values. Asking "What's my purpose?" can be a heavy question. For some, the answer is obvious. For others, it's nebulous; and the process of finding the answer is agonizing, riddled with overthinking and self-doubt. One study found that 85 percent of people feel they have a purpose, but only about 65 percent of them believe they can actually articulate it.[10] As part of this mindset shift, it's important to allow a pause for self-compassion if the question of "What's my purpose?" bubbles up some difficult emotions.

Here's a fact: Your life purpose can be your work purpose. Here's another fact: Your work purpose can align with your organization's purpose. And here's yet another fact: Your life purpose can have nothing to do with work or organizational purpose. If there's one thing we want to free you from with this book, it's the idea that you're somehow "doing it wrong" if you don't think that work is your whole purpose for being.

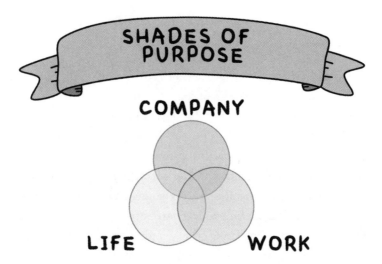

Instead, think of it like this: When we have a clear understanding of where our purpose intertwines with our work, we can better advocate for the future we want and know where to seek help along the way. Try on the exercise of discovering where your purpose lies in each of these categories and if there is crossover.

PURPOSE IS NOT STATIC: IT, AND WE, CAN CHANGE OVER TIME (OR, HOW WE LEARNED TO STOP WORRYING AND LOVE THE SEARCH)

Hannah used to believe that finding her work purpose was critical to finding overall life happiness and fulfillment. Every couple of years, she'd attend a workshop and reflect on that good ol' question of "What is your why?" After a brief life crisis panic, she'd complete the exercise and reference what she'd written two years prior. It was always different. One year, it was "empowering new keynote speakers." Another, it was "sharing cool research to shift mindsets." Then the panic would return. If her why statement changed, did she even have a purpose to begin with? Or was it all a lie, and Hannah was destined to walk the work world, *pretending* to know why she was there?! Whew, the drama. Hannah relayed this story to a mentor, who scoffed, "Hannah, of course it's changed. You've changed. Just roll with it and stop overthinking everything." Wise words: Purpose can change if and when a person changes. It doesn't have to, but it can.

Research backs this. When any person (much like Hannah) gains experience and/or circumstances change, they grow and their purpose evolves. Life events are a prime example of why this happens. When people enter the workplace for the first time, they may have one purpose. Ten years later, when they have their first kid, they may have a new perspective. A family illness could shift how someone wants to spend their time at work. Or, a pandemic could hit, and seven out of ten people reconsider their purpose at work.[11] One of our interviewees, Angelica, described working hard and spending a lot of money on her master's degree. Therefore, she was always looking for work that would utilize it. After years in for-profit organizations and considerable time spent working within her local community, Angelica decided a change was necessary and moved to go into the nonprofit sector with little care about whether her master's degree was used.

This is why a reflection practice of any kind can be incredibly helpful. Whether it's journaling, discussing life changes with friends, or consulting a career coach, changes in life (large and small) are bound to make someone ponder why they do what they do.

CALLOUT: Rethink the Norm

The Passion/Work Trap

"Follow your passion and you'll never work a day in your life" is a common idiom, usually told by experienced generations to those who are less experienced. (It's an especially common message shared by Baby Boomers to Millennials.) And while the intention behind the advice is noble, following it can leave some people feeling empty. When the consensus is that work equals passion, people may either enmesh work and personal life to the extreme, where identity becomes entirely wrapped up in work, or they may get drained and lost in the pursuit of passion because no matter what they do, they aren't sure if they're finding their passion at work. Also, work is work. Even people who feel deep purpose also can feel burned out and need a break. Pretending otherwise leads people to feel like they are "failing" if they're tired. Nope, not in our book.

OUR WHY CAN BE NUMEROUS

There is a reason why the search for purpose is a profitable business. Books, seminars, videos, and workshops all exist to help people find their defining life mission. And while the argument stands that corporate investment in such an endeavor could have some dubious intent (i.e., increased production as the end goal), it can create a sense of personal calm in the chaos. When our why is clear, we have a guiding principle to serve as a compass for decision-making.

That said, clarity is not to be confused with simplicity. A singular purpose at work is, for some, enough. And for others, it is far from enough. They need to create a tapestry of purpose from all avenues of their life.

This might not shock you: Humans have layers, so the way we live our meaning will also be layered, especially when we're embracing the fundamental truth that it's normal to not find all of it at work. If we do, it can lead us to feel lost when work is done. And while we may always have a guiding focus, daily challenges may ignite a new why for that day—or send us down a path to a whole new why for our lifetime. That's why we advocate so much for providing space and time for reflection about what really matters before we reach an age when we're looking back, wishing we could have done it differently.

At GCC, we always return to our purpose. As keynote speakers, we often have to push back on the assumption that we just want to be on stage talking and entertaining because, in reality, we don't need that! What we want to do is communicate information that helps people and makes work suck just a little bit less. So we ask ourselves if what we write, share, and present is truly helping create better workplaces. And in the best scenarios, we hear from clients shortly after a speaking engagement and learn just how much our work has impacted them.

During a recent presentation, Lisa introduced the idea of work-life harmony as described in chapter 4. It was referenced a couple of times in a panel she led afterward, but then we didn't hear anything for a few weeks until the client sent an email that read, "Hello Lisa, I am excited to share a confidential draft of our revised Values Statements, I call your attention to the third statement to see the lasting impact of your presentation on our organization." The third statement? Work-life harmony. This is what drives us: knowing that our work, in some way, for some people, is changing work for the better.

We all need to find this connection to meaning in some way throughout the third of our lives we spend working. Some may need it more than others, but it's guaranteed that if at some point you hear that you helped someone or improved their life in some small way, it'll feel pretty awesome. The more we connect those dots, maybe everyone will feel a little more (or maybe a whole lot more) contentment and value at work.

✦ THE GIST ✦

PRE-PORTAL STANDARD

Over the past few decades, there's been a positive shift from motivating employees mainly through increased pay and promise of promotion to motivating by creating a deeper sense of meaning and purpose in their work.

PORTAL LESSONS

When employees mostly gathered in one space and place, it was easier to maintain a unified message and rally people behind a collective mission. With virtual work options thrown into the mix, it takes a bit more intentional effort to keep that through line of purpose.

NOW WHAT? STEPPING THROUGH THE PORTAL

Meaning can be woven in at every level of the organizational hierarchy:

- ✦ **Individuals**, define your life purpose and work purpose, and map out the overlap between the two. Are you clear on how you contribute to the company's purpose?

- ✦ **Leaders and managers**, make it a daily practice to help employees connect their work to the bigger picture: the team, the business, and the overarching organizational mission.

- ✦ **Organizations**, write a purpose statement if you don't yet have one—and make sure it's not just lip service but authentic and embedded into every layer of the business. Do the work and design the systems and messaging to ensure that the statement is well-known and aligned with people in the company.

CHAPTER 9

Leading with Compassion, No Matter Your Role

✦ *When leaders can honor the humanity not only of those they lead but also their own, that's when the heart of compassionate leadership truly clicks.*

Leadership is an art that baffles many. People have devoted their entire lives to the quest to understand the special, magical alchemy that makes for a truly great leader.

What further complicates matters is that there's no one mold or model that singularly defines great leadership. Awesome leaders can look and act quite differently. There's the friendly leader, the stalwart and stoic leader, the hands-off leader, the quiet leader, the bold leader, the goofy leader, and the brainiac leader. Different leaders are also the right fit for different employees.

And yet, despite all this variety and the fact that there is no one tried-and-true set of instructions defining exactly what to do and how to act, at GCC we believe there's a uniting thread across all truly great leadership—and that is compassion.

We use this word intentionally. More commonly, we've seen the case made for empathetic leadership, and certainly empathy is a great quality. But compassion takes it one step further.

While empathy is rooted in feeling for the other person, compassion is feeling *with* other people. The Latin root for *compassion* literally means to suffer together or "to feel sorrow or deep tenderness for one who is suffering or experiencing misfortune."[1] In modern interpretations of the word *compassion*, a call to action is implicit. Because think about it: If a person not only acknowledges others' suffering but also feels it with them, of course they'll be driven to act and find relief.

For those in formal leadership roles, compassion looks like acting in employees' best interests. These leaders regularly feel not only empathy, but also compassion for what their reports are going through. They don't wait until employees bring problems or frustrations to their doors. Instead, they proactively ask questions that will keep employees happy and healthy. How heavy are the workloads? How strong is the

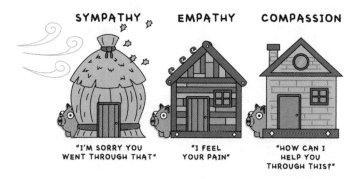

sense of belonging? What voices need to be heard more often? Whose potential needs to be nourished? How are people doing as a group? How can the company better support not only employee output, but also employee well-being?

These questions (and many more) are all within the purview of the compassionate leader. Because compassionate leaders understand that if you don't care for the humans doing the work, then the work quality will diminish and the culture will eventually unravel. Most of all, they understand that tapping into each person's humanity to build engaging, motivating, and supportive workplaces is an act as important as—if not more than—company growth and market success.

But the idea of compassionate leadership should not be reserved only for those who hold formal titles. If you look for it, we think you'll find that leadership (like love) is all around. (High five to those who get this reference!) We're serious, though. Leadership in action doesn't only come from CEOs, directors, VPs, managers, and executives who drive strategy and make decisions for the company—you know, the usual suspects. In our opinion (and experience), it's possible for every contributor to step up and act as a leader within their sphere of influence. We call this low-key leadership, and anyone can act as a low-key leader. When we're part of a team and an organization, we play vital roles as listeners, challengers, includers, doers, and innovators. Our actions, in any role we take on, impact the people around us. We can lead through the behavior we model. We can lead by embracing a compassionate approach to work. We can lead by speaking up for ourselves and for those who might, for one reason or another, be reluctant to do so.

How we show up as leaders—in whatever form that takes—is paramount. Because leading with compassion will keep us focused on the humans at work. Isn't that the goal in the end anyway?

✦ PRE-PORTAL

Even though there's no singular, evergreen, or finite definition for what "good leadership" looks like, attempts have been made to define characteristics under that umbrella. We've all anxiously clicked on the headline "Ten Traits You Need to Have to Actually Be the Best Leader Ever" in hope that we already have eight of them (and can work on the other two). But these lists are usually disappointing because they're always different and changing, which makes sense. As the workplace has evolved over the past century, that list has evolved as well.

There was a time not too long ago when the notion of a good leader was modeled after military commanders. Coming out of World War II, many of the men (yes, they were predominantly men) populating the workforce were trained in that command-control style that was mission-critical when lives were quite literally at stake.

At work, a hierarchical organizational structure and the corresponding leadership methodology meant that there was a clear order of command, defined roles, and levels of accountability. This style of leadership held sway for quite a while and was certainly effective in its time. But in the past few decades, the way we work has changed drastically, and so have the people doing the work.

THE DIGITAL REVOLUTION AND THE DEMOCRATIZATION OF WORK

With the digital revolution came a new era of leadership. With widespread access to the Internet, we witnessed a democratization of information. There's the popular adage that "knowledge is power." Pre-Internet, few had widespread, easy access to said knowledge, so few had power. And getting access to knowledge was hard! You needed plentiful resources and time. That information might be gained at college, within the pages of the Encyclopedia Britannica collection that your eccentric uncle had through a network of the right people or passed down from family members or mentors. But suddenly, with the Internet, knowledge was for everyone! Now, people can take online college courses for free. No need to hire a plumber, because YouTube has thousands of step-by-step tutorials to help you figure out how to unclog a sink. Or do your taxes. Or ace job interviews. Information is more accessible than it's ever been.

This democratization of information caused ripple effects, with a major one being its influence on organizational models at work. More and more, we saw that organizational structures started to mimic the networked informational world that we now live in. Like the World Wide Web, in network models, the information flowed easily from team to team (like node to node). Just as the Internet's social media platforms both gave everyone a voice and granted access to those in positions of power ("You can tweet at the president!? Whoa!"), network organizational models encouraged even the newest employees to share their input. Clusters of teams shared information freely and leaders invited employee connection through open-door and feedback-friendly policies.

And, of course, no description of a changing work world is complete without talking about the new generations showing up to do the work. Fresh crops of talent always bring new expectations and demands. Gen Xers, unlike the post-WW2 Traditionalists, the Silent Generation, and even the Baby Boomer pipeline, demanded efficiency so that they could get work done and go home to their families. Then came the digital revolution, and Millennials (aka the digital explorers) questioned the why behind traditional structures and mindsets, wondering out loud, "If there was a better way." Now, Gen Zers (aka the digital natives) are shining a light on the absolute necessity of diversity at all levels and see representation and equity at work not as a "would be nice to have" but as a baseline expectation.

With a new environment, tools, modes of thinking, and talent pool, the leadership techniques that once effectively engaged, motivated, and inspired aren't working as well as they used to. The shifts in the general working condition have opened the door for conversations around revising the previously held idea of what effective leaders look like.

For example, here are the leadership traits that were valued pre-digital revolution:

- Has a commanding presence
- Carries a wealth of institutional knowledge
- Directs employees
- Enforces rules and regulations
- Relies on top-driven decision-making
- Appears to be all-knowing
- Has a keen eye for competency
- Manages risk
- Is driven by competition
- Invests in tools

Now, here are the leadership traits that are valued post-digital revolution:

- Has an inspiring presence
- Exhibits emotional intelligence
- Supports employees
- Builds trust and transparency
- Is driven by collaboration

LEADING WITH COMPASSION, NO MATTER YOUR ROLE

- Is always learning
- Has a keen eye for potential
- Encourages calculated risk-taking and innovation
- Relies on consensus-driven decision-making
- Invests in people

LEADERS AT ALL LEVELS

As the digital revolution ushered in new expectations for leadership, so, too, has it created more opportunities for employees to show up as low-key leaders. No longer competing for the same one or few seats at the top, people could leave behind hypercompetition, fear of vulnerability, and aversion to failure (all elements of a scarcity mindset) in favor of collaboration and information sharing, authenticity, and bold attempts at innovation (more akin to a generosity mindset). With more visibility and access to those in positions of leadership and less need for professional politicking and diplomacy, employees are closer to those with the power to effect change. And they've been bolder about voicing their opinions, whether it agrees with those leaders with a capital *L* or not.

For some, these changes to our workplace power dynamics have been unsettling and uncomfortable. They've been resistant to these changing tides and have held tight to the more established ways of thinking and leading: enforcing compliance over building trust, butts-in-seat management over flexibility, and hewing to bureaucratic norms instead of innovative change. If this clinging to the past did them a disservice before the 2020s hit, now they may be actively causing damage to their organization.

✦ THE PORTAL

Enter the pandemic portal, and the leadership shifts that had started taking root became supercharged.

The conditions that old-school leaders were used to operating under were ripped out from under them. In 2020, they had to learn to lead in a whole new world. Under pressure, leaders were put to the test as change became inescapable. As Mara, a career counselor, so thoughtfully put it, "You realize people's leadership in times of crisis."

Leaders who were used to an authoritative style of leadership found it difficult to acclimate to the new predominantly WFH environment. When the ever-reliable rules and regulations to "keep people in line" were suddenly stripped away and leaders lost their ability to oversee employees (both literally and figuratively), many were at a loss. "How do we know they're getting their work done?" they would ask. "How can we maintain the same level of output and accountability?" There were those who didn't trust their employees to take work as seriously from home, much to the detriment of company culture.

On the flip side, the pandemic years showed employees that the statements of "We could never do that" or "That just wouldn't work for our organization" were simply untrue (even though they might have felt true at the time). Eyes opened to the reality that in this new landscape, where evolution is more important than sticking to the tried-and-true, some leaders and companies were still unwilling to bend, insisting everyone return to the office and conduct business as pre-pandemic usual. In response, swaths of people jumped ship, seeking out the places where leadership was open to shedding outdated workplace norms and mindsets for newer, more modern, more relevant ones. This dynamic played a key role in The Great Resignation.

In our survey, one frustrated employee commented, "We're not asking for WFH as a way to be lazy.... It's a quality-of-life boost. I want them to realize that the more they push their own ideology on all of our employees, the further away they are pushing us."

In our research, we heard multiple accounts of people saying "I'll never forget how this company and its leaders treated me." In some cases, this was an expression of frustration. But in others, it was actually one of gratitude. There were organizations and leaders who made accommodations for the challenges of the time. There was a real sense of grace for people's lives mid-pandemic, as well as flexibility, support, and a scaling down of expectations. There was humanity. Something as simple as a leader's email response to an employee's mistake with the spirit of "It's 2020, we all get a pass, don't be too hard on yourself. . . ." made people feel a sense of understanding.

In other cases, it was quite the opposite. Some people left jobs with nothing else lined up, even with all the mid-pandemic uncertainty because they realized, simply, that *life is short. I can't keep being treated like this. It's just not worth it*. Others, with very real and understandable fears about making ends meet, hung on tighter and worked harder to prove their worthiness. But many kept the memory of how they were treated, by organizations and leaders alike, close to heart.

Clara, a middle manager at a paper packaging company, pointed to a moment she'll never forget. She shared how, in March 2020, she received a multiple-page HR memo right as the organization was transitioning to WFH.

We read this and cringed. It seemed like it should have been followed by a "jk" or "psych!" It wasn't.

For Clara, "it felt like a misunderstanding of people's lives, and it dehumanized the experience of the

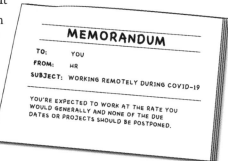

chaos of living right now. It made me really troubled." (Spoiler: she left the organization nine months later.)

While the professional world was already en route to more human-centric workplaces, the pandemic years have made compassion a must-have skill for leaders and managers. Still skeptical? Compassionate leadership is not a fluffy feel-good concept. Rather, it has real, concrete, data-driven implications at work:

- 88 percent of employees said they value bosses who listen to them.[2]

- Employees are more confident, productive, and self-aware when leaders focus on their strengths instead of weaknesses .[3]

- People who work in a culture where they feel free to express affection, tenderness, caring, and compassion for one another are more satisfied with their jobs, committed to the organization, and accountable for their performance.[4]

In short, employees are hungry for compassion, grace, and humanity from their leaders.

✦ NOW WHAT?

Leaders, remember that what you do and how you impact organizational change trickles down to the individual level. You carry the brunt of the weight when it comes to transforming workplaces for the better. For people reading this who aren't in a leadership position, if you don't see your current boss or organization represented in what we cover next, think about ways to ask for what you need. And don't be afraid to be bold in your critique and push for change.

CALLOUT: For Your Consideration

When Good Intentions Go Bad

It's only natural for leaders to try to do the best for their teams, but sometimes the implications that spring from that goal don't play out as intended. The best way to prevent unintended negative consequences is to foster a feedback-heavy culture, one where it's common to share praise and criticism, even when it's hard. Watch out for these commonly well-intentioned approaches to leadership that can often cause more harm than good.

INTENTION	IMPACT
"I'm a leader who's always on and available for my people!"	Employees think they need to mirror the leader's behavior and are always on, too.
"I don't want to tell my people what I want. I coach them to get the 'right answer.'"	There's a "right answer," so people become wary about what they say or suggest.
"I'm there at every step because I don't want my people to fail."	Failure is something that's looked down upon, so employees opt to operate in a safe, measured way.
"I want to be an empathetic, kind leader, so I cushion feedback."	People aren't held accountable.
"I'm going on vacation, but I'll still be reachable!"	Employees feel that leaders don't trust them to adequately handle problems on their own.

MAKE COMPASSIONATE LEADERSHIP AN ACTION

A quick note about what compassionate leadership is not. Compassionate leadership is not about "kids glove" management. It is not about sugarcoating feedback, letting people walk all over you, avoiding tough conversations, and letting employees with toxic behavior or consistently poor results linger.

It is about helping everyone at work see the shared humanity in one another. It's about leaders offering support, kindness, and encouragement to help employees maximize their potential in a measured, balanced way. It's about having the courage to be direct but kind in feedback, saying no with love (yes, love), inviting self-feedback (even—no, especially—when it's hard to hear), and being open to growth and change. Far from a soft, laissez-faire approach to leading, compassionate leadership is really hard. It requires a high degree of emotional intelligence and deep self-awareness.

Speaking of which, we've identified three cornerstones to a compassionate leadership approach, each of which builds off the other:

- Self-awareness and self-compassion
- Awareness of and compassion for others
- Inspiring people to action

So what do these cornerstones look like at work?

CORNERSTONE 1: SELF-AWARENESS AND SELF-COMPASSION

Even excellent leaders often fall short of offering themselves the same grace and compassion they give others. It doesn't matter how kind, generous, or giving a leader is to their employees. If they don't reflect the same back onto themselves, their efforts lose much of their potency. Self-awareness and self-compassion should not be the last boxes ticked. They should be the first. If leaders don't honor their own humanity first, they won't be able to lead in a truly compassionate way. This takes vulnerability.

When we say the word *vulnerability* to clients, we can almost see them physically tense up before we explain what that looks like. Vulnerability does not mean weakness. It doesn't mean being soft or a pushover. What it means is that you're open to others seeing that you are not, in fact, infallible. Not being afraid of being revealed to be human.

Human leaders will (naturally) have vulnerabilities and growing edges. By owning up to this simple fact, they invite those they lead to work alongside them, not just report to or defer to them. As Violet, a graphic designer, told us when describing the characteristics of her ideal leader, "Meet people where they're at. Have a normal conversation like a regular human, and not an email that sounds like it went through five different people and four different drafts."

> **LEADING WITH SELF-AWARENESS LOOKS LIKE . . . INVITING REGULAR FEEDBACK ON YOUR LEADERSHIP STYLE**

What's more open and vulnerable than inviting feedback about how you lead? It's so brave, because you have no idea if people are going to shower you with compliments or list your many flaws—and it's so necessary. Also, it's really hard to do this properly. Employees might not be open and honest for fear of potential backlash. They also might be uncomfortable with the power differential. Leaders must create an environment where employees feel comfortable expressing candid feedback to anyone and everyone. Make it a practice to avoid defensiveness, be gracious in receiving comments, and thank employees for their thoughts.

In practice, we suggest the following:

+ **Set the Expectation that You'll Be Soliciting Feedback** on your performance as a leader and the organization at large, at regular, predetermined intervals that work for you and your organization (e.g., once a week, once a month). This expectation, for maximum impact, is best paired with an explanation of how leaders hold themselves accountable to turn what they learn into action.

+ **Nurture a Healthy Mix of the Ways You Solicit Feedback**: one-on-ones, surveys, anonymous surveys, town halls, team meetings, etc.

  - For one-on-ones, come prepared with questions (both pointed and open-ended) to direct the conversations.

  - Follow up on surveys you conduct. Don't make employees feel like they're wasting time and effort responding. Be as transparent as possible in sharing the responses; and for each survey, make sure you're addressing how the feedback will be digested and, ideally, acted upon.

  - For town halls and team meetings, setting expectations is once again key. Establish a clear process for how these gatherings are conducted. Do attendees anonymously submit questions beforehand? Do you want to hear from every employee in the room? Be clear about the meeting standards, and communicate them beforehand.

+ **Operate by the Platinum Rule** (introduced in chapter 3) to solicit the best feedback from your employees. Know that each person may require a slightly different approach to coax out direct feedback. For example, Lisa had a direct report who never had any critiques during their one-on-one meetings. When review time came around, Lisa found that the person she managed actually had quite a lot to say! After approaching her directly (and with curiosity, not defensiveness), she discovered that this person felt uncomfortable giving critical feedback in person. She much preferred writing out responses to the questions Lisa was asking during those one-on-one meetings. From then on, Lisa set up a recurring email to go out shortly after their touch-base conversations, prompting this employee with three simple questions:

- What can I do to better support you?
- Any frustrations from the past week?
- What changes would you like to see from me? From the organization?

CALLOUT: BEWARE!

The Not-So-Anonymous Survey

Anonymous surveys should be an excellent tool to solicit critiques that, for understandable reasons, employees might be wary of sharing directly with a leader or manager. But they often fall short of being as anonymous as they proclaim. Many people question the true anonymity of those surveys, knowing that their critiques will spotlight who shared what or that the technology can actually track who says what. We've even heard stories of people who have been punished for feedback delivered on an "anonymous" survey. Before any anonymous survey can be successful, trust must be established by the organization so it's understood that they will not try to uncover who said what (even when they promised they wouldn't) and will not reprimand participants for their criticisms and critiques.

This written format made it much easier for the direct report to relay important critiques, which meant that there were no surprises at the next feedback session and that Lisa was able to adjust her management style in real time.

LEADING WITH SELF-AWARENESS LOOKS LIKE... COMMUNICATING WITH TRANSPARENCY

Want to alienate your employees? Communicate with bravado, not authenticity. Or, perhaps even worse, confidently present information without a proper amount of certainty. During the pandemic years, leaders who tried to cover up unknowns about the organization's future quickly lost employee buy-in. People wondered, "How can you try to predict when we'll be back in the office when even epidemiologists don't know what course this pandemic will take?" The more successful messaging was transparent, even if the answer was "I don't know." Leaders who acknowledged the challenges ahead and admitted that the road was uncertain but that they were committed to being thoughtful and strategic every step of the way were the leaders who earned people's trust.

In practice, we suggest the following:

- ✦ **Own Up When You Don't Know the Answer**, and invite others in to help find the solution.

- ✦ **Openly Acknowledge Issues or Areas of Weakness Within Your Organization**, and (when possible) share plans to improve them. Yes, it's scary, but it's okay. Employees are much more willing to trust (and follow) leaders who aren't trying to sweep all the bad or "in the works" stuff under the rug while highlighting all the areas that they're confident about.

- ✦ **Communicate Regularly with Updates**, even if they're just to say, "We're keeping a pulse on the situation, and we want to let you know our eyes are still on this." It's common practice for leadership to have meetings behind closed doors. It's also common for employees to question what happens behind those doors (or panic about the conversations they aren't hearing, even if they're about a bonus). No matter the news discussed within the room, it doesn't take long for a closed door to symbolize "We don't trust you with this information." Asana, a project management tool company, publishes internally what happens in upper management and board meetings so that there are few questions as to why decisions are being made. It also empowers people with the information they need to make decisions about their work. So, ultimately, this transparent communication is a win for everyone.[5]

LEADING WITH SELF-COMPASSION LOOKS LIKE . . . ACKNOWLEDGING YOUR HUMANITY

Yes. It's true. As leaders, you're not superheroes. You are, in fact, mere mortals. Even the Arianna Huffingtons and Bill Gateses of the world . . . well, they're brilliant, but they're also human beings who sleep, cry, laugh, and make their fair share of mistakes. Too often leaders feel they need to present this foolproof front, don their armor without chinks or weaknesses. Leaders who openly embrace their humanity are more relatable and better equipped to build a stronger foundation of trust.

In practice, we suggest the following:

- ✦ **Let Your Personality Shine**. Share those weird quirks and idiosyncrasies that make you . . . well, you. One interviewee we spoke with said that his boss spent twelve years deejaying and only told the team after years of leading them. So surprised and tickled by this new image of their boss, they asked to see a video for proof. Instead of sending a clip, their leader decided to host a DJ night during WFH pandemic times to bring people together.

+ **Don't Smother Your Emotions.** Not always—and not all emotions, obviously. But showing emotion—whether a tearful moment, excitement, worry, or even exasperation—can help humanize you, the leader, to your direct reports and aid in the strengthening of connection and sense of team loyalty.

+ **Admit When You're Struggling.** Whether you've failed, or whenever you're buckling under a particularly heavy workload, admitting it doesn't make you look weak. It makes you human. (Quick note: There's a fine line between admitting struggles and emotional dumping. You shouldn't be dumping all your problems on your employees, but acknowledging that you, too, have moments where you fail and fall short can be powerful.)

CORNERSTONE 2: AWARENESS OF AND COMPASSION FOR OTHERS

Compassionate leaders don't think of themselves as the most informed company mouthpiece or font of wisdom. Instead, they see themselves as great observers, people who learn from their employees and constantly seek to understand (and to remove those leadership perspective goggles that are such a danger). By tapping into their employees' experiences, what they're struggling with, where their potential lies,

and how they interact with teammates, only then will leaders have the requisite information to behave empathetically and compassionately toward those they lead.

> **LEADING WITH AWARENESS OF AND COMPASSION FOR OTHERS LOOKS LIKE . . . TENDING TO YOUR EMOTIONAL CULTURE**

Emotions have always been like the f-word at work: to be avoided at all costs. But we are constantly processing emotions, and they nearly always influence the way we work unless we're the most emotionally intelligent humans of all time. (Pro tip: If someone says they are the most emotionally intelligent human of all time, they most likely are not.) We have to grow more comfortable with discussing emotions at work and how they impact us if we want to work in a space of compassion. Doing so is a way to tend to the emotional culture in our work.

What is emotional culture? We're glad you asked. According to Sigal Barsade and Olivia A. O'Neill in their piece for HBR, emotional culture is "the shared affective values, norms, artifacts, and assumptions that govern which emotions people have and express at work and which ones they are better off suppressing."[6] Or, as we like to think of it, it is about comfort with discussing, expressing, and managing emotions at work. There once was a time when people wouldn't talk about therapy, much less answer honestly to the question "How are you?" (The common, unspoken answer? "Pretty awful.") Now, we refer to our therapists by name in conversation with colleagues and are ready for leaders who dip their toes into the feelings pond.

In practice, we suggest the following:

- ✦ **Acknowledge and Hold Space for Trauma.** This has always been a thing; it's not just the continued pandemic trauma that people will be healing from. Life has always been fraught with individual challenges, traumas, and tragedies because the all-time lows (and all-time highs) are part of human existence. But it's been a century since the masses experienced a pandemic at this scale, and the fallout from these pandemic years will likely play out through the 2020s. Invest in training to learn how to best hold space and have these conversations.

+ **Get Specific with Naming Your Feelings**. It can be challenging to name how we're feeling beyond angry, sad, happy, or fine. But sometimes we say we're feeling sad, but we're actually feeling helpless. Other times, we say we're happy, but we're actually feeling hopeful. Specificity is key in getting the help we need, and finding the right word is usually just a thesaurus search away.

+ **Ask, "How Are You Doing, Really?"** This is not just, "How are you doing?" We've heard many stories about people who said that when someone asked this question—like, actually asked it and wanted to know the real answer—a small bit of ease entered the nervous system because they didn't have to hide so much anymore.

Compassionate leaders normalize conversations about well-being and mental health for the sake of the team. Every single person endures hardship in their lives; and while they don't need to detail what's causing their feelings, they should feel safe to say, "I'm having a tough day, and I'm going to need some grace."

> **LEADING WITH AWARENESS OF AND COMPASSION FOR OTHERS LOOKS LIKE . . . EMBRACING THE PLATINUM RULE**

Remember our old friend, the Platinum Rule? Well, it's back (yet again!), because it is extremely important in a leadership context. Even when leaders are making an effort to understand others and lead in a way that's motivated by compassion, they tend to follow

LEADING WITH COMPASSION, NO MATTER YOUR ROLE

CALLOUT: BEWARE!

The Danger of Compassion Fatigue

There is such a thing as too much compassion; and those who are naturally inclined to be empathetic, compassionate people can be at risk of compassion fatigue. Leaders are balancing many different responsibilities. They feel the weight of keeping the organization healthy and growing, with not only the bottom line but also employees' livelihoods at stake. Leading can sometimes feel like taking on the weight of the world. This topic of compassion fatigue is a big area of interest in health care fields and, unsurprisingly, for occupational therapists. Taking a page from their book, there is a cap to how much empathy and compassion a person can give. The trouble is, when a person burns out, they'll reach a point at which they no longer have the capacity to care for anyone. If this is you, or if you're feeling overwhelmed by taking on too many people's challenges and emotions, boundaries are your best friend. Be aware of when you're feeling overwhelmed with overcare, ask for support from other leaders, and take a step back for self-nourishment.

---

the guidance of the Golden Rule. But to lead more effectively, it's much more useful to treat others the way *they* wish to be treated. This is why it's so vital for leaders to listen, observe, and understand those they lead. It helps you customize and individualize your approach so that you can motivate and engage with precision, rather than with a self-focused lens. This does not mean abandoning authenticity. It does mean moving the needle slightly to accommodate others' preferences.

In practice, we suggest the following:

- **Develop the Habit of (and Even Better, a Process for) Asking Your Reports How They Like to be Managed.** Ask about their preferred frequency of check-ins, the best way for you to deliver feedback, how much instruction they like to receive for projects, what they loved about a past manager, what they didn't enjoy about a past manager, and anything that's important to know about their style of work and how they're best led. Lisa, for example, doesn't enjoy receiving praise in public forums. Picture someone saying to Lisa, "Wow! This is incredible work. You're very talented." Then picture Lisa freezing, nervously laughing, and saying something like, "What? Oh, no, hey *you* are talented. Am I right?" She prefers getting positive feedback in a private setting, where there's much less awkwardness.

- **Have Your Team Take Assessments (or Participate in Team Exercises) to Learn More About Who They are and How They Work.** Two of our favorite assessments are Kolbe (which measures the instinctive way you take action at work) and CliftonStrengths (which identifies natural talents, such as ways of thinking, feeling, and behaving). We've taken almost every assessment you can imagine, including the ones like "Which *Twilight* character do you lead like?" So we boldly stand behind our two recommendations.

- **Defer to Chapter 3's Concept of Empathetic Listening.** The more informed you are as a leader, the better equipped you'll be to individualize your approach and lead more effectively. One bit of pushback we hear sounds a little something like this: "If I made myself available to listen to every employee, direct report, or person who wanted to share something, I would be working eighty-hour weeks and doing nothing but that." We get it. No one has a Time-Turner, and thoughtful engagement can seep into other to-dos and urgencies. This fear of the time crunch can be avoided if clear parameters and expectations are defined. Leaders can set weekly office hours where their door (be it virtual or physical) is open for people to come to chat with them. Perhaps a digital feedback system (i.e., a modern version of the suggestion box) where employees can submit feedback, either anonymously or not, at their leisure can be created and utilized. There is a multitude of microways to invite feedback and listening moments, without making it your full-time job.

CALLOUT: A Generational Moment

Generational Compassion

Oh, the tales we could tell about generational frustration (bordering on resentment) in the workplace. "Gen Xers are blunt and mean!" "Baby Boomers are too old-fashioned!" "Millennials are entitled!" "Gen Z can only communicate in emojis!" The stem of all the butting of generational heads boils down to a lack of understanding and compassion for each generation. A brief overview of the why behind generational identities and the unique challenges each generation currently faces almost inevitably dissolves tension between these cohorts and helps to foster cross-mentorship and a supportive working environment. When compassionate leaders approach challenges with curiosity (like asking questions such as, "Why does it seem like Millennials are entitled? Where is that perception coming from? And what might really be at play?") instead of painting with the broad stroke of "They just don't know what hard work looks like," it sets the stage for others to follow suit and employ the same understanding, compassion, and grace that the leader is displaying.

> **LEADING WITH AWARENESS OF AND COMPASSION FOR OTHERS LOOKS LIKE . . . BALANCING GRACE WITH ACCOUNTABILITY**

Whenever we work with clients, this is one of those messages that sticks. CEOs, leaders, and managers alike come to us and say, "That piece about grace . . . I think that was the single most important thing I've heard in a long time." It seems that giving others grace has not been the norm. Instead, accountability is the norm, where getting the most out of every employee means driving productivity and holding people to results.

But what if grace were added to the mix? What if, when something goes wrong, leaders respond with curiosity instead of a desire to reprimand or even fix it themselves? If an employee is showing up late consistently, instead of jumping to write them up or admonish them, they ask with care and sincerity, "Is everything okay? Can I help?" We can never know what any one person is going through in their private lives—and it's often so much more complicated and challenging than we could even imagine.

All this being said, there is no grace without accountability. *Balance* is key. Sometimes, with all the best intentions, leaders extend grace, kindness, compassion, and understanding to the detriment of those they're trying to help. When someone constantly and consistently drops the ball, lashes out at other team members, proves unreliable,

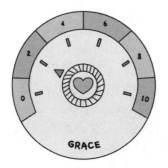

negatively affects team morale, and shows a lack of integrity, then keeping this person onboard becomes damaging to others and the organization.

Balancing grace with accountability can look like firing an underperforming employee. It can also look like being radically candid, as articulated by Kim Scott, challenging directly while caring personally.[7] Sometimes grace simply means offering accountability where there is none.

In practice, we suggest the following:

- **Determine if the Grace or Accountability Dial Needs to be Turned Up** in a given situation by asking yourself the following:

  - Is this the first time this behavior or situation has come up? Or the first few times?

  - Do I understand the why behind the behavior?

  - Is it negatively impacting other teammates? Or morale?

  - Has this person earnestly made good faith attempts to improve?

  - Are we, as an organization, dropping the ball in some way?

  - Are my actions as a leader motivated by a desire to help (e.g., the person, the team, the organization) or to defend (e.g., my actions, the rules, something else)?

Honestly, this is great advice for all coworkers regardless of their level in the organization. However, we're aware that due to power dynamics, it might be riskier to be radically candid when you're not in a leadership position with a capital L and P yet.

CORNERSTONE 3: INSPIRING EMPLOYEES TO ACTION

One of the magical things about compassionate leadership is that, rather than telling employees what to do and exactly how to do it (whatever "it" is), the compassionate leader motivates through inspiration. Their teams are, in large part, intrinsically motivated and committed to the mission at hand. These employees are moved to act because they feel supported (by leadership and fellow employees), they know their voices matter and are heard, and they sense they have the autonomy to act on their intuition and creativity without fear of negative consequences if something goes a little off course. They are, in short, the kinds of employees who most leaders wish they had more of. (They're also the kinds of colleagues everyone wishes they had more of!) And the good news is, a shift in leadership style can help create an environment that attracts and retains them.

> **LEADERS CAN INSPIRE EMPLOYEES BY . . . EMBRACING A COACH/MENTOR MINDSET**

Coach-like leaders inspire people to be their best. They remove barriers and spot potential. They watch and listen to truly understand where and how to best position employees. They care about people's overall careers and development, not just how they contribute to the company.

These types of leaders lean into the role of "mentor" more than "boss." They will offer accountability in a way that encourages and does not seek to tear people down. They refrain from leading strictly with rules and regulations; and rather than issue explicit directives from on high, they work to influence their team's work. Old-school leadership believes that productivity is a priority, but the modern leader knows that to be truly efficient (and not simply productive), you must put people first.

That's why coaches will seek to maximize employee engagement and satisfaction over productivity. In general, spend more time observing and listening than talking. Coaches will own what they don't know, gather people around them who know more, and empower everyone to utilize their knowledge and skills. They know that caring for people's well-being means everyone wins. This may sound like the fictional, wonderful coach from Hollywood stories (oh, hey, Coach Lasso). But they're real, we promise. They are the great leaders at work who many of us have had the opportunity to work with.

In practice, these coach leadership-style environments look like the following:

- Feedback is given and embraced up and down the ladder.
- Everyone knows what is expected of them.
- Failure (within reason) is expected (and even encouraged).
- People feel free to say no.
- A network of support runs through the team.
- Employees feel comfortable approaching their leaders.

LEADERS CAN INSPIRE EMPLOYEES BY . . . PUTTING FEAR IN ITS PROPER PLACE

Fear is a destructive ingredient at work. Even so, its presence is not uncommon in modern workplaces. A common fear is that of losing one's job. This is, of course, entirely understandable. A job is a paycheck that provides financial stability. We get it! Unfortunately, this underlying fear is accompanied by many others that feed into all sorts of workplace behaviors that stunt both individual and enterprise growth.

Some common workplace fears include:

- ✦ Fear of trying something new
- ✦ Fear of failure
- ✦ Fear of being shut down
- ✦ Fear of going against the grain
- ✦ Fear of ruffling feathers
- ✦ Fear of upsetting others
- ✦ Fear of being or appearing uninformed
- ✦ Fear of not playing the work politics game

The first step toward putting this fear in its proper place is to address it head-on. Leaders who don't shy away from addressing fears out loud can better take steps of reassurance and encouragement. It's true that depending on the fear, there may be certain unknown factors, complex interpersonal dynamics, or potential legal barriers to what can and can't be shared. Even so, leaders can address these fears by shedding light on what is and isn't known, what they can and can't share, and how they plan to move forward.

The second is to root out the more harmful causes of workplace fear and tame them. In our experience, these are some of the most damaging fear-inducing elements within workplace cultures. We sometimes call them the Four Horsemen of the Fearpocalypse.

Depending on the leader's level of influence, they may not be able to overhaul their organization's culture. What individuals can do on their own, though, is to establish a safe microculture within their team. One of the most powerful ways to do this is through the oft-discussed (for good reason) concept of creating an environment

THE FOUR HORSEMEN OF THE FEARPOCALYPSE

of psychological safety, popularized by Google. At its most basic level, psychological safety is about team members feeling safe to take risks and be vulnerable with each other. With that safety established, they feel free to bring up ideas without worry of being heckled, stirring the pot, or creating some sort of weird political dynamic.

For psychological safety to be realized, there needs to be a deep level of trust among the group. And it's not just that an individual trusts the group. They're also secure in the knowledge that the group trusts them. Within the bounds of psychological safety, people feel empowered and emboldened to take risks, to innovate, to ideate. It frees them from the cage of fear that can paralyze even the brightest, most dedicated minds at work.

In practice, we suggest the following:

+ Model curiosity.

+ Praise calculated risks, even if the result isn't as desired.

+ Coach through failures, and praise the efforts where praise is due.

+ Quickly shut down harmful pessimism and negativity.

+ Embrace the "Yes, and . . ." mindset of the improv world.

+ Regularly ask for feedback on your thoughts or ideas.

LEADERS CAN INSPIRE EMPLOYEES BY . . . RALLYING PEOPLE AROUND A CORE MESSAGE

This is a callback to chapter 8: There is nothing that will inspire a team to action faster than believing in a uniting core mission. Shortsighted leaders get mired in the minutiae (hence behaviors like micromanaging and being miserly about people taking "too much" PTO). The best leaders look to the horizon and paint a picture of what is possible. They see and can tap into their employees' aspirations and hopes. They illuminate the way forward in an emotionally compelling and purpose-driven way. Their messaging is less about the how and more about the why. They rally people around their mission by being authentic, accessible, and what Liz Fosslein and Mollie West Duffy coined in their book *No Hard Feelings: The Secret Power of Embracing Emotions at Work* as "selectively vulnerable."[8]

In practice, we suggest the following:

+ **Weaving the Uniting Company Why into Your Work**, whether it's at meetings, through feedback sessions, or connecting employees with customers. There's never an opportunity too big or small to reiterate that uniting message.

LEADING WITH COMPASSION, NO MATTER YOUR ROLE

✦ **Adapting to the Why of the Moment in Times of Crisis** instead of clinging to the tried-and-true. The pandemic years proved that sometimes a purpose of the moment is the best kind of rallying cry.

In 2020, that infamous year that tested all of our mettle, one CEO proved his own in a pretty spectacular way. On March 19 of that year, at the onset of the pandemic and mid-battle with pancreatic cancer, Marriott CEO Arne Sorenson spoke to employees in a worldwide video address. His advisers counseled him against appearing on camera, worried that his bald head and thin frame would convey a message of weakness instead of strength. Sorenson pushed back and pushed forward. The five-minute video that followed is one of the most compelling testaments to true, compassionate leadership that emerged in the midst of the crisis.

While it's worth taking in every minute, the sign-off pulls it all together. That's when Sorenson uttered his rallying cry, uniting employees around a core mission for the times. He said, "While it's impossible to know how long this crisis will last, I know we as a global community will come through the other side, and that when we do, our guests will be eager to travel this beautiful world again. When that great day comes, we will be there to welcome them, with the warmth and care we are known for the world over."[9]

To this day, that closing sentiment gives us chills when we read it. And even though, tragically, Arne passed less than a year after this all-company address, his words and transformative leadership style continue to resonate.

Never has there been a better, more auspicious time to shift how we lead at work. When we spoke with Joe, a restaurant industry manager, he said, "Everything about the pandemic is a microcosm like when a herd sees a threat. Either you can go out on your own and then suffer those consequences alone in isolation, or you can understand what your responsibility is in your community or to the people dependent on you and take care of them."

Leadership, whether formal or informal, is about community and compassion. What lies at the end of this portal? Borrowing from Arne, we hope that we step into a world where warmth and care are the first descriptors of successful leaders the world over.

✦ THE GIST ✦

PRE-PORTAL STANDARD

The slow but steady evolution from an authoritarian, top-down style of leadership to a more supportive, coach-like leadership methodology was a welcome change to the managerial landscape.

PORTAL LESSONS

The many hardships of the pandemic years hypercharged the call for more human and humane leaders. Those who are having the greatest success with employees are the ones who are embracing a compassionate approach.

NOW WHAT? STEPPING THROUGH THE PORTAL

Leaders, keep in mind the compassionate leadership cornerstones (and their action items):

Self-awareness and self-compassion, because compassion begins with the self:

- ✦ Invite feedback on your leadership style.
- ✦ Communicate with transparency.
- ✦ Acknowledge your humanity.

Awareness of and compassion for others, without being overwhelmed by compassion fatigue:

- ✦ Tend to your team's emotional culture.

THE FUTURE OF WORK IS HUMAN

- ✦ Lead through the Platinum Rule.
- ✦ Balance grace with accountability.

Inspiring employees to action instead of leaning on directives.

- ✦ Embrace a coach/mentor mindset.
- ✦ Put fear in its proper place.
- ✦ Rally people around a core message.

CONCLUSION

A MORE HUMAN WORKPLACE

From the time we entered the working world to now, the "I hate my job" chant has been consistent—and loud. Listening to people share anecdotes about the why behind that statement has been the fuel that's fired the work we do.

The default shouldn't be that people hate their jobs. Do they need to be obsessed with their work? No, absolutely not. We actually don't think that's healthy. But we do believe that people should at least be working in a happy medium—a place in the middle where the work gets done, but not at the cost of well-being and joy. Where individuals can invest in their personal lives while still developing their careers and meeting professional goals.

The great work awakening has taken hold, whether or not organizations, business owners, and leaders are ready for it. The Great Reassessment was a sign of the times. Long gone are the days when people sit back and just work at the pace and style that their forefathers had. Now, they're demanding a more human, more realistic approach to work.

While this book instructs you on how to lead and operate a more human workplace, there are several essential lessons that we hope you take away from it.

THE HUMAN WORKPLACE REVOLUTION IS HERE

We've been working in a business world that has centered on profit and growth. But that centering has come at a considerable cost: People have been disengaged, stressed, and lonely. Now, a shift is occurring where businesses can reorient toward people and reap the benefits in the process. And contrary to what the fear-induced voices may say in your head that this could cost the company success, it can actually be the just the thing to nourish flourishing bottom lines and employees. It's not an either-or proposition. You can have both a productive, humming workplace and one where human beings are prioritized.

Now, for the first time in a long time, power lies with the people at work, not the leaders and organizations. This shifting balance of power shows up differently in the people at work. There's the person who says it's only temporary and we should just wait it out, the person who is scared of what it means for themselves, and the person who cheers for the change and wants to be a part of it.

Consider what role you will play in this human workplace revolution. If you are a leader, are you going to be the one championing changes to paid leave policies? Or will you opt for the status quo? Will you read about changes at work and listen to people's ideas? Or think about every idea that won't work? Consider how a leadership workplace evolution is happening alongside the human workplace evolution. Leaders, you do not have to fit the mold of what once was successful. You can shape a new one.

If you are an individual contributor, do you see one thing you can do to be a part of this workplace revolution? We understand that in many situations, unfortunately, people can't change systems by themselves. They often may be reprimanded for speaking against the norm. And we also know that there is strength in numbers! Often, when one person notices a problem, there are many other people who do, too. Find another one of the many, if you can. Control what you can control, advocate for each other, and help each other in the process of workplace evolution.

ON THE PRIORITY LIST, WORK DOESN'T NEED TO BE NUMBER ONE

Being professionally successful has usually gone hand in hand with sacrifice—of time, health, family, friends, and even joy. Whether going on vacation, leaving early to head to a basketball game, or taking a day off to spend the day with Mom, if a work obligation comes up, then those personal experiences are a no-go. But people are done choosing work over everything else. Sure, there may be some late nights and working weekends, but it should no longer be treated as an expectation.

For those of you who are leaders, that means choosing people over productivity, opting at times to stay the course instead of scale, and centering employees in every decision. In practice, this looks like taking vacations (seriously, drain those PTO banks) and being unavailable when you're out. It looks like creating a flexible work culture so that when employees go about their lives, they know that personal matters take precedence over work ones. It looks like allowing a hybrid work model that works for most instead of demanding people return to the office.

This also looks like knowing when to take care of yourself so that you can take care of others. It is not easy to be a leader. We understand this. We've been leaders. We've been non-leaders, too, and we know the challenges that come from moving from one role to another. For those of you who are leaders, take care of yourself. When you take the steps to nurture your own mental, emotional, and physical well-being, you are setting a standard for how you expect others to care for themselves. Consider the long-term benefits of this: Leaders should not be expected to put in forty more hours a week just because they are a leader!

For individuals, that means making choices that put you first. Work does not have to be your identity—or your purpose. It does not have to be the thing that fuels your existence. Healthy boundaries with work are... well, healthy! And even if others around you ridicule your priorities or want to punish you for them, remember why work isn't always your number one.

YOU DON'T GET ANYWHERE ALONE

Humans are not designed to live and operate solely as individuals, especially at work. We know that this can feel in conflict with the notion that the American identity is one of individualism. We also know that this conflicts with age-old professional advice to make yourself irreplaceable. But it's essential to think beyond the individual most of the time.

Living through the pandemic years illuminated the importance of people as a collective. In some ways, people felt profound grief, depression, and anxiety from the isolation of quarantining and foregoing social gatherings to keep others safe. While this may have been particularly felt on a personal level, people also felt it professionally. There was (and is) an integral need to focus not just on people at work, but also on relationships with people. It moves the focus from "what I need" to "what we need."

When you, as a leader or an individual, operate from a place of we rather than I, it can increase compassion—even compassion and understanding for the person who is not in your mental space. And herein lies the power to transform workplaces: by leaning on and listening to each other.

Leaders, seek input from those whose perspectives are different. Make informed decisions about the direction of your company, the statements you make, and the accountability you accept. Set a goal to foster relationships with a variety of people: those who are near you every day, and workers you'd otherwise not interact with. Nurture a work environment that lends well to relationships. Make time for personal check-ins, infuse play and fun into the day, and invest in connection. Build a circle of people who look and think differently than you.

Individuals, learn from colleagues whose experiences are different from yours. Ask one another for help. Set goals for yourself and bring people along with you as you achieve them. When someone new is added to the team, reach out and get to know them. Lean on trusted colleagues to effect change.

All of the work that we do is a web of connection. We don't get anywhere alone. Famous CEOs and executives achieved nothing by themselves. Succeeding on a project is rarely (if ever) done without the research, idea, execution, or input of another person. Even consider that to write a report of your findings requires a computer that was designed, manufactured, and built by many other people.

We started this book with a quote by Arundhati Roy, in which she wrote that the pandemic is a portal. The door has been opened to a new work world of possibility, where people are thriving and happy instead of hurting and dreading the Sunday scaries.

It's time for you to walk through the portal and decide what you want to create. What do you want to leave behind? What are you going to reimagine? How can you make that a reality? This portal is not going to be open forever. Sure, there is always an opportunity to change (and, in fact, we should seize those more often). But this one-of-a-kind moment, where the ripple of change is actually a tidal wave, is not going to be here for long.

At the time of this writing, we're seeing a faction of people clinging to what once was. Leaders are demanding office time. People are refusing to continue the conversation about how the pandemic is affecting the workplace. Another surge is occurring, supply chains are backed up, and people are quitting their jobs in droves. To deny the power of this moment is to turn your back on necessary change.

Opt to see this time—at present, and as you look upon its history—as a powerful period of transformation. Where individuals take it upon themselves to change their mindset, or work differently to create a better work world.

We hope you'll join us in our belief that work doesn't have to suck. Not now, not ever. And to bring back one more thought from Arundhati Roy, "Another world is not only possible, she is on her way. On a quiet day, I can hear her breathing."[1]

What do you hear?

REFERENCES

INTRODUCTION

1. Jim Clifton, "The World's Broken Workplace," *The Chairman's Blog*, Gallup, June 13, 2017, https://news.gallup.com/opinion/chairman/212045/world-broken-workplace.aspx.

2. "Monster Job Index," Monster, last modified August 2021, https://learnmore.monster.com/job-index-in-the-time-of-coronavirus.

3. Deloitte and the Female Quotient, *Shift/Forward: Redefining Leadership—The Inclusion Imperative*, June 2018, https://www2.deloitte.com/content/dam/Deloitte/us/Documents/about-deloitte/us-shift-forward-redefining-leadership.pdf.

4. Heather Long, "It's not a 'labor shortage.' It's a great reassessment of work in America," *The Washington Post* (online), May 7, 2021, https://www.washingtonpost.com/business/2021/05/07/jobs-report-labor-shortage-analysis/.

5. Arundhati Roy, "Arundhati Roy: 'The pandemic is a portal' | Free to read," *Financial Times*, April 3, 2020, https://www.ft.com/content/10d8f5e8-74eb-11ea-95fe-fcd274e920ca.

THE FUTURE OF WORK IS HUMAN

CHAPTER 1: HUMANS, NOT ROBOTS

1. National Humanities Center, "Frederick Winslow Taylor: The Principles of SCIENTIFIC MANAGEMENT, 1910, Ch. 2: 'The Principles of Scientific Management' excerpts," published 2005, http://nationalhumanitiescenter.org/pds/gilded/progress/text3/taylor.pdf.

2. Sarah Gallo, "Microchipping Employees: A Rising Trend in the Future of Work?", *Learning Technologies* (blog), Training Industry, January 28, 2020, https://trainingindustry.com/articles/learning-technologies/microchipping-employees-a-rising-trend-in-the-future-of-work/.

3. Margaret Heffernan, "Treat workers like robots and they might behave like them," *Financial Times*, February 24, 2020, https://www.ft.com/content/a6e4b886-56e8-11ea-abe5-8e03987b7b20.

4. Judith Magyar, "Mental Health Day: SAP Offers Employees a Chance to Recharge," *SAP News Center* (blog), SAP, March 4, 2021, https://news.sap.com/2021/03/mental-health-day-sap-employees/.

5. Travis Bradberry, "Why You Need Emotional Intelligence To Succeed," *Forbes* (online), January 7, 2015, https://www.forbes.com/sites/travisbradberry/2015/01/07/why-you-need-emotional-intelligence-to-succeed/?sh=ef5a22f62468.

6. Brita Belli, "Emotionally intelligent bosses make for happier, more creative employees," *Yale News* (blog), Yale University, March 6, 2020, https://news.yale.edu/2020/03/06/emotionally-intelligent-bosses-make-happier-more-creative-employees.

7. Kyle Benson, "The Magic Relationship Ratio: According to Science." *The Gottman Institute*, accessed November 3, 2022, https://www.gottman.com/blog/the-magic-relationship-ratio-according-science/.

8. Beth Bratkovic, "Feedback and the Power of the 5:1 Ratio,"

REFERENCES

LinkedIn (blog), LinkedIn, November 15, 2018, https://www.linkedin.com/pulse/feedback-power-51-ratio-beth-bratkovic/.

9. Annamarie Mann. "Why We All Need Best Friends at Work." *Gallup.* January 15, 2018. https://www.gallup.com/workplace/236213/why-need-best-friends-work.aspx.

CHAPTER 2: DEFEATING PERFECTIONISM

1. Anne Lamott, *Bird by Bird* (New York: Bantam Doubleday Dell Publishing Group, 1980), 27.

2. Thomas Curran and Andrew P. Hill, "Perfectionism Is Increasing Over Time: A Meta-Analysis of Birth Cohort: Differences From 1989 to 2016," *American Psychological Association* 145, no. 4 (2019): 410 – 429, https://doi.org/10.1037/bul0000138.

3. Curran and Hill, "Perfectionism Is Increasing Over Time," 410 – 429.

4. Jane Adams, "More College Students Seem to Be Majoring in Perfectionism," *The New York Times* (online), January 18, 2018, https://www.nytimes.com/2018/01/18/well/family/more-college-students-seem-to-be-majoring-in-perfectionism.html#:~:text=New%20data%20from%20American%2C%20Canadian,by%2033%20percent%20since%201989.

5. Maria Cohut, "Perfectionism on the rise among millennials, but to what effect?", *Medical News Today*, January 6, 2018, https://www.medicalnewstoday.com/articles/320513#Too-much-pressure-on-millennials.

6. Rachel Genevieve Chia and Qayyah Moynihan, "More millennials feel pressure to be perfect. It's causing depression, anorexia, and suicide rates to spike," *Business Insider*, September 16, 2018, https://www.businessinsider.com/perfectionism-causing-more-early-deaths-and-suicides-among-millennials-2018-9.

7. Aysa Gray, "The Bias of 'Professionalism' Standards," *Stanford Social Innovation Review*, June 4, 2019, https://ssir.org/articles/entry/the_bias_of_professionalism_standards.

8. Hannah L. Ubl, Lisa X. Walden, and Debra Arbit, "Managing Millennials For Dummies Cheat Sheet," *Dummies*, updated April 26, 2017, https://www.dummies.com/article/business-careers-money/business/management/managing-millennials-dummies-cheat-sheet-238734/.

9. Emily Kleszewski and Kathleen Otto, "The perfect colleague? Multidimensional perfectionism and indicators of social disconnection in the workplace," *Personality and Individual Differences* 162, 110016 (August 2020): https://doi.org/10.1016/j.paid.2020.110016.

10. Katharine Brooks, "Your Career and the Tyranny of the Shoulds," *Psychology Today* (online), March 8, 2017, https://www.psychologytoday.com/us/blog/career-transitions/201703/your-career-and-the-tyranny-the-shoulds#:~:text=German%20psychoanalyst%20Karen%20Horney%20(1885,out%20inner%20critic%20comes%20out.

11. Lisa Heffernan, "In defense of participation trophies: Why they really do teach the right values," *Parents* (blog), Today, August 31, 2015, https://www.today.com/parents/defense-participation-trophies-kids-t40931.

12. Ron Carucci, "Are Your High Expectations Hurting Your Team?", *Harvard Business Review* (online), January 15, 2019, https://hbr.org/2019/01/are-your-high-expectations-hurting-your-team.

CHAPTER 3: THE POWER OF EMPATHETIC COMMUNICATION

1. Francisco Sáez, "Micro-Tasks. The Pleasure of Checking Off," *FacileThings* (blog), FacileThings, accessed February 3, 2021. https://facilethings.com/blog/en/micro-tasks.

REFERENCES

2. David Grossman, "The Cost Of Poor Communications," *PRovoke Media*, July 16, 2011, https://www.provokemedia.com/latest/article/the-cost-of-poor-communications.

3. Patricia M. Buhler and Joel D. Worden, "The Cost of Poor Communications," *Society for Human Resource Management* (SHRM), accessed March 2, 2021. https://www.shrm.org/resourcesandtools/hr-topics/behavioral-competencies/communication/pages/the-cost-of-poor-communications.aspx.

4. SMB Communications Pain Study Whitepaper. *SIS International Research*. Accessed October 20, 2022. https://www.sisinternational.com/smb-communications-pain-study-white-paper-uncovering-the-hidden-cost-of-communications-barriers-and-latency/.

5. Scott, Kim. *Radical Candor: How to Get What You Want by Saying What You Mean*. Pan Books, 2019.

6. "SBAR Tool: Situation-Background-Assessment-Recommendation," Institute for Healthcare Improvement, accessed March 3, 2021. http://www.ihi.org/resources/Pages/Tools/SBARToolkit.aspx.

7. Explorance, *Employee Feedback: Survey Report*, 2021, https://explorance.com/wp-content/uploads/explorance-resource/employee-feedback-survey-report-explorance.pdf.

8. Marcel Schwantes, "Why Are People Really Leaving Their Jobs? The Whole Reason Can Be Summed Up in 4 Words," *Inc.*, accessed April 4, 2021. https://www.inc.com/marcel-schwantes/why-are-people-really-leaving-their-jobs-whole-reason-can-be-summed-up-in-4-words.html.

CHAPTER 4: OUR BURNOUT EMERGENCY

1. "ICD-11: International Classification of Diseases 11th Revision," World Health Organization, accessed June 4, 2022, https://icd.who.int/en.

2. Sara Berg, "WHO adds burnout to ICD-11. What it means for physicians," *Physician Health* (blog), American Medical Association, July 23, 2019, https://www.ama-assn.org/practice-management/physician-health/who-adds-burnout-icd-11-what-it-means-physicians.

3. "Chronic stress puts your health at risk," Mayo Clinic, July 8, 2021, https://www.mayoclinic.org/healthy-lifestyle/stress-management/in-depth/stress/art-20046037.

4. InformedHealth.org, "Depression: What is burnout?", *National Library of Medicine*, June 18, 2020, https://www.ncbi.nlm.nih.gov/books/NBK279286/.

5. Michael Blanding, "National Health Costs Could Decrease if Managers Reduce Work Stress," *Working Knowledge* (blog), Harvard Business School, January 26, 2015, https://hbswk.hbs.edu/item/national-health-costs-could-decrease-if-managers-reduce-work-stress.

6. Mark Royal and Val Olson, "COVID-19 Burnout: Four Ways to Deal with It," *This Week in Leadership* (blog), Korn Ferry, accessed April 13, 2022. https://www.kornferry.com/insights/articles/coronavirus-burnout-four-ways-to-handle.

7. George Anders, "Burnout signs have risen 33% in 2020; here are seven ways to reduce risks," *LinkedIn* (blog), LinkedIn, October 7, 2020, https://www.linkedin.com/pulse/burnout-signs-have-risen-33-2020-here-seven-ways-reduce-george-anders/.

8. Trevor Wheelwright, "2022 Cell Phone Usage Statistics: How Obsessed Are We?", *Mobile* (blog), Reviews.org, January 24, 2022, https://www.reviews.org/mobile/

REFERENCES

cell-phone-addiction/#Smart_Phone_Addiction_Stats.

9. Daphne K. Lee (@daphnekylee), "Learned a very relatable term today," Twitter, June 28, 2020, https://twitter.com/daphnekylee/status/1277101831693275136.

10. Thomas, Rachel et al. "Women in the Workplace 2022." LeanIn,org, McKinsey & Company, accessed October 3, 2022.

11. The American Institute of Stress. Accessed on November 10, 2022. https://www.stress.org/workplace-stress

12. Indiana University, "Worked to death? Study says lack of control over high-stress jobs can lead to early grave," *Science News* (blog), ScienceDaily, October 17, 2016, https://www.sciencedaily.com/releases/2016/10/161017084123.htm.

13. Margaret M. Quinn and Peter M. Smith, "Gender, Work, and Health," *Annals of Work Exposures and Health* 62, no. 4 (May 2018): 389–392, https://doi.org/10.1093/annweh/wxy019.

14. Dnika J. Travis and Jennifer Thorpe-Moscon, "Day-to-Day Experiences of Emotional Tax Among Women and Men of Color in the Workplace (Report)," *Research* (blog), Catalyst, February 15, 2018, https://www.catalyst.org/research/day-to-day-experiences-of-emotional-tax-among-women-and-men-of-color-in-the-workplace/.

15. Martha Tesema, "Why We Need to Talk About—and Recognize—Representation Burnout," Shine, February 1, 2019, https://advice.theshineapp.com/articles/we-need-to-talk-about-and-recognize-representation-burnout/.

16. Tiana Clark, "This Is What Black Burnout Feels Like," *Culture & Criticism* (blog), BuzzFeed News, January 11, 2019, https://www.buzzfeednews.com/article/tianaclarkpoet/millennial-burnout-black-women-self-care-anxiety-depression.

17. LeanIn.Org and SurveyMonkey, "Women are maxing out

and burning out during COVID-19," *Research* (blog), LeanIn.Org, May 7, 2020, https://leanin.org/article/womens-workload-and-burnout.

18. Randall J. Beck and Jim Harter, "Why Great Managers Are So Rare," *Workplace* (blog), Gallup, accessed December 13, 2021, https://www.gallup.com/workplace/231593/why-great-managers-rare.aspx.

19. Emily Nagoski and Amelia Nagoski, B*urnout: The Secret to Unlocking the Stress Cycle* (New York: Ballantine Books, 2019), xii.

20. Emily Nagoski and Amelia Nagoski, *Burnout: The Secret to Unlocking the Stress Cycle* (New York: Ballantine Books, 2019), 14-21.

CHAPTER 5: FLEXIBILITY OR BUST

1. Evan DeFilippis, Stephen Michael Impink, Madison Singell, Jeffrey T. Polzer, and Raffaella Sadun, "Collaborating During Coronavirus: The Impact of COVID-19 on the Nature of Work" (working paper, National Bureau of Economic Research, Cambridge, Massachusetts, July 2020) https://www.nber.org/papers/w27612.

2. Ankur Modi, "The Untold Side Of Remote Working: Isolation And Lack Of Career Progression," *Forbes* (online), September 27, 2021, https://www.forbes.com/sites/ankurmodi/2019/12/26/the-untold-side-of-remote-working-isolation-and-lack-of-career-progression/?sh=4ebbaa5068c7.

3. Quentin Fottrell, "'I'm very outspoken about my desire to never work in an office again': CEOs and employees are locked in a battle of wills over when they return to the office," *The Human Cost* (blog), MarketWatch, updated June 7, 2022, https://www.marketwatch.com/story/

REFERENCES

workers-dont-want-toys-or-free-food-they-want-a-higher-quality-of-life-the-great-resistance-is-here-companies-struggle-to-get-workers-back-to-the-office-11653281432.

4. "State Of Remote Work 2021," Buffer, accessed October 12, 2021, https://buffer.com/2021-state-of-remote-work.

5. Carolyn Kylstra, "10 Things Your Commute Does to Your Body," *Time* (online), February 26, 2014, https://time.com/9912/10-things-your-commute-does-to-your-body/.

6. "Work-at-Home After Covid-19 – Our Forecast," Global Workplace Analytics, accessed May 12, 2021. https://globalworkplaceanalytics.com/work-at-home-after-covid-19-our-forecast.

7. Jessica Howington, "6 Ways Working From Home Can Save You $6,000 or More Annually," *FlexWorkers* (blog), FlexJobs, accessed March 21, 2022, https://www.flexjobs.com/blog/post/does-working-remotely-save-you-money/.

8. Julian Birkinshaw, Jordan Cohen, and Pawel Stach, "Research: Knowledge Workers Are More Productive from Home," *Harvard Business Review* (online), August 31, 2020, https://hbr.org/2020/08/research-knowledge-workers-are-more-productive-from-home.

9. "It's time to reimagine where and how work will get done: PwC's US Remote Work Survey," PricewaterhouseCoopers, January 12, 2021, https://www.pwc.com/us/en/library/covid-19/us-remote-work-survey.html.

10. PA Media and Kelly Earley, "Barclays scraps tech that warned employees to 'avoid breaks,'" *Business* (blog), SiliconRepublic, February 21, 2020, https://www.siliconrepublic.com/companies/sapience-software-barclays-employee-data.

11. Gloria Mark, Daniela Gudith, and Ulrich Klocke, "The Cost of Interrupted Work: More Speed and Stress," in *CHI '08:*

Proceedings of the SIGCHI Conference on Human Factors in Computing Systems (New York: Association for Computing Machinery, 2008). Available online at https://www.ics.uci.edu/~gmark/chi08-mark.pdf.

12. "No ego," GitLab Values, GitLab, accessed January 13, 2022, https://about.gitlab.com/handbook/values/#no-ego.

13. "It's impossible to know everything," GitLab Values, GitLab, accessed January 13, 2022, https://about.gitlab.com/handbook/values/#its-impossible-to-know-everything.

14. Vignesh Ramachandran, "Stanford researchers identify four causes for 'Zoom fatigue' and their simple fixes," *Stanford News* (blog), Stanford University, February 23, 2021, https://news.stanford.edu/2021/02/23/four-causes-zoom-fatigue-solutions/.

15. Matt Richtel, "Don't Like What You See on Zoom? Get a Face-Lift and Join the Crowd," *The New York Times* (online), August 13, 2020, https://www.nytimes.com/2020/08/13/health/coronavirus-cosmetic-surgery.html.

16. Jena McGregor, "Remote work really does mean longer days — and more meetings," *The Washington Post* (online), August 4, 2020, https://www.washingtonpost.com/business/2020/08/04/remote-work-longer-days/.

17. Stephen Shinnan, "Just How Fair Is Remote Work?", *HR* (blog), WorkTango, December 5, 2020, https://worktango.com/2020/12/05/just-how-fair-is-remote-work/.

CHAPTER 6: CARING FOR CAREGIVERS

1. Simon Workman and Steven Jessen-Howard, "Understanding the True Cost of Child Care for Infants and Toddlers," *Building an Economy for All* (blog), The Center for American Progress (CAP), November 15, 2018, https://www.americanprogress.

org/issues/early-childhood/reports/2018/11/15/460970/understanding-true-cost-child-care-infants-toddlers/.

2. Mary Ann Mason, Marc Goulden, and Karie Frasch, "Keeping Women in the Science Pipeline," *The ANNALS of the American Academy of Political and Social Science* 638, no. 1 (2011): 141–162, https://doi.org/10.1177/0002716211416925.

3. Joseph B. Fuller and Manjari Raman, *The Caring Company: How Employers Can Cut Costs And Boost Productivity By Helping Employees Manage Caregiving Needs* (Boston, Massachusetts: Harvard Business School, updated January 17, 2019). Available online at https://www.hbs.edu/managing-the-future-of-work/Documents/The_Caring_Company.pdf.

4. Gretchen Livingston and Deja Thomas, "Among 41 countries, only U.S. lacks paid parental leave," *Short Read* (blog), Pew Research Center, December 16, 2019, https://www.pewresearch.org/fact-tank/2019/12/16/u-s-lacks-mandated-paid-parental-leave/.

5. Caitlyn Collins, "Two New Moms Return to Work — One in Seattle, One in Stockholm," *Harvard Business Review* (online), March 3, 2020, https://hbr.org/2020/03/two-new-moms-return-to-work-one-in-seattle-one-in-stockholm.

6. "New Study Reveals Paid Family Leave Policies Lead to 20 Percent Fewer Women Leaving the Workforce," The Institute for Women's Policy Research (IWPR), January 3, 2020, https://iwpr.org/media/press-releases/new-study-reveals-paid-family-leave-policies-lead-to-20-fewer-women-leaving-the-workforce/.

7. Patricia Cohen, "Recession With a Difference: Women Face Special Burden," *The New York Times* (online), November 17, 2020, https://www.nytimes.com/2020/11/17/business/economy/women-jobs-economy-recession.html.

8. *Enough Already: How The Pandemic Is Breaking Women*

(blog series), National Public Radio (NPR), last updated October 28, 2020, https://www.npr.org/series/928323746/enough-already-how-the-pandemic-is-breaking-women.

9. Chip Cutter, "The Pandemic's Toll on Women's Careers," *The Wall Street Journal* (online), updated September 27, 2021, https://www.wsj.com/articles/womens-careers-pandemic-toll-11632520837.

10. Jessica Grose, "America's Mothers Are in Crisis," *The New York Times* (online), February 4, 2021, https://www.nytimes.com/2021/02/04/parenting/working-moms-mental-health-coronavirus.html.

11. Nicole Bateman and Martha Ross, "Why has COVID-19 been especially harmful for working women?", 19A: *The Brookings Gender Equality Series* (blog series), Brookings, October 2020, https://www.brookings.edu/essay/why-has-covid-19-been-especially-harmful-for-working-women/.

12. Carey Oven, "Peace of mind: Inclusive culture + paid family leave," *Life at Deloitte* (blog), Deloitte, accessed April 2, 2022 https://www2.deloitte.com/us/en/pages/about-deloitte/articles/inclusion-family-leave-well-being-parental-caregiver.html.

13. Sammer, Joann. "Improving the Lives of Caregivers Makes Good Business Sense," SHRM (blog), January 6, 2020. , https://business.bofa.com/en-us/content/workplace-benefits/why-us/latest-insights.html.

CHAPTER 7: A CULTURE OF CONNECTION

1. Alan Kohll, "5 Reasons Social Connections Can Enhance Your Employee Wellness Program," *Forbes* (online), January 31, 2018, https://www.forbes.com/sites/alankohll/2018/01/31/5-ways-social-connections-can-enhance-your-employee-wellness-program/?sh=6455d85b527c.

REFERENCES

2. "Cigna Takes Action To Combat The Rise Of Loneliness And Improve Mental Wellness In America," *Newsworthy* (blog), Cigna, January 23, 2020, https://www.cigna.com/about-us/newsroom/news-and-views/press-releases/2020/cigna-takes-action-to-combat-the-rise-of-loneliness-and-improve-mental-wellness-in-america.

3. Marianna Pogosyan, "On Belonging," *Psychology Today* (online), April 11, 2017, https://www.psychologytoday.com/us/blog/between-cultures/201704/belonging.

4. Karyn Twaronite, "The Surprising Power of Simply Asking Coworkers How They're Doing," *Harvard Business Review* (online), February 28, 2019, https://hbr.org/2019/02/the-surprising-power-of-simply-asking-coworkers-how-theyre-doing.

5. Cigna, *Loneliness and the Workplace: 2020 U.S. Report*, January 2020, https://www.cigna.com/static/www-cigna-com/docs/about-us/newsroom/studies-and-reports/combatting-loneliness/cigna-2020-loneliness-report.pdf.

6. Richard Eisenberg, "Who's Lonely at Work and Why," *In Good Company* (blog), NextAvenue, February 25, 2020, https://www.nextavenue.org/whos-lonely-at-work-and-why/.

7. Kathryn Vasel, "Why workplace loneliness is bad for business," *CNN Business* (blog), *CNN*, December 5, 2018, https://www.cnn.com/2018/12/05/success/workplace-loneliness.

8. Jessica Grose, "Is Remote Work Making Us Paranoid?", *The New York Times* (online), January 13, 2021, https://www.nytimes.com/2021/01/13/style/is-remote-work-making-us-paranoid.html.

9. Nelson D. Schwartz, "Working From Home Poses Hurdles for Employees of Color," *The New York Times* (online), September 6, 2020, https://www.nytimes.com/2020/09/06/business/economy/working-from-home-diversity.html.

10. Jonah Lehrer, "Your Co-Workers Might Be Killing You," *The Wall Street Journal* (online), August 20, 2011, https://www.wsj.com/articles/SB10001424053111903392904576512233116576352.

11. Joshua Pham, "Is Venting Good for Us?", Future Minds Lab, November 27, 2019, https://www.futuremindslab.com/blog/2019/11/27/is-venting-good-for-us.

12. Larry Hirschhorn and Thomas Gilmore, "The New Boundaries of the 'Boundaryless' Company," *Harvard Business Review* (online), reprinted from the original article in the magazine's May–June 1992 issue, https://hbr.org/1992/05/the-new-boundaries-of-the-boundaryless-company.

13. Ron Ashkenas, "Jack Welch's Approach to Breaking Down Silos Still Works," *Harvard Business Review* (online), September 9, 2015, https://hbr.org/2015/09/jack-welchs-approach-to-breaking-down-silos-still-works.

14. Kendra Cherry, "What Is the Sense of Belonging?", *Psychology* (blog), Verywell Mind, updated March 5, 2021, https://www.verywellmind.com/what-is-the-need-to-belong-2795393.

15. Colleen Bordeaux, Betsy Grace, and Naina Sabherwal, "Elevating the Workforce Experience: The Belonging Relationship," *Capital H: Human Capital Blog*, Deloitte, November 23, 2021, https://www2.deloitte.com/us/en/blog/human-capital-blog/2021/what-is-belonging-in-the-workplace.html.

16. Cigna, *Loneliness and the Workplace*, January 2020. https://www.cigna.com/static/www-cigna-com/docs/about-us/newsroom/studies-and-reports/combatting-loneliness/cigna-2020-loneliness-report.pdf

17. Holly Althof, "Viewpoint: Belonging is the Missing Piece in the Fight for Inclusion," Society for Human Resource Management (SHRM), August 21, 2020, https://www.shrm.org/resourcesandtools/hr-topics/behavioral-competencies/

REFERENCES

global-and-cultural-effectiveness/pages/viewpoint-belonging-is-the-missing-piece-in-the-fight-for-inclusion.aspx.

18. Barbara Palmer, "Priya Parker: Don't Skip Over Purpose," Professional Convention Management Association (PCMA), October 31, 2018, https://www.pcma.org/priya-parker-dont-skip-over-purpose/.

19. Kristen Senz, "Rituals at Work: Teams That Play Together Stay Together," *Working Knowledge* (blog), Harvard Business School, March 24, 2022, https://hbswk.hbs.edu/item/rituals-at-work-teams-that-play-together-stay-together.

20. RingCentral, Inc., "New Study Reveals Boost in Employee Productivity and Well-Being Among Companies That Foster a 'Connected Culture' in Work from Anywhere Environment," Business Wire, November 11, 2020, https://www.businesswire.com/news/home/20201111005284/en/New-Study-Reveals-Boost-in-Employee-Productivity-and-Well-Being-Among-Companies-That-Foster-a-'Connected-Culture'-in-Work-from-Anywhere-Environment.

21. Thomas J. Saporito, "It's Time to Acknowledge CEO Loneliness," *Harvard Business Review* (online), February 15, 2012, https://hbr.org/2012/02/its-time-to-acknowledge-ceo-lo.

22. PricewaterhouseCoopers, *Work-life 3.0: Understanding how we'll work next*, PwC Consumer Intelligence Series, published 2016, https://www.pwc.com/us/en/industry/entertainment-media/publications/consumer-intelligence-series/assets/pwc-consumer-intellgience-series-future-of-work-june-2016.pdf.

CHAPTER 8: MEANING MATTERS

1. Jonathan Emmett, Gunnar Schrah, Matt Schrimper, and Alexandra Wood, "COVID-19 and the employee experience: How leaders can seize the moment," *Capabilities* (blog),

XV

McKinsey & Company, June 29, 2020, https://www.mckinsey.com/business-functions/people-and-organizational-performance/our-insights/covid-19-and-the-employee-experience-how-leaders-can-seize-the-moment.

2. Naina Dhingra, Andrew Samo, Bill Schaninger, and Matt Schrimper, "Help your employees find purpose—or watch them leave," Capabilities (blog), McKinsey & Company, April 5, 2021, https://www.mckinsey.com/business-functions/people-and-organizational-performance/our-insights/help-your-employees-find-purpose-or-watch-them-leave.

3. The Science of Purpose (home page), accessed December 6, 2021. http://scienceofpurpose.org.

4. Harvard Business Review and EY, *The Business Case for Purpose* (Boston, Massachusetts: Harvard Business School Publishing, 2015). Available online at https://assets.ey.com/content/dam/ey-sites/ey-com/en_gl/topics/digital/ey-the-business-case-for-purpose.pdf.

5. Harvard Business Review and EY, *The Business Case for Purpose*.

6. Ranjay Gulati, "The Soul of a Start-Up," *Harvard Business Review* (online), reprinted from the original article in the magazine's July–August 2019 issue, https://hbr.org/2019/07/the-soul-of-a-start-up.

7. Maddy Savage, "Has the meaning of work changed forever?", *The Life Project* (blog), BBC.com, November 16, 2020, https://www.bbc.com/worklife/article/20201112-has-the-meaning-of-work-changed-forever.

8. Vincent Stanley, "How Patagonia Learned to Act on Its Values," interview by Ted O'Callahan, *Yale Insights* (blog), Yale School of Management, April 22, 2021, https://insights.som.yale.edu/insights/how-patagonia-learned-to-act-on-its-values.

9. Dhingra, Samo, Schaninger, and Schrimper, "Help your employees

find purpose."

10. Dhingra, Samo, Schaninger, and Schrimper, "Help your employees find purpose."

11. Dhingra, N. D., & Schaninger, B. (2021, June 3). *The Search for Purpose at Work*. McKinsey & Company. https://www.mckinsey.com/capabilities/people-and-organizational-performance/our-insights/the-search-for-purpose-at-work

CHAPTER 9: LEADING WITH COMPASSION, NO MATTER YOUR ROLE

1. "Compassion," Dictionary.com, accessed November 3, 2020. https://www.dictionary.com/browse/compassion.

2. Max Klein, "Here's What Makes an Amazing Boss," Medium, November 2, 2021, https://emaxklein.medium.com/heres-what-makes-an-amazing-boss-1bc8439ea0e.

3. Gallup. Accessed by authors on November 10, 2022. https://www.gallup.com/learning/248405/strengths-development-coaching.aspx

4. Sigal Barsade and Olivia A. O'Neill, "Employees Who Feel Love Perform Better," *Harvard Business Review* (online), January 13, 2014, https://hbr.org/2014/01/employees-who-feel-love-perform-better.

5. Laura Macpherson, "10 bold examples of transparency in the workplace," *FrontPage* (blog), Front.com, February 16, 2021, https://front.com/blog/10-bold-examples-of-transparency-in-the-workplace.

6. Sigal Barsade and Olivia A. O'Neill, "Manage Your Emotional Culture," *Harvard Business Review* (online), reprinted from the original article in the magazine's January–February 2016 issue, https://hbr.org/2016/01/manage-your-emotional-culture.

7. "Our Approach," Radical Candor, accessed January 25, 2022, https://www.radicalcandor.com/our-approach/.

8. Mollie West Duffy, "How to Embrace Emotions at Work During a Difficult Time," interview with Arielle Shipper, Donut, April 8, 2020, https://www.donut.com/blog/embracing-emotions-at-work-during-covid-19/.

9. "VIDEO: Marriott CEO Arne Sorenson on COVID-19 "never seen anything like it in 92 years" Hospitality and Catering News. March 21, 2020. https://www.hospitalityandcateringnews.com/2020/03/video-marriott-ceo-arne-sorenson-on-covid-19-never-seen-anything-like-it-in-92-years/.

CONCLUSION: A MORE HUMAN WORKPLACE

1. Roy, Arundhati. *War Talk*. South End Press, 2003.

ABOUT THE AUTHORS

HANNAH L. UBL is an author, researcher, and thought leader on the future of work. As the cofounder of Good Company Consulting, she's committed to creating workplaces that don't suck by putting the focus where it matters: the people at work. As a keynote speaker, she has been trusted to deliver her findings to thousands of leaders, new hires, and everyone in between.

Hannah is the coauthor of *Managing Millennials for Dummies* and *The Future of Work is Human: Transforming Work for a Post-Pandemic World*. Find more of her workplace wisdom at goodcompanyconsulting.com.

LISA X. WALDEN is a speaker, author, and consultant dedicated to helping people create authentic, empowering workplaces. Lisa has been studying people at work for over a decade, and her insights have been featured in publications including *Forbes*, *The Wall Street Journal*, *Fast Company*, and *Fortune*.

Lisa is the coauthor of *Managing Millennials for Dummies* and *The Future of Work is Human: Transforming Work for a Post-Pandemic World*. Find Lisa's actionable tools and insights online at goodcompanyconsulting.com.

HERE IS WHAT SOME OF THEIR CLIENTS HAVE TO SAY:

Lisa was everything we asked for and more. Not only did she engage and energize the crowd— she spoke to every meaningful objective and brought new material that was relevant to the event. Fantastic! We couldn't be happier.

—S<small>YNTELLIS</small>

Hannah is just incredible. This is my second experience, and it was even better than the first. The content is spot-on, and her presentation skills are unmatched. Wonderful experience all around. We will definitely work with her again.

—A<small>SSOCIATION OF</small> S<small>UPPLIERS FOR THE</small> P<small>APER</small> I<small>NDUSTRY</small>

To book Hannah or Lisa for your next event, head to www.goodcompanyconsulting.com.

SPEAKING ENGAGEMENTS

For over a decade, Hannah L. Ubl and Lisa X. Walden have delivered compelling, actionable keynotes that help people foster top-notch cultures, from small mom-and-pop shops to Fortune 100 companies.

Their approach includes a unique customization process to ensure that the content is tailored to each audience's distinct challenges. By scanning the latest data and reports, speaking with employees within the organization, and scanning social media to get a pulse of collective attitudes towards work, Hannah and Lisa ensure that their presentations leave people empowered and excited to change their workplace for the better.

THEIR POPULAR KEYNOTE TOPICS INCLUDE:

- ✦ Creating a Workplace That Doesn't Suck
- ✦ Leadership Reimagined
- ✦ Recruiting and Retaining in Today's Workplace
- ✦ Connecting Across Generations